BRITAIN AND THE OLD DOMINIONS

BRITAIN AND THE OLD DOMINIONS

J. D. B. Miller

Professor of International Relations
Australian National University

THE JOHNS HOPKINS PRESS : BALTIMORE

Published in Great Britain by
Chatto & Windus Ltd.
42 William IV Street
London, W.C.2

*

Library of Congress Catalog Card Number: 66–27471

To the memory of
N. P. J.

*Such ways, such arts, such looks
hadst thou!*

CONTENTS

PREFACE

AN Australian ought to apologize in advance to Canadians, New Zealanders and South Africans for his native inability to understand the fine print of their social contracts. He ought perhaps to apologize to the British for the same reason, but, having lived for ten happy years in their midst, I shall risk the consequences of not doing so.

My thanks are due to St. Antony's College, Oxford, which asked me to write this book, and to the Leverhulme Trustees, for advice and for making it possible for me to make my first visit to Canada. They are also due to the numerous Canadians who found time to talk to me about their country's relations with Britain.

Mr. D. M. Bensusan-Butt and Dr. P. S. Cohen have kindly read the manuscript and given me the benefit of their criticisms. Professor James Eayrs did the same for a portion. I am grateful to these friends, who must not be held responsible for the faults which remain. Professor K. S. Inglis made available material on the fate of the Anzac memorial at Port Said which he had collected for his forthcoming work on the Anzac tradition. Mrs. Joan Davidson looked up many details for me; her help was of great value.

I would like to make acknowledgment to the following for the use of copyright material: Thomas Nelson & Sons for John Buchan's *Prester John*; Messrs Heinemann and the Viking Press for Wallace Stegner's *Wolf Willow*; Hamish Hamilton Ltd. for Graham McInnes' *The Road to Gundagai*; Allan's Music (Aust.) Pty. Ltd., and Leo Feist Inc. for J. D. Burns' "The Bugles of England"; the Contract Press, Montreal, for F. R. Scott's "W.L.M.K." (from *The Eye of the Needle*); Angus and Robertson Ltd., Sydney, for R. D. Fitzgerald's "Transaction", and the estate of A. R. D. Fairburn and Mrs Amber Blanco White for quotations from poems by A. R. D. Fairburn and William Pember Reeves respectively (all from *The Penguin Book of New Zealand Verse*).

My wife has suffered much in confusion of arrangements and lack of my company because of this book. Even so, she read the manuscript and corrected errors and infelicities. My debt to her cannot be calculated, but it should at least be acknowledged.

J.D.B.M.

INTRODUCTION

CANADA, Australia, New Zealand and South Africa make an awkward but natural grouping. Historically, they have been associated with one another in British minds by their colonization in the nineteenth century, by their possession of "Dominion status", and by their participation with Britain in two world wars. Even since 1945, when the Commonwealth of Nations has expanded to take in a great many Asian and African members, these countries have been widely thought of as having more in common with each other, and with Britain, than with the newer members: they form the "Old Commonwealth". It was a shock to many people when South Africa left the Commonwealth, but a common character is often thought to cling to the other three. This view is not entirely correct, but it is understandable. In each of these countries British parliamentary government has been firmly established, and British ways still impress the visitor. Canada, Australia and New Zealand provide the most remarkable examples in history of the relations that can develop between a metropolitan country and its settler colonies.

It may be asked why, in a series on Britain in the World Today, this book still includes South Africa, which left the Commonwealth in 1961 and does not now stand in the same relation to Britain as the other three. South Africa has always stood apart, because of its Afrikaner traditions and its black majority; moreover, it will probably play a steadily declining part in Britain's future affairs. But it is included here for several reasons. One is that South Africa is still bracketed with the other three in the minds of people in many countries besides Britain. Another is that South Africa participated in the same historical development as Canada, Australia and New Zealand down to 1961. A third is that Britain's relations with South Africa did not cease when it left the Commonwealth. There are still significant connections in trade, investment and other fields, including Britain's right to use the Simonstown naval base.

There is thus some justification for treating these four countries as a group with which Britain has had a certain common relationship; but we must also remember that each is a different entity, and that each has striven to impress its own character and importance upon Britain in their mutual relations. In terms of policy, they have banded together when they could find something to agree on, but they have mostly sought separate advantages. Their economic development has never been subject to any overall plan; they have grown up in their own separate ways. Set apart by great distances from one another and from Britain, they have all been insular in thought and domestic in their preoccupations. Each has woven its own strand of contact with Britain from the diverse elements of migration, investment, geography, trade, language and the balance of elements within its own society.

The need to combine general consideration of the Old Dominions with awareness of the different relations of each one with Britain has influenced the plan of this book. It starts with the growth of the common background of the Four in the century after Waterloo. Then there are chapters on their individual development. A chapter on the situation of Britain and the Four between 1918 and 1945 is followed by an examination of post-war events. These are dealt with in two ways. The first is by discussion of changes in the structure of Commonwealth relations, in defence and foreign affairs, and in economic and social connections. The second is through consideration of the attitudes taken by Britain and the Four in certain critical situations affecting them in recent years—the Suez crisis of 1956, South Africa's departure from the Commonwealth in 1961, Britain's attempt to enter the European Economic Community in 1961–2, and the Southern Rhodesia problem of 1964–5. Finally, there is an attempt to summarize and project Britain's relations with the Four.

Perhaps something should be said about the kind of relations that are dealt with here. I am mainly concerned with those between the British Government and the governments of the Four: this is primarily a political study. I describe these relations, but also attempt to explain them by reference to social, political, demographic, economic and other relevant factors. In other words, the non-governmental relations are discussed in order to illuminate the governmental relations. In addition, however, they are considered because they are important in their own right: they have often mattered most in the general relations between Britain and the Four.

This is not a story of international politics at its full stretch, but of the satisfactory settlement of occasional differences; with now and then a major problem such as the racial policy of South Africa. Britain and the Old Dominions have usually been friends with one another. The fact that the Four gained their independence by imperceptible degrees meant that they shared with Britain the over-lay of mysticism occasioned by first a common Crown and then a common Monarch; there was room for disagreement within this relationship, but it did not require the full formalities of diplomacy. All the same, the Four have been for a long time more than parts of 'Greater Britain'. Their international personalities have been discernible since World War I, although the assertion of these per-sonalities has not always been a success. They are now firmly established as forces in their own right, though with some lack of assurance about the future.

To some extent, their futures will depend on what is thought of them in Britain, where attitudes towards them, while usually benevolent, have often been fuzzy. Some British people may well share Mr. Auden's view that "the Dominions are for me *tiefste Provinz*, places which have produced no art and are inhabited by the kind of person with whom I have least in common". Others may identify themselves with those he calls the Low-Brows : "for them, the Dominions are inhabited by their relatives and people like them-selves, speaking English, eating English food, wearing English clothes and playing English games, whereas 'abroad' is inhabited by immoral strangers".* There is something in each of these views, but neither will do as a full assessment.

* W. H. Auden, "Going into Europe", *Encounter,* Vol. XX, No. 1, January 1963, p. 54.

I

THE COMMON BACKGROUND

THE Old Dominions are only a small part of the total British experience, but to them Britain is a massive and significant element in their whole range of existence. Historically, it is the principal determinant in many spheres that matter to them. In the chapters immediately following this one we shall see something of the indigenous elements contributing to their present state; but here the emphasis is on the common element which Britain has represented in all four. Some aspects of this common element are uniform throughout the four countries (e.g. British parliamentary practice). Some mean little or nothing to Afrikaners and French-Canadians (e.g. Anglicanism). But there are others which are woven into the whole texture of Dominion experience, and others again which have been influential but are now losing their power. The important things to remember about the general British connection with the Dominions are that, as modern communities, these countries are largely the product of British migration and investment in the nineteenth and twentieth centuries; that, as new lands with new resources, their trade developed largely on a basis of exchange with Britain (except in the case of Canada); that their social and political institutions bear many of the marks of British descent; that their status in the world, and their defence against enemies, used to be essentially dependent on Britain; and that all these connections were given formal expression by a common Crown and a number of institutions clustered around it. I shall try to show how each of these aspects grew in importance in the century or so after 1815.

SETTLEMENT AND INVESTMENT

The central fact is that in the hundred years between the battle of Waterloo and the outbreak of World War I over twenty million people left the British Isles to migrate to countries beyond Europe, and that, while about thirteen millions of these went to the United

States, four millions went to Canada, one and a half millions to Australia and New Zealand, and a very much smaller number to South Africa.* This was the biggest outpouring of people in British history. Most of it was explicable in terms of inadequacies in Britain itself, from potato famines to unemployment, but it was also due to the vision of opportunity in new lands which spoke English and held out the promise of a life like that in Britain, only better. To the United States and the Four also went substantial British investment. Money and people strengthened one another's impact on the economies of the overseas countries, and forged a multitude of personal links between the old country and the new ones. British investment was not, however, confined to the countries of emigration; vast amounts were invested in India and Argentina without any corresponding increase in settlement. Trade was not confined to the countries of emigration either. Of the overseas countries which received people and money from Britain, the United States was subject to many other influences; but it was migration and investment from Britain that decisively shaped the outlines of the present economies of Canada, Australia, New Zealand and South Africa.

Before about 1840 mass emigration from Britain was largely a matter of either transportation or the efforts of poor and dispossessed people to avoid indigence. There had been schemes for the mass emigration of paupers, in order to avoid their remaining a charge on the rates, and more ambitious schemes, such as those of Edward Gibbon Wakefield, for the transfer to the colonies of people with capital who would be able to provide themselves with equipment and labour to pioneer adequately. There were some group settlements, as with Scots in Canada. Emigration was viewed as a means of getting rid of surplus population, rather than as a way of building up strong nations overseas. The attractions of the overseas countries were difficult to prove, in any case, since they had little to offer except empty land until the gold discoveries of the 1850's in Australia and the 1860's in New Zealand. But land was, in itself, a magnet to many people in Britain who had been either dispossessed through political or economic change, or thought of land as basic property which they could never hope to gain in the land of their birth. In Canada, Australia and New Zealand, but especially the first two, immigration throughout the century was skewed in terms of the distribution of peoples in the British Isles:

* N. H. Carrier and J. R. Jeffery, *External Migration* (London, 1953), p. 33.

the proportions of Scots and Irish amongst the immigrants were much higher than in Britain itself, since these were the odd men out in the distribution of nineteenth-century British wealth. The Scots are still distinctive in each of these countries, especially in Canada and New Zealand.

The Irish formed even more of a special case, especially after the Hungry Forties. The torrent of their emigration spilled overwhelmingly into the United States, but left enough over for Canada, Australia and New Zealand to provide a distinctive strain in each of those: proletarian and small farming, Catholic, and potentially discontented. Their preference for the United States, so near across the water and with Irish colonies rapidly multiplying in New York and Boston, was understandable; but the growing colonies in the farther countries tempted them there too.

The 1860's were years of development in the British countries abroad, with the disruption of immigration into the United States by the Civil War; the 1870's and 1880's were also boom years; there was a decline in the 1890's, but a very substantial increase in migration between 1900 and the start of World War I. Some comparable figures, roughly averaged, will indicate the swings of favour amongst emigrants in trying to decide where to settle. In the 1880's the United States was taking between 100,000 and 150,000 British migrants a year, Canada about 25,000, Australia and New Zealand together about 30,000, and South Africa 2,000 or 3,000. The drop in the 1890's was marked. The American figure fell to about 50,000, the Canadian to about 10,000, the Australian and New Zealand to about 5,000, while the South African, in the era of the booming Rand, rose to about 5,000. Between 1900 and 1910 the preference for the United States began to diminish. Between 50,000 and 100,000 migrants went there each year, but much the same numbers went to Canada. Australia and New Zealand varied greatly between 5,000 and 25,000 a year, and South Africa varied between the same extremes, with a spate after the Boer War ended and then a substantial return traffic as it became clear that South Africa would not, after all, develop as a paradise for the British at the expense of the Boers. The period from 1910 to 1914 saw the high tide of emigration to the countries with which we are concerned. The United States still took about 50,000 each year, but the Canadian figure rose to 150,000, the combination of Australia and New Zealand to 50,000, and the South African to about 5,000. World War I saw the end of emigration for five years;

by its resumption in the 1920's, the British had changed their ways, no longer emigrated in such numbers as before, and, when they did, preferred the Dominions to the United States. In the 1920's some 75,000 to 100,000 British people emigrated each year, of whom 25,000 to 50,000 might go to Canada and something like the same number to Australia and New Zealand. Only 1,000 or 2,000 went to Southern Africa. Emigration ceased in the 1930's; the 1940's were years of war; but when emigration began again in the 1950's, its pattern was much the same as in the 1920's.*

To this picture of varying emigration from the British Isles we may add one of the investment of capital abroad. Rounding off Professor Cairncross's rough figures,† the following is instructive:

British Investment Abroad: Totals in £m.

Area	1870	1885	1911
India	160	270	350
Australasia	74	240	380
Canada	20	113	375
South Africa	less than 16	35	350
U.S.A.	200	300	690
Europe and Near East	230	175	?
South America	85	150	585

In the forty years covered by these figures, British investment in the countries of emigration (including the United States) increased more rapidly than in Europe, the earlier area of investment, and in India, the jewel in the Imperial crown. The rapid expansion of population in the new countries led to demands for railways, housing, public works, banks, insurance; there was no planning about either investment or migration, but they tended to go together, in both direction and size.‡ The big exception was South America. Another, which concerns us more, was South Africa: here, as we have seen, migration was a much smaller matter than to Canada, Australia and New Zealand, but investment in the mining industry in the 1890's and 1900's was particularly heavy.

British investment provided the indispensable resources without

* B. R. Mitchell with Phyllis Deane, *Abstract of British Historical Statistics* (Cambridge, 1962), pp. 50–51.

† A. K. Cairncross, *Home and Foreign Investment* 1870–1913 (Cambridge, 1953), pp. 183, 185.

‡ Ibid., p. 209.

which the British colonies of settlement could have managed little but subsistence agriculture. The growth of the goldfields, the wheat-lands, the metal mines, the extensive pastures, the banking systems, the shipping lines and the local transport networks was largely a matter of British money. It took the forms of loans to govern-ments, investment in private companies, and extension to the colonies of the activities of British companies such as those in shipping and insurance. In addition, there were the savings which many migrants took with them. Although the mass of migrants were people without means, and before 1900 were predominantly from the rural areas of Britain, there were always middle-class people with money to invest and careers to make; "the colonies" appealed to the "remittance man" (or his parents), but they also appealed to many thousands of people with capacities and skills which they felt they could not use to the full in Britain.

By the standards of today, the century of emigration from 1815 to 1914 is epical in its hardships and miseries, in the courage of those who took ship, in the massive economic transformations which it effected. The people endured conditions on the voyage which would now be objected to by the representatives of the "under-developed" countries as intolerable; the lies put about by govern-ments and land sharks to tempt migrants abroad were so blatant that the British Government set up an Emigrants' Information Office to provide truthful information about the colonies; the sufferings of disappointed settlers were often heartbreaking.* But the economic structure which arose in each of the four countries was substantial. It provided a sound basis for later investment, which still produces dividends for British capital. Where now is the British investment in South America, on any count? Dilke might grumble in 1868 that

"We at present tax our humblest classes, we weaken our defences, we scatter our troops and fleets, and lay ourselves open to panics such as those of 1853 and 1859, in order to protect against imaginary dangers the Australian gold-digger and Canadian farmer";†

* One of them was George Lansbury, who left a vivid account of his ex-periences in Queensland in the 1880's. When he returned, his oratory helped to get the British Government to take action. See Raymond Postgate, *The Life of George Lansbury* (London, 1951), pp. 22–30.

†Sir Charles Wentworth Dilke, *Greater Britain* (8th edition, London, 1890), p. 385; the words quoted are retained from the 1st (1868) edition.

after his trip twenty years later he was no longer concerned about the few million pounds a year which it had cost to provide local defence for the colonies, but was glad to find the peoples of those countries

> "differentiated from the people of the old country and from the Americans of the United States by a healthier cheerfulness of life. To the generosity, breadth, self-reliance, readiness of resource, and proneness to wander which . . . our colonists share with our American descendants, they add a happiness in the act of living which is their own. [The defects which he saw] are inevitable in the early life of peoples which have rapidly pushed themselves into a foremost position in the world".*

It would be a mistake, however, to read too much British intention into either investment or migration. As already suggested, these were not planned. In their period of greatest abundance, they were the product of a free market in labour and money. The British Government kept the ring, but no more. Voluntary bodies helped with the migration process; colonial governments did their best to encourage it. But, as we have seen, it was not till after World War I that the superior attractions of the United States disappeared. British investors went on putting their money into South America, in spite of the reproaches of their colonial cousins. It took a long time for the analogy with the American colonies to fade: the Cobdenite notion of colonies dropping off the parent stem like ripe fruit had great support in nineteenth-century Britain. No matter how much colonial politicians might press for special advantages, they got very little except the classification of their loans as trustee securities. Throughout the period of the greatest growth of what were later called the Dominions, British private and official opinion was largely incurious about them. But the spread of men and money meant the diffusion of more than bodies and investment; the point was occasionally made in Britain by an enthusiastic publicist such as J. A. Froude or Anthony Trollope, but it did not strike home.

* Sir Charles Wentworth Dilke, *Problems of Greater Britain* (London, 1890), p. 696.

TRADE

One reason was the pattern of trade. One sometimes meets the myth that Britain's trade was once primarily with the Dominions, and that only contemporary wickedness, and the trade policies of the United States as exemplified in G.A.T.T., have altered this. The following figures, spaced at thirty-year intervals, tell a different story:

British Trade with selected Areas. 1871–1931* £m.

Area	1871		1901		1931	
	Imports	Exports	Imports	Exports	Imports	Exports
Europe, North Africa, M. East	155·9	155·7	243·4	152·7	390·1	188·2
U.S.A.	61·1	39·7	141·0	37·7	104·0	26·2
Latin America	22·5	20·6	26·7	22·5	82·7	30·3
All Africa but North	7·4	5·3	9·5	26·9	29·7	42·5
Australia	12·0	9·6	24·2	23·6	45·7	15·1
New Zealand	2·5	1·5	10·6	6·1	37·8	11·7
Canada	9·3	9·2	20·4	9·6	34·9	22·7

At no time did Britain's trade with the settler colonies predominate. Europe and its environs overshadowed all other areas of trade throughout the period covered. In the hey-day of Gladstone and Disraeli, the countries which we are considering hardly mattered in British trade. By the time of Balfour and Campbell-Bannerman, imports from them had begun to count: the wheat from Canada, wool from Australia, meat and dairy products from New Zealand were effective commodities in the British trade balance. Even so, Europe's pre-eminence remained undisturbed; and imports from the United States far outweighed those from the four countries of this study. When the significant pair in British politics were Baldwin and Ramsay Macdonald, the overseas Dominions had greatly increased their sales, but so had Europe. Imports from Latin America equalled those from Australia and

* Adapted from B. R. Mitchell and Phyllis Deane, *Abstract of British Historical Statistics* (Cambridge. 1962), pp. 315–26. Totals for exports include re-exports.

New Zealand. Imports from the United States were three times those from Canada. On the export side the situation was even more pronounced. Exports to Australia, Canada and New Zealand never equalled imports from them, but the disparity became more marked in the twentieth century as all four countries accentuated the protection of local industries at the expense of British, in spite of the fact that they gave (and still give) British goods preference over those from foreign countries. The heavily protectionist policy of the United States, which by 1931 had reached its dizziest heights under the Smooth-Hawley tariff, still permitted Britain to sell as much to that country in that year as to Australia and New Zealand together.

Thus, trade with the old Dominions was never sufficient to meet Britain's needs, and never came near to this position. The Ottawa agreements of 1932 made some alteration in this state of affairs, but not much; more is said about them in Chapter 5. For our purposes here, it is important to note the subordinate but solid part which the Dominions came to play in British trade, and to relate the character of that trade to the development of their economies.

The fact of the matter was that, while the colonies of settlement represented only a small part of British trade, Britain bulked very large indeed in theirs. They did not sell only to Britain; other countries also bought Canadian wheat, Australian wool, and South African gold and diamonds. But the paths blazed by settlement and investment were natural ones along which to organize trade; the English language was a bond of great importance; banking and shipping connections conduced to a concentration upon the British market wherever possible. Some industries, such as the grassland industries of New Zealand, grew up with the British market as their only goal. It was natural that, when the settler colonies struck hard times, or when they encouraged new developments which required an expansion of existing markets, they should think of Britain as the place to which they had a right to sell things. This, however, was not the view taken in Britain itself. By the 1860's Free Trade seemed to have shown such beneficial effects on the British standard of living, that hardly anyone in British politics was prepared to question it for forty years. Free Trade was obviously of benefit to Britain; it was difficult for British people to see that it might not benefit everyone else. The Free Trade view was echoed in the colonies by merchants and others who stood to gain from imports from Britain and Europe. However, it was contested by some colonial farmers, who wanted their local markets protected and their exports to Britain safeguarded by tariffs against foreigners, and by local manufacturers and their workers, who wanted local industries protected against British goods as well as foreign. For some considerable time the appearance of this protectionist view in the colonies was solemnly brought forward in Britain to show how economic madness might seize the working classes if they ever got political power; the example was often used as a warning in the debates on the franchise before the Second Reform Bill. Free Trade was a self-evident truth. It did not require demonstration.

When the young Alfred Deakin, later to be a notable Australian Prime Minister, went to the Colonial Conference of 1887 as a representative of Victoria, he met at lunch the ageing John Bright and recorded the event in a letter home:

"John Bright was there also—a smaller man in body and head than I had thought—very old, very good-looking, very dogmatic. Told me we ought to cut the painter, and when I replied that we were attached to the Mother Country, rejoined that we proved this by taxing our parent's goods, to which in my turn I answered that this was because, instead of treating us as children she only put us on the same footing, in her markets, as her enemies and rivals."*

Deakin did not record Bright's reply; nevertheless, this must have been a highly representative conversation. It is true that Deakin was an enthusiastic young protectionist in a colony in which protectionism was the road to political preferment, and that Bright was a fading force. But they were representative of self-righteous British Free Trade opinion and self-centred colonial protectionist zeal; the two attitudes were to break upon one another at Colonial and Imperial conferences for another forty years. Moreover, the fact that the colonial attitude was essentially two-sided—demanding both protection against foreigners in the British market and protection against Britain in the local one—left plenty of room for difference of emphasis within the colonies themselves. Canada was a special case, in that the debate there was between some form of local protection plus British preference, and reciprocity in trade with the United States. Local circumstances varied a good deal. Yet, when Joseph Chamberlain made his bid to disengage Britain

* Walter Murdoch, *Alfred Deakin: A Sketch* (London, 1923), p. 103.

from Free Trade and institute some form of reciprocal Empire preference, he met with strong support from all four major colonies. It was the determined opposition of the Liberal Government at the Imperial Conference of 1907 that banged the door on prospects of reciprocal preference for a quarter of a century; that opposition was based on a traditionalist Liberal conviction that cheap food was Britain's first need. If it could be got from Europe, no amount of phrase-making about "kith and kin" beyond the seas was going to lead to the denial of Free Trade principles.

In any case, whether the colonies got preference was not a major factor in the growth of their economies. It was rather a matter of whether they would be able to preserve their existing high living standards in times of bad trade. Each of the four developed a roughly similar economy. The base was massive exports of primary products from the fields, pastures and mines; these earned foreign exchange to pay for imports, and enabled rapid development to take place in the building of cities (all four countries expanded these to a size somewhat unexpected in view of their ultimate dependence on rural industries). Capital from abroad helped to develop the infrastructure of the economy; local capital provided for many of the service industries, and for the gradual growth of manufactures. The continual availability of untapped resources was a constant goad towards economic growth. It also worked against subsistence farming and the emergence of a peasantry, except in French Canada, where the peasantry ante-dated the period of rapid development of the other parts of Canada and of Australia, New Zealand and South Africa. Of the four countries, South Africa remained an exception in the composition of its population: the existence of a vast potential proletariat in the Bantu created many different patterns from those forming elsewhere. All four evolved economies which ran at a high rate when export prices were high, but were liable to acute disruption if these fell for any length of time.

SOCIAL AND POLITICAL INSTITUTIONS

The practice of responsible government on the British pattern was, in many ways, the most notable of the gifts from Britain to the Old Dominions. It remains a distinguishing mark. While each has made minor changes in the practice—the abolition of a Second

Chamber in New Zealand, for example—the essentials of responsible government remain : a cabinet responsible to the elected House, a civil service which is subordinate to the cabinet, a Prime Minister whose strength comes from party and public support, but who is essentially a parliamentary figure. Settlers in each of the Four agitated for responsible government as soon as they found their feet; protests against government from Downing Street became endemic as soon as local interests felt themselves impeded by Colonial Office control through a governor. One need not glorify the motives of the men who sought responsible government in Australia and New Zealand and tried to remove "the Imperial factor" from South Africa; the important thing is that, once the matter had been effectively argued in Lord Durham's Canadian report of 1839, only local expediency could prevent the assertion of the doctrine that

> "It needs no change in the principles of government, no invention of a new constitutional theory, to supply the remedy which would . . . completely remove the existing political disorders. It needs but to follow out consistently the principles of the British constitution, and introduce into the government of these great colonies those wise provisions, by which alone the working of the representative system can in any country be rendered harmonious and efficient."*

Ever since the middle of the nineteenth century, a common political style and language in the Old Dominions have provided a universe of discourse for them and for Britain.

Much the same is true of the English legal system and the prevalence of the common law. Roman–Dutch law in South Africa amongst the Afrikaners, and the civil *Coutûme de Paris* amongst French-Canadians, are marks of the essential differences between these two non-British groups and the British elements which gave the Dominions their characteristics as developing countries; everywhere in the Old Dominions, with these two exceptions, the English legal system prevailed. Its connection with the system of responsible government has remained close, largely through the prominence of lawyers amongst politicians, which was characteristic of the colonies in the nineteenth century and is still important. The fact that the

* *The Report of the Earl of Durham* (reprinted London, 1902), p. 204.

constitutions of Canada, Australia and South Africa implied judicial review of the enactments of their central parliaments, thus negating the supremacy of parliament which was basic to British practice, did not prevent either courts or parliaments from maintaining very much their characteristic British roles. English precedents continued to be quoted; English professionalism prevailed amongst lawyers; legal training reflected the peculiar habits of the English tradition. It is easy to become lyrical about the common law, even to the extent of claiming for it virtues which a critical examination does not always support; but there is no doubt that it has formed an immensely important link between Britain and the Four, in the language and frame of reference which it carried with it, and in the character of the legal profession and of the courts which it established so firmly in settler communities.

Whereas the British took overseas only one sort of law (Scots law is not for export), they carried with them a number of forms of the Christian religion. These have been a significant element in building connections between Britain and the Four. The Church of England, the Presbyterian Church, the Methodist Church, the Baptist Church: these, with variations, comprise the colonial component of British Protestantism, with the Roman Catholic Church in its Irish aspect as their counterpoise. As already indicated, migrants left Britain in proportions different from those of the population of Britain itself, with the Scots and Irish taking a bigger part. Despite dreams of establishment by some Anglican bishops, it was impossible to sustain abroad the official primacy which the Church of England enjoyed at home; similarly, it was impossible to maintain the anachronistic form of choice of bishops which still obtains in England. The Church of England was effectively decentralized, its local congregations providing its finance and government. The process was less difficult for the Presbyterians, Methodists, Baptists and Congregationalists, already accustomed to autonomy and local choice; the problem did not arise for the Roman Catholics. In spite of local independence, however, the links with the churches in Britain remained very close. The various branches of the Church of England clung for long to the practice of importing Archbishops; Presbyterian theologians went out from Glasgow and Edinburgh to Toronto, Sydney and Dunedin; the flow of Irish priests still continues, in spite of the substantial localization of the Roman Catholics in Australia, New Zealand and Canada.

Apart from similarity of religious belief, the export of the churches from Britain to the old Dominions had important social effects. In spite of the Church of England's lack of establishment, it remained, in most places except sternly Scottish localities like Otago in New Zealand, the church of respectability and the upper classes. The Presbyterians shared this characteristic in some measure. Methodism, the Baptist churches and the Salvation Army carried on abroad their nineteenth-century roles in Britain, as the natural tabernacles of the middle and respectable working classes. Roman Catholicism was the mark of Irish poverty improving itself. These divisions could have political consequences when religion was called into aid over social issues: in nineteenth-century Australia and New Zealand, Protestant and Catholics were arrayed against each other over drinking and gambling legislation, and on state aid to church schools. In Canada the position of the Catholics was complicated by the existence of French-Canadians as well as Irish-Canadians; as in the United States, episcopal organization had to take account of ethnic origins. In South Africa, the entrenched position of the Dutch Reformed Church among the Boers made it impossible for any of the British churches to attain a significant position, except where concentrations of British settlers were heavy, as in Natal and Capetown.

A further aspect of social life affected by the transplantation of the churches from the British Isles was education. Despite early efforts to confine primary education to church sources, as in nineteenth-century England, each Dominion developed its own state-operated system. But at the secondary and tertiary levels there was room for religious influence. Schools on the English public school pattern, both Protestant and Catholic, often having links with similar schools in Britain, were established by the local churches, and provided, for many years, the main avenue to the professions and to higher education. The early influence of the churches is still to be seen in the older Canadian and Australian universities: denominational colleges were common, and still retain some importance, although the twentieth-century development of universities has been more along the lines of those in the English provinces. The English-speaking universities of Canada and South Africa shared with those of Australia and New Zealand the habit of recruiting large numbers of their staffs from Britain, or from amongst local men who had been to the English and Scottish universities; this habit persists, and has meant a continual living link between Britain and the Four. In medicine, law and engineering, the

Dominion universities kept close connections, so that professional qualifications obtained there were valid in Britain, and *vice versa*; the extension to the Dominions of professional bodies of such diverse people as accountants, veterinary surgeons and optometrists meant further links. The move towards professionalization of this kind in Britain in the nineteenth century was easily extended to the colonies. It was natural to think of them as further fields in which expanding professions might be carried on. The extension of a British qualification might lead to local training and the demand for primacy of local talent; even so, connections were usually retained with the parent bodies in Britain.

In the less easily assessed fields of sport and recreation, the links with Britain are also demonstrable. Cricket is only a fringe game in Canada, but the main summer game in Australia, New Zealand and South Africa. Soccer is a specialized sport in the Old Dominions, but Rugby Union quickly conquered New Zealand and South Africa, and has kept up a strenuous opposition in Australia to the popularity of Australian Rules; Australia and New Zealand also play Rugby League. Canada has remained the only bulwark against British sport: climate and the proximity of the United States have conspired against it.

One is on more general ground in stressing the importance of the English language as a common background of culture against which only French in Canada and Afrikaans in South Africa have managed to prevail. The classics of English literature, the habit of British philosophy, and the fashion of British economics, history and political ideas, have all been transmitted wholesale to the Dominions. There are local literatures of consequence in a great many fields, but these took a long time to grow. The essentially provincial character of intellectual life in new countries was one reason; another was the paucity of local outlets for local work. Even now, however, when these particular difficulties have gone some way to being remedied, reading matter from Britain is still highly influential amongst the English-speaking peoples of the four countries.

An Australian Prime Minister has summed up, in romantic yet specific terms, the heritage of influence and practice which British connection with his country meant. It is the lyrical statement of a man determined that the connection with Britain shall be maintained. A more nationalistic representative of one of the Old Dominions might put the relation in harsher terms, and dwell on the influence of British capital and the corruption of British ideas of social class. Yet there is point in what Sir Robert Menzies said:

"To me the British Empire means (and here you will find a curious jumble in both time and place) a cottage in the wheat lands of the North West of the State of Victoria, with the Bible and Henry Drummond and Jerome K. Jerome and 'The Scottish Chiefs' and Burns on the shelves. It means the cool green waters of the Coln as they glide past the church at Fairford; the long sweep of the Wye Valley above Tintern, with a Wordsworth in my pocket . . . It means King George and Queen Mary coming to their Jubilee in Westminster Hall . . . It means, at Chequers, Winston Churchill, courage and confidence radiating from him . . . It means Australian boys in tired but triumphant groups at Tobruk and Benghazi . . . It means, at Canberra, at Wellington, at Ottawa, at Pretoria, the men of Parliament meeting as those met at Westminster seven hundred years ago; at Melbourne the lawyers practising the Common Law first forged at Westminster. It means Hammond at Sydney, and Bradman at Lord's, and McCabe at Trent Bridge, with the ghosts of Grace and Trumble looking on . . ."*

Such thoughts have been expressed many times by Australians, Canadians, New Zealanders and South Africans who were happy about Britain; as we shall see, this happiness has not always been unalloyed, and there have been other Dominion people to whom British actions were an offence. Nevertheless, influences persist.

FOREIGN POLICY AND DEFENCE

Till late in the nineteenth century, there were British garrisons in all four countries. Only in Australia had they not had to fight. In Canada they had helped to put down Papineau's rebellion in 1837 and Riel's in 1870; in New Zealand they were heavily engaged in the Maori Wars, especially those of the 1860's; in South Africa the Anglo-Boer wars were formidable affairs. Moreover, each country harboured British naval bases. In due course the British regulars left, but the naval bases remained. It was assumed that, while each colony ought to make arrangements for local

* R. G. Menzies, *The British Commonwealth of Nations in International Affairs* (Roy Milne Memorial Lecture, Adelaide, 1950), pp. 25–26.

defence, the protection of the British Empire as a whole was a matter for the Royal Navy. The Empire was thought of as a single state for purposes of peace and war. There was no substantive difference in this regard between self-governing colonies (such as the Old Dominions were) and Crown colonies under direct British control. The self-governing colonies' responsibilities did not extend to issues of peace and war; British power in the world was a unified conception, typified by the R.N.

Such a state of affairs was probably welcome to most English-speaking people in the Dominions before World War I. They were not called upon to pay heavy taxes for defence; they had the guarantee of automatic British involvement if their coasts were in danger; they could look on the Royal Navy as both a symbol and a shield. Nevertheless, to nationally-minded Canadians and Australians, the situation was not entirely welcome. It was, after all, a contented parasitism. Decisions about the kind of naval defence their countries needed were necessarily made in London. There was no assurance that a particular kind of vessel, or a fleet of a particular sort, would be available in the Pacific if there was trouble in the Atlantic. Moreover, there was little to fire the spirit of the local nationalist in the presence of R.N. ships in his harbours. There arose a demand for Dominion navies which would be ancillary to the R.N. The demand was resisted in both Canada and Australia by those who regarded it as evidence of "separatism"; it was also resisted by the Admiralty, which was understandably preoccupied with the task of keeping a fleet in being, and did not want any ships under its control to be inhibited in their movements by the need to be stationed permanently in this or that spot. The alternatives suggested by the Admiralty were colonial contributions to the cost of the R.N., and the enlistment of colonial sailors into its ships. Both were acceptable to some sections of opinion in the self-governing colonies; to some others they were not. At the outbreak of war in 1914, however, only one Dominion force of significance, the Royal Australian Navy, had made its appearance.

If the pattern of imperial defence had continued to be that of the Maori and South African Wars—a pattern of operations in the country itself, directed by British generals and involving continual disruption of local affairs—later developments would certainly have been different from what they were. In fact, however, a different pattern asserted itelf in 1914. There were no further examples of pitched battles on Dominion soil, with British troops actively engaged. Instead, the conflict of 1914 led to the dispatch to Europe and the Middle East of contingents of Canadians, Australians and New Zealanders which were vast in proportion to the populations of those countries, and which created quite new problems in relations between Britain and these countries. (The South African effort was smaller and more confined to the African continent, but similar problems arose.) Contingents had been sent from the other colonies to South Africa between 1899 and 1902, but they were fairly small and proved fairly easy to incorporate into the British forces. In France between 1914 and 1918, however, the problem of the identity of the Dominions' national forces, and the responsibility for their deployment, became a real one; it was not humanly possible to have hundreds of thousands of such troops quietly absorbed into the British Army without concern and protest from the countries which they represented. The problems were not simply those of technical military control. They also involved national pride. Countries which could put so many fighting troops into the field could not be treated as children in the disposition of them; moreover, they could not be regarded as solely appendages of Britain itself. Considerations such as these caused widespread discussion of the future of the Dominions during World War I. Much of it took place in London, where Dominion Ministers came to discuss the conduct of the war. Borden of Canada, Hughes of Australia and Smuts of South Africa were all striving, in their characteristic ways, for a relationship with Britain which would recognize the stature of their countries and yet ensure that there was no break in the universality of the Crown or the unitary character of major policy on foreign affairs and defence. It was impossible to arrive at a satisfactory solution, since the Dominions were, in effect, trying to eat their cake and have it too. At the Paris Peace Conference they wanted to be treated as separate powers in their quest for mandates and in other matters that touched them closely, but as parts of the British Empire in the context of Great Power relations. The ambiguous fashion in which they signed the Treaty of Versailles and joined the League of Nations—as simultaneously separate and parts of a whole—reflected the disturbed situation in which their circumstances and inclinations had placed them.

From the British standpoint, there was no disposition to coerce the Dominions into this or that arrangement, but some uneasiness about the implications of their actions. Much of British prestige rested on the notion of a unified empire; also, British assumptions about defence, citizenship, trade and law were based upon the unitary character of the British Crown, and the supremacy of the British parliament. It had been recognized for many years that the self-governing colonies could not be prevented from legislating on tariffs, and from taxing goods from Britain; it had also been recognized that Canada had special problems with the United States, and that there must be scope for agreements between these two countries, even if, in form, they were made by the British Government on Canadian advice. On issues of peace and war, however, successive British governments had taken the view that if the Monarch was at war, all his subjects were at war; the decision on such a grave matter had to be in the hands of the British Government, which bore the primary risks and must therefore take the primary responsibility. This view had been widely accepted in the Dominions, even if Sir Wilfrid Laurier in Canada had been prepared to accept it only on the understanding that their belligerency could be passive if they wished. In 1914 they all wished it to be active. But the sobering experiences of four years of war caused many Dominion leaders to wish for the right to restrain and advise Britain in the choice of peace or war, or at any rate to be continuously informed about the course of events. Conversely, they caused others to seek for the right of neutrality.

In the face of these difficulties, the British Government maintained, throughout the 1920's and 30's, one of its typical postures: a bland refusal to spell out the logical implications of what it was doing. In naval and air defence it continued to maintain forces which assumed a world-wide role, including major defence for the Pacific Dominions. In foreign policy it took its own major decisions, sometimes consulting the Dominions, sometimes not. In constitutional matters it contrived the Statute of Westminster, a masterpiece of ambiguity. In legal terms it asserted that relations between itself and the Dominions were not international relations as generally understood; but it continued to encourage the Dominions to take a full part in the League of Nations. It was able to act in this way because of the almost universal refusal to tamper with the notion of a common Crown.

THE CROWN AND ITS ACCOMPANIMENTS

The Monarchy has been, at the constitutional level, the strongest and most inescapable tie between the Old Dominions and Britain.

Today Canada, Australia and New Zealand remain monarchical. Symbolically, it was the proposal that South Africa should become a republic which precipitated South Africa's departure from the Commonwealth and the consequence that it became officially 'foreign' in the eyes of the British Government. It is easy to see why the Monarchy should have such importance. In traditional British practice, the whole operation of government is the King's personal affair. The courts are the King's courts; the ministers are his ministers; the armed forces swear allegiance to him and derive authority from him; the Lords and Commons compose his parliament; his enemies are the country's enemies, and treason to the country is treason to him in person. He declares war, and it is in his name that diplomacy is carried on. The colonies are his possessions. It is true that responsible government in Britain transformed the reality of power within this framework of formal authority, but it left the framework undisturbed. When responsible government came to the colonies of Canada, Australia, New Zealand and South Africa, it came in a form that left monarchical authority unaltered. The powers of the monarch were exercised in the local situation by a Governor or Governor-General, who was appointed by the British Government. The constitutions of the colonies were either drawn up under the royal prerogative or enacted by the British parliament. Colonial responsible government was derivative government: the colonists governed themselves in their local affairs, but did so by virtue of royal authority granted through the action of the British Government, and dependent ultimately upon the will of the British parliament. In the legal understanding of the time, the colonists possessed no initiating authority of their own; to have admitted any right of constitutional origination on their part would have been to allow them the position asserted defiantly by the American colonists in the eighteenth century.

The Monarchy thus possessed immense significance in the legal sense. "The Crown" comprised the whole authority of government. To prevent inconsistency of approach, ultimate authority had to be in the hands of the British Government. The Monarch could not be made to seem to be in two minds in his conduct, especially where foreigners were concerned; thus, Britain retained the right of veto over the behaviour of governments in the colonies, and recognized no original power of diplomacy on their part. They, in their turn, bowed to the legislative supremacy of the British parliament. As they grew in stature, such a position could be sustained only by mutual forbearance.

However, even more important than the legal significance of the Monarchy was its political importance as a symbol of loyalty. This was recognized at an early stage by Lord Balfour, whose views in 1901 on an occasion when the new King Edward VII wished to prevent his son (later King George V) from going to open the first national parliament in Australia deserve to be quoted:

"Mr Balfour (he wrote) cannot help feeling there are on the other side reasons to be urged which touch the deepest interests of the Monarchy. The King is no longer merely King of Great Britain and Ireland and of a few dependencies whose whole value consisted in ministering to the wealth and security of Great Britain and Ireland. He is now the greatest constitutional bond uniting together in a single Empire communities of free men separated by half the circumference of the Globe. All the patriotic sentiment which makes such an Empire possible centres in him or centres chiefly in him; and everything which emphasizes his personality to our kinsmen across the seas must be a gain to the Monarchy and the Empire.

Now the present opportunity of furthering the policy thus suggested is unique. It can in the nature of things never be repeated. A great commonwealth is to be brought into existence, after infinite trouble and with the fairest prospects of success. *Its citizens know little and care little for British Ministries and British party politics. But they know, and care for, the Empire of which they are members and for the Sovereign who rules it.* Surely it is in the highest interests of the State that he should visually, and so to speak corporeally, associate his family with the final act which brings the new community into being; so that in the eyes of all who see it the chief actor in the ceremony, its central figure, should be the King's heir, and that in the history of this great event the Monarchy of Britain and the Commonwealth of Australia should be inseparably united."[*]

This might serve as a text for all Royal Tours. Its immediate significance lay in Balfour's recognition that the Monarch, an essentially mystical element in the context of colonial affairs, could be

[*] Balfour in a letter of February 6, 1901; given in Harold Nicolson, *King George the Fifth* (London, 1952), pp. 67–8. The italics are mine.

made to stand for the unity of the Empire, which in its turn could serve the interests of Britain. Balfour and those who thought like him did not visualize any difference of ultimate interest between Britain and countries like Australia. Balfour, as a realist, could undoubtedly see immediate differences over money and markets, over colonial policy in the Pacific and the treatment of Australian soldiers in South Africa; but he looked beyond these immediate matters to a wider community of interest between Britain and the "communities of free men" who were Britain's "kinsmen". Monarchy could do what no attempt at coercion by the British Government could do. Moreover, Balfour saw that thoughts of coercion were out of date. Spontaneous loyalty, nourished by the monarchical principle in its living forms, could cement relations where no amount of legislation could hope to do so.

It is important not to isolate the Crown in our attempt to understand the common background which the Old Dominions shared in the late nineteenth and early twentieth centuries. Its influence was buttressed in a variety of ways. To start with, the Governor-General of each of the four was from Britain and usually a peer, nominated by the British Government and understood to be its representative. This practice showed remarkable staying power. New Zealand has not yet had a native-born Governor-General;* Canada did not have one until 1952; South Africa waited until World War II; Australia appointed one in 1931, reverted to British appointments in 1935, swung back to an Australian in 1947, and stuck to British appointments from 1952 until 1965. The Governor-General had two main functions in regard to Britain. Socially, he provided a court: it was possible to emulate the circumstances of royalty in some degree, and to invest with British splendour the affairs of Government House. The presence of the Governor-General's personal staff, so heavily impregnated with English social standards, contributed to this effect. Politically, the Governor-General was, until 1926, the means through which the British Government conveyed its views to the Dominion government; he was a political officer expected to weigh British views in deciding any matter which involved his discretion. Ordinarily this did not amount to much. Governors-General were expected to avoid any impression of coercion from Downing Street, and

* Lord Freyberg, who was Governor-General from 1946 to 1952, had been educated in New Zealand and was G.O.C. New Zealand Forces in World War II; but he was born in London.

usually managed it.* But they were a constant reminder of continuing British upper-class attitudes and standards.

Along with Governors-General went honours. Knighthoods are still granted in Australia and New Zealand, where the O.B.E. is a familiar set of letters after a name. Canada repudiated honours in 1918, and has not admitted them since. South Africa continued to provide them until the advent of the Nationalists in the late 1940's under Dr. Malan. Like imported Governors and Governors-General, honours became something of a symbol of the link with Britain, praised by their supporters as evidence of the Royal contact with the far-off Dominions, attacked by their opponents as rewards for servility and encouragement of social snobbery. It is only fair to add that the most determined opposition was often on grounds which did not affect Britain, those of the likelihood that knighthoods would be recommended for men who had paid to get a particular government elected. The general system of honours, however, pertaining so much to the atmosphere of Monarchy, undoubtedly gave a special sort of substance to the link with Britain.

In similar ways one can mention the common citizenship which British subjects were assumed to have, wherever they might come from, and the summit of the imperial legal system, the Judicial Committee of the Privy Council as a court of appeal. Citizenship arose from common allegiance; the Privy Council was visible evidence that British justice prevailed throughout the countries of the Empire. More important, perhaps, were the use of a common flag (the Union Jack) for many purposes, and its incorporation in the four national flags. "God Save the King" as an anthem was also influential. All of these things were imperial symbols. It is not surprising, therefore, that they should have been brandished in any clash between nationalists and imperialists. Canada was still arguing about flags in 1964; Australia still has no anthem of its own; flag and anthem were for decades bones of contention in the struggle for republicanism in South Africa. Only New Zealand has escaped this sort of hubbub. The Judicial Committee has caused some argument, Canada abolishing appeals to it in 1949. Common citizenship lasted till 1946, after which a bewildering variety of laws in the various Dominions produced results which

---

* The position was sometimes different with the Governors of Australian States, who, unlike comparable officials in Canada and South Africa, have remained vice-regal in a special sense, and have usually been imported from Britain.

the layman cannot understand, but which included the disappearance of the British passport as a common phenomenon. However, some Dominion passports continued to look like British ones.

So far in this section we have considered some of the accompaniments of a common Crown, and have seen how these could be both actual institutions and symbolic representations of the British connection. In both aspects they could be attacked and defended by those to whom the British connection was a source of pride or annoyance. Britain stood for many things. To some people it was "home", even if they had never been there; this usage died out first in Canada but still lingers in New Zealand. To others it was the place from which they had escaped to take up a new life, unfettered by rigid social distinctions and poor prospects or permanent poverty. To others again it was the source of a variety of conflicting influences, the embodiment of "tradition" and of the old-established practices which colonial nationalism might challenge but to which it had to pay tribute by its very opposition. All of these contrary possibilities could be caught and focused in the Crown; Monarchy was the British thing.

It is appropriate at this point, before attempting to sum up the effect of the common background, to refer to those aspects of imperial organization which were the expression of the changing common relationship.

Before 1887 there was little or nothing of a common meeting-place for the self-governing colonies. They might be spoken of as constituting a notable group, but the group was never seen together. Britain's relations with the Canadian colonies, with Natal and the Cape, with New Zealand and with the six colonies of Australia, were direct and bi-lateral in each case. The Colonial Office provided common supervision, but it had to deal with Crown Colonies as well, and its concern for the self-governing colonies was relatively slight once they gained control of their internal affairs. Nevertheless, there were theorists to whom the idea of a united empire, on some sort of federal basis, was an inspiration. Stimulated in part by what seemed to be the inherent defeatism of the Cobdenite view that colonies would "cut the painter", and aware of the possibilities for trade and investment latent in the overseas countries, these men laboured for a solution which would preserve and enhance the links that already existed. But the nearest the Empire ever came to possessing its own representative institutions was the series of conferences, first Colonial and later Imperial, which began in 1887 with Queen Victoria's Golden Jubilee.

At first these occurred simply through the accident of colonial politicians' presence in London for great ceremonial occasions such as those of 1887 and 1897. By 1907, with Australia federated into a single nation and South Africa about to be unified, the time had come to recognize some special status for the Four, which were henceforward to be known as Dominions. The Imperial Conference, held regularly from 1911 onwards, was their forum. Their Prime Ministers came to London to hear the British Foreign Secretary outline the foreign policy of the Empire; they also discussed interminably questions of imperial defence, and had muttered to them suggestions for a closer union of the Empire, through the transformation of the conference into some sort of Council, and the creation of a secretariat to conduct its business when it was not sitting. Schemes such as these had been in the mind of Joseph Chamberlain as Colonial Secretary at the turn of the century. They appealed to New Zealand representatives and sometimes to Australian; but they broke first against the immovable force of Sir Wilfrid Laurier's suspicion of institutions which might restrict Canada's freedom of action, and then against the conviction of General Botha that South Africa would not stand such an arrangement. Later Mr. Mackenzie King and General Hertzog enacted the same two roles.

Nevertheless, Imperial Conferences did much to strengthen ties between Britain and the Dominions. They might not have succeeded in creating an entirely satisfactory scheme of imperial defence, but they did pave the way to some extent for 1914.* Their ideas for Imperial cables, shipping lines and airways bore considerable fruit, not least in ensuring, through the cheap cable rate, that news of the outside world should mainly be filtered through London for consumption in South Africa, Australia and New Zealand. They familiarized Dominion leaders with some of the trappings of international intercourse, and encouraged a certain camaraderie. Since the Dominions had little else in the way of foreign relations, their leaders would have been condemned to a steady diet of domestic questions if they had not had to go to an Imperial Conference every four years. It was perhaps a poor substitute for the genuine cut and thrust of international politics; on the other hand, one can argue

---

* However, the Committee of Imperial Defence provided the machinery for a great deal of joint professional effort.

that some training was better than none. Also, the Conference provided an opportunity for slowly and painfully revising constitutional understandings about the status of the Dominions.

The most notable conference from this standpoint was in 1926, when, under pressure from Canada and South Africa, a new definition of the Dominions' status was adopted. It spoke of them and Britain as

"autonomous communities within the British Empire, equal in status, in no way subordinate one to another in any respect of their domestic or external affairs, though united by a common allegiance to the Crown, and freely associated as members of the British Commonwealth of Nations".*

This particular statement, already referred to as a masterpiece of ambiguity, was repeated in the Statute of Westminster of 1931, which attempted to set beyond doubt the legislative competence of the Dominions, and to affirm that the British parliament would not exercise its right to legislate about them unless they asked it. The statute sufficed (and, indeed, still suffices, since no official attempt has been made to change it) to define the status of Canada, Australia and New Zealand. It sufficed for South Africa until that country left the Commonwealth. However, its initial reception differed according to the dominant notion in each Dominion of what relations should be with Britain. In Canada R. B. Bennett, the Conservative Prime Minister, spoke of feeling "the utmost pleasure because I realize that it is the culmination of the long, long effort that has been made since we were a colony to become the self-governing dominion that we now are."† General Smuts in South Africa praised Lord Balfour and Lord Birkenhead for their part in the definition on which the Statute was based:

"These men were not afraid. These men wrote down the grand equation of the commonwealth which equates Great Britain with the dominions. Do not let us boggle over the words. If Great Britain is a sovereign state, then by the laws of Euclid, by the

* From the Report of the Inter-Imperial Relations Committee, Imperial Conference, 1926, Cmd. 2768, p. 14.

† From Bennett's speech of June 30, 1931, moving the request to the King for the enactment of the Statute of Westminster; reprinted in Walter A. Riddell (ed.), *Documents on Canadian Foreign Policy 1917–1939* (Toronto, 1962), p. 153.

laws of thought, the same thing can be applied to any of the dominions. This was not only great statesmanship, but it was great faith in the future of the Empire, of the commonwealth . . . Although some of us may not like the word, some of us may hark back to the past and to what my hon. friend has somewhat ungenerously called the 'Crown colony mentality'—do not let us here in this country do that. Let us have equal faith and equal pride in British institutions and in the nature of the great group to which we belong. Freedom, equality are the essence of it."*

New Zealand's ministers, however, liked none of this development, and the Statute was not adopted there until 1947. It was not accepted in Australia until 1942, when it owed its adoption to an Attorney-General whose approach to Britain was somewhat cooler than his predecessors'. The line taken by the Australian governments of the 1920's was put in harsh terms by R. G. Casey, who had been their liaison officer in London :

"The dominant feature of these post-war Imperial Conferences has been the insistence by certain Dominions of their right to be regarded by the rest of the world as independent entities, or, conversely, their strenuous insistence that none of their business, domestic or internationl, should be decided or even influenced by any suggestion, not to say decision, of the British Government.

The attitude of these Dominions has been implacable and uncompromising—but the narrow logic and relentless insistence of their arguments has (sic) won the day. Thus the common interests of the whole Empire have gone down before the individual claims of the component Dominions. At these four post-war Imperial Conferences we have torn down a castle to build a row of villas . . . Foreigners watched this rapid and pathetic post-war evolution with evident delight."†

But a more directly British view was voiced by Winston Churchill who related his experiences in 1926 :

"I had misgivings that we were needlessly obliterating old, famous landmarks and signposts, which, although archaic, have

---

* General Smuts in the South African House of Assembly on the Status of the Union Bill, April 11, 1934; reprinted in Nicholas Mansergh, *Documents and Speeches on British Commonwealth Affairs 1931–1952* (London, 1953), I, p. 17.
† R. G. Casey, *Australia's Place in the World* (Melbourne, 1931), pp. 9–10.

a historic importance and value. I remember that that great statesman, the late Lord Balfour, with whom I talked this matter over very often, answered me, and to some extent reassured me, by saying, 'I do not believe in wooden guns.' I thought that a very pregnant remark. He saw no advantage in preserving an assertion of rights and powers on which, in practice, we should not find it possible effectively to base ourselves. I still repose faith in the calm, lambent wisdom of that great man in his later years."*

As has often been remarked, the achievement of equal status with Britain did not give the Dominions equal stature; they remained small and inexperienced states on the world scene, and their ties with Britain continued to be effective. What the Statute of Westminster and the achievement of Dominion status did, however, was to render easier the knotty question of the unity of the Crown. When the 1926 statement spoke of them as "united by a common allegiance to the Crown", it did not assert any primacy in the *British* Government's advice to the Monarch in the exercise of the authority of the Crown; and in saying that they were "freely associated" it left open at least the possibility that one or more of them might freely dissociate if it wished. No longer could it be asserted with any confidence that there was only one Crown, that it was indivisible and that it could legitimately operate only through the agency of the British Government. The path lay open for the separate approaches to peace and war which the Dominions were to display in 1939.

The constitutional changes which the Imperial Conferences of the inter-war period agreed on were very much a matter of Dominion pressure, mainly from Canada and South Africa. Australia and New Zealand were mostly opposed, although the Australian Labour Government of 1929–31 (the only one between the wars) was responsible for the clear statement that a Governor-General should be appointed on Dominion advice. What were British attitudes during this time? No significant study has been made in answer to this question; but, if one were made, it would almost certainly reveal that the Dominions were not news in Britain, except as regards sport, and that they were not politics

* Winston Churchill in the House of Commons, November 20, 1931; reprinted in A. Berriedale Keith (ed.), *Speeches and Documents on the British Dominions 1918–1931* (London, 1932), pp. 275–6.

either, in the sense of raising contentious issues. So far as the British political parties were concerned, the Dominions had outgrown argument. They might still be children, in a sense, but their whims must be humoured and their vagaries borne. Their continued growth in population and prosperity, and the intensity with which discussion of the link with Britain often intruded into their politics, made them dangerous creatures to provoke. They could not be coerced, yet it would be a direct blow to British prestige if they absconded. No votes were to be gained by alienating them. It is not surprising, therefore, that British parties preserved a discreet silence about most Dominion issues, and that British governments acquiesced in the demands for status, though always in a manner which prevented the worst consequences from following. The enduring links were retained; troublesome new ones were not forged.

THE POLITICAL PARTIES

The preceding paragraph expresses the state of British politicians' behaviour towards the Four in the inter-war period; but it does not do justice to their attitudes, which were uniformly favourable, except when an occasional Australian politician threatened to default on interest payments or South Africa showed itself especially brutal towards native rights. It is worthwhile noting some of the origins of these favourable attitudes. They arose largely from the general identification of the British people with communities which they did not regard as foreign, but also from special associations. To the British parties of the Right, the Dominions had shown themselves worthy in 1914–18. There were also a good many Conservative and Liberal politicians with associations in the Dominions, especially in South Africa; L. S. Amery was the most active and prominent of these. The Round Table movement, initiated by Lionel Curtis before World War I with the objective of unifying the Empire into a single political unit, had had no success in political persuasion, but continued to exercise an influence out of all proportion to its numbers, through the personal connections between its groups in Britain and those in the Dominions, through *The Round Table* itself, and through another of Curtis's creations, the Royal Institute of International Affairs with its counterparts overseas. The Conservative and Liberal Parties did not have official connections with corresponding parties in the Four (although there were Liberal links with Canada at times), but institutions such as those associated with Curtis, and the growth of bodies like the Empire Press Union and the associations of Chambers of Commerce, enabled men of importance on the Right to make contact.

For the British Labour Party there were special bonds with Labour movements in Australia and New Zealand, and, to a lesser extent, in South Africa. The early leaders of the Australian and New Zealand Labour Parties had in many cases learnt their rudiments from the I.L.P. and its predecessors; Australian trade unions had saved the day with an opportune £30,000 in the great Dock Strike of 1889; a number of people influential in British Labour circles, from Hyndman and H. H. Champion to Tom Mann, the Webbs and George Lansbury, had visited or lived in Australia. Trade Union movements in Australia, New Zealand and South Africa owed their whole structure to British example, sometimes to direct transfer, in distinction from Canada, where the dominant influence became that of American unionism. The achievements of Australian Labour Governments had often been cited as examples (though sometimes awful examples) in the British Labour movement. Efforts to achieve a common front, as for example at the Inter-Commonwealth Labour Conference of 1925, were usually not effective, because each national party was preoccupied with its own people's interests; but George Lansbury was right in referring to

"the genuine traditional affection of the population of the Dominions of Britain and the reciprocating feeling at home. It is a fact, which is true of all classes, that the British people would at all times wish to do good to and to protect in the case of danger, the people whom they still insist on calling colonials. They are pleased at the thought of closer economic, political and military relations with them, though the amount of sacrifice they are prepared to make for this is, despite propaganda, not very great."*

Assessment of the Common Background

Increasingly, in this summary of the common background between Britain and the Four, evidence of divided approaches to that

* George Lansbury, *Labour's Way with the Commonwealth* (London, 1935), pp. 21–2.

background has accumulated. In the chapters immediately following we shall see how those differences arose within the context of each Dominion. Differences of circumstances and social composition often expressed themselves in the context of the British tie, especially since it was often taken to represent established and exploitative economic forces. Just as today there is resentment against "neo-colonialism" in former African and Asian colonies, so in the formative years of the old Dominions there was repulsion as well as attraction in British investment and markets. The "Hoggenheimer" of Afrikaner cartoonists and the "Fat Man" drawn by radicals in Australia might not have much in common, but they both had British money. This kind of underlying resentment against the British, capable of breaking out on the Canadian prairies as well as in the Australian mines, was supplemented in particular situations by Afrikaner and French-Canadian sentiment, by Irish hostility, and by the growth of national feeling and local interests in each of the Four. At the same time, strong "pro-British" feelings also existed. These might in part be encouraged by sheer opposition, e.g. the expressions of loyalty by English-speaking South Africans in the face of Afrikaner nationalist extremism. They might also be aroused by simple protection of property rights: the right wing in Australia and New Zealand has always made more of the Union Jack than the left wing in these most "loyal" Dominions. They might be nourished again by historical experience, as in World War I. But it was fair to say, as Churchill said in 1931 :

> "In all our self-governing Dominions there have been for many years two parties on Imperial questions. One party has set the Imperial connection at its highest; the other has set it at the minimum; and these two parties have disputed against each other in Canada, in Australia, in New Zealand, and in South Africa."*

Yet it is important to recognize how substantial was the British atmosphere within which that dispute took place. Countries which had been mostly settled from Britain, which spoke English, which were parliamentary in their form of government, which had unconsciously absorbed ideas and customs in a great many fields, could not argue about Britain as they might about Russia or Germany or Spain, supposing that their economic connections with those

* A. Berriedale Keith (ed.), *Speeches and Documents on the British Dominions 1918–1931* (London, 1932), p. 275.

countries had been substantial. Even in the case of Afrikaners and French-Canadians, the absence of living contact with the Nether-lands and France meant a divorce from the habits of mind and action of those countries, and some degree of espousal of British modes. Laurier and Botha were symbols of how this reluctant union might bring forth the best fruit.

There was, of course, a fundamental imbalance in the matter of influence. Britain's influence on the Dominions was great, theirs on Britain was only slight. The cricketers came every few years, an occasional comet like Olive Schreiner or Katherine Mansfield streaked across the literary sky, a Bonar Law or Max Aitken might force his way into British politics; but there was no steady impact of Dominion thought or feeling upon the British public. There were caricatures in plenty, of the Mounties getting their man, of the rich uncle from Australia, of

> *the sun that never blisters,*
> *the rain that never chills—*

but there was not much genuine understanding of how the Dominions were developing. An ex-Governor or businessman or general might return to tell the Royal Empire Society what he had seen, but otherwise the English vision of the four was largely re-stricted to their propaganda for markets and migrants, their deeds in war, and the inarticulateness of family connections. All of these things had reality (they were not just fancy), but they had hardly enough reality to create a lasting impression. Britain had, in any case, so much else to worry about. Even in the context of imperial problems, India absorbed far more official attention; outside that context, Europe commanded consideration. There is a sense, still current, in which Britain not only acquired an Empire in a fit of absence of mind, but also retained the beginnings of a Common-wealth through inattention.

2

CANADA

IN this and the next two chapters, I shall deal with the four countries separately, trying to emphasize the special characteristics of each and to indicate those aspects of history and society which have been of direct importance to the connection with Britain. I assume that it is not necessary to provide a complete potted history of any of the Four.

Canada is the oldest of the four Old Dominions, and the one which has figured most prominently in shaping the common relationship between Britain and the Four. The Canadian colonies posed the first problem of free colonists' connection with Britain at the time of the American Revolution; it was in Canada that Lord Durham produced his Report; Canada provided in 1867 the first example of voluntary federal union between self-governing colonies; Canada appointed the first High Commissioner in London; Canadian governments were foremost in the moves which led eventually to some definition of "dominion status"; the relationship with Canada was the model which the British Government offered to Ireland in negotiations for the Treaty of 1921; it is to Canada that the greatest number of British migrants have gone, apart from those who went to the United States. Canadians often sound proprietorial about the Commonwealth of Nations. To a considerable extent they have a right to. But Canada's circumstances, not any particular genius in Canadians as such, have been the main agent in deciding these matters.

As a physical entity, Canada's significant aspects in the context of our concern are its vast size, its relatively small population, its climate, its proximity to the United States, and the fact that it could be reached by emigrant ships more quickly than any of the other Dominions. In human terms, its most significant aspects are again its proximity to the United States, and its possession of some millions of French-Canadians whose cultural traditions are those of New France, not Old England.

The vastness of Canada, bigger than the United States but with only a tenth of the population, has made it constantly aware of the possibilities of growth, and eager for the means to promote that growth. It has had a succession of frontiers. Western Ontario, the North-West, the prairies, the Yukon, the west coast and more lately the recesses of the Laurentian shield have all served as magnets for people and money. There have always been too few people and too little money to perform the task from Canada's own resources; yet Canadians have responded with enthusiasm to schemes such as Sir John Macdonald's "National Policy", which promised to get the task done under Canadian control. The attempt to employ the federal government as a nation-making agent, stimulating econ- omic growth and through it national identity, has been a theme in Canadian affairs for a century. The rationale of it is that, if Canada is to mean anything as a nation, it must not be simply an extension of the U.S. economy.

This cogent position has frequently been undermined by the facts of Canadian economic life. Apart from the fact that Canadian industry owes most of its modern growth to American money and management, much of the Canadian economy can be understood only in terms of parallel development in the United States. For example, the settlement of the prairies is of a piece with that of the Dakotas: the stress of vacant land in combination with a rising world demand for wheat explains both. It would be ludicrous for any "National Policy" to claim all the credit. The main difference, in the absence of a nationalistic Canadian Government, would have been that the railways which carried the wheat ran to American instead of Canadian terminals. Much the same settlement would have taken place, financed in much the same way and carried out by much the same people. To satisfy the urge towards national identity, Canadians have had to find reasons why activity north of the border should be regarded as distinctively different from similar activity south of it. The difficulty has been heightened because, in spite of Macdonald's national policy, the lines of action have run north-south rather than east-west: the Maritime Provinces tradi- tionally trade with New England, the economy of Ontario owes much to that of the Middle West, the prairies have their counter- parts to the south, and British Columbia's closest affinities are with Oregon and Washington. The situation is dramatized by Wallace Stegner in his account of his boyhood in the 1910's in western Saskatchewan, near the frontier.

"In winter, in the town on the Whitemud, we were almost

totally Canadian. The textbooks we used in school were published in Toronto and made by Canadians or Englishmen; the geography we studied was focused on the Empire and the Dominion, though like our history it never came far enough west, and was about as useless to us as the occasional Canadian poem that was inserted patriotically into our curriculum . . . The songs we sang were 'Tipperary' and 'We'll Never Let the Old Flag Fall' and 'The Maple Leaf Forever' and 'God Save the King'; the flag we saluted was the Union Jack, the heroes we most revered belonged to the Canadian regiment called the Princess Pats, the clothes and Christmas gifts we bought by mail came from the T. Eaton mail-order house . . . Our holidays apart from Thanksgiving and Christmas, which were international, were Dominion Day, Victoria Day, the King's birthday."

This was in the winter, when the family sought the shelter of town. But in the summer it went to its homestead on the plains, and

". . . our lives slopped over the international boundary every summer day . . . The magazines to which we now subscribed were American magazines, the newspapers we read were published in Havre, Great Falls, even Minneapolis. The funny paper characters to whom I devoted charmed afternoons were Happy Hooligan, the Katzenjammer Kids, Hairbreadth Harry, Alphonse and Gaston—all made in the U.S. Our summer holidays were the Fourth of July and Labor Day . . . when we bought anything by mail, we bought it not from T. Eaton but from the lavish and cosmopolitan catalogs of Sears Roebuck and Montgomery Ward . . .

Winter and summer were at odds in us. We were Americans without the education and indoctrination that would have made us confident of our identity, we were Canadians in everything but our sentimental and patriotic commitment."*

The realities of closeness and economic interdependence have meant that only an economic policy which was rigidly self-denying could have forced Canadians to orientate themselves east to west instead of north to south. Such a policy would have been self-defeating as well as self-denying if carried out with any rigour, since those Canadians who did not accept its postulates could readily have

* Wallace Stegner, *Wolf Willow* (London, 1964), pp. 80–82.

found homes for themselves across the border; emigration from Canada to the United States is the easiest in the world.

All the same, there have been continual attempts to circumvent economic tendencies at the political level, though never too harshly. Reciprocity in one form or another has been defeated whenever the Canadian electorate was actually offered it. Macdonald's triumph in 1891 and Borden's in 1911 were paralleled by Diefenbaker's in 1958. Canadians have, it seems, seen no reason to make consistency an over-riding political virtue: faced with their economic dependence on the United States, they have refused to accept what many Americans would regard as the logical consequences. They have remained obstinately Canadian, different enough to be distinct.

First amongst the reasons for this obstinacy is the composition of the Canadian population. English-speaking Canadians are the residue of a very substantial immigration into Canada from the British Isles; between 1871 and 1951 their numbers grew from just over two millions to rather more than eight millions. To call them a residue, however, is historically accurate, since something like the same number of migrants moved on to the United States as stayed in Canada. Those who remained can be presumed to have done so because, in one way or another, Canada suited them. Much the same is true of the million or so of "new" stock (German, Dutch, Italian, Ukrainian, Scandinavian, Polish, etc.) by which the Canadian population was enriched in the same period. The French-Canadians, who increased in the same ratio as the English-speakers (from just over one million to just over four) between 1871 and 1951, did so entirely through natural increase; immigration from France has been negligible.* They showed a much greater readiness to stay in Canada than the English-speakers, although some have disseminated themselves into neighbouring states of the U.S.A. It seems fair to suggest that the English-Canadians† are in Canada because they prefer it to the United States, on grounds of either traditional attachment or individual advantage; that the "new" Canadians are there because of connection with existing settlements of their own peoples and individual advantage; and that the

* These rough figures on Canadian population are from the graphs in A. R. M. Lower, *Canadians in the Making* (Toronto, 1958), p. 386.

† This inaccurate expression will be used hereafter as Canadians use it, to describe the Canadians whose mother-tongue is English, in spite of its implied insult to Canadians of Scots, Irish and Welsh descent.

D

French-Canadians are there because of a French Canada which shares its characteristics with nowhere else.

The next relevant point about the population is that English and French-Canadians have, by their juxtaposition over two centuries, achieved a set of relationships which has no counterpart in the United States. These relationships have set the tone and habit of most Canadian politics. There is a sense in which Canadians have had to spend so much time worrying about relations amongst themselves that they have not been able to spare much attention for issues relating to the United States. Despite Goldwin Smith's belief in union with the U.S.A. because "the primary forces will in the end prevail",* they have given more attention to getting on together than to finding a more directly logical connection with the United States. Put another way, the "primary forces" have not been those which seemed obvious to Goldwin Smith, but those of immediate and local concern in Canada itself.

The lines of these primary forces were set soon after the British conquest of New France in 1760. As Lower says,

> "The English-Canadian schoolchild has always been told about the way in which the Highlanders, that first hard winter, cut firewood for the nuns and the nuns knitted long stockings for the Highlanders; but French schoolchildren have probably had the seamier side of conquest carefully explained to them, and many French historians have stressed it. Tales of the ravaging and burning that accompanied the last campaigns are said to be still repeated round the winter fire . . ."†

The defeated French soon became set in a defensive posture, in which the preservation of their laws, church, language and customs remained a prime objective. English-Canadians, as they grew more numerous, often identified their position as legatees of the conquest with an innate superiority over their French-speaking neighbours. It was easy to ally oneself with Lord Durham: "And is this French-Canadian nationality one which, for the good merely of that people, we ought to strive to perpetuate, even if it were possible? I know of no national distinctions marking and continuing a more hopeless inferiority."‡

* Goldwin Smith, *Canada and the Canadian Question* (London, 1891), p. ix.
† Lower, op. cit., p. 117.
‡ *The Report of the Earl of Durham* (reprinted London, 1902), pp. 215–16.

In the ensuing hundred years it became all too easy for the two sections to fail to comprehend one another, in spite of a good deal of coalition at the level of national politics. Baldwin and Lafontaine were able to work together in the Reform Party of the 1840's, to win responsible government after the Durham Report. During the period of the Union of Upper and Lower Canada, which ended with Confederation in 1867, the parties were not divided on a strict English–French basis, and Macdonald owed his success in putting through Confederation to his ability to work with the Quebec leader, George Cartier. In 1896 Canada achieved its first French-Canadian Prime Minister, Laurier. In the 1920's and 30's Mackenzie King owed much of his success at perpetual government to his alliance with Lapointe. In all these cases there was a "composite party, with membership from the two races", but "always in a state of internal tension . . . frequently torn by dissension. Its unity [was] always somewhat doubtful, for French and English find it difficult to understand each other even when they can speak one another's language."* In 1940 the American Minister to Ottawa recorded in his diary that "to one unfamiliar to Canada the gulf between French-Canadian and British-Canadian is a constant source of wonder".† In spite of the century's tradition of the "composite party", he thought Mackenzie King the only one of the outstanding English-Canadian leaders who trusted, and consequently was trusted by, the French-Canadian.‡

The roots of this lack of trust lay in difference of economic function, of religious belief, of basic philosophy. More has been made of the latter two of these than of the first, yet one can argue that it was the first which perpetuated and intensified the division between the two sorts of Canadians. In 1867, when the British North America Act was passed, the two groups were not so different in economic function and standards of living as they later became. The small farmer was the mainstay of both. In the decades of development which followed, the English-Canadians spread out, both in area and in function, while the French-Canadians stayed more in Quebec. Their movement was from country to town or from Quebec to neighbouring states of the U.S.A., rather than to other parts of Canada. They were to be found in the western

* Frank H. Underhill, *The Image of Confederation* (Toronto, 1964), p. 54.
† Nancy Harvison Hooker (ed.), *The Moffat Papers* (Cambridge, Mass., 1956), p. 339.
‡ Ibid., pp. 339–40.

provinces at first, but others soon outnumbered them. As the rest of
Canada moved into the first stages of industrialism, Quebec tended
to hug its isolation and make a distinctive virtue of its rural and
Catholic background. *Notre maître, le passé* could be seriously
propounded as a slogan by Canon Lionel Groulx. The simplicities
of *Maria Chapdelaine* expressed French-Canadian orthodoxy with
charm and fervour. English-Canadian businessmen outdistanced
their French-Canadian counterparts; Montreal might be governed
by those who spoke French, but its money spoke English. In reply,
French Canada seemed to reject the modern world. Its propagandists stressed its other-worldly characteristics, its concern for
home, church and family, its devotion to language and custom, both
at variance with the North American norm, its emphatic disavowal
of the secularist tendencies in France itself.

Yet this propagandist stereotype should not be accepted as entirely factual. Whatever might be true of the other parts of the
traditionalist picture, the rural aspect became less so. "In 1901,
40 per cent of the population of Quebec lived in cities; in 1911,
the proportion had risen to 48 per cent; another 8 per cent had
been added in 1921; the figure was 63 per cent in 1931 and 67 per
cent in 1951."[*] Urbanization set up tensions between French- and
English-Canadians; eventually it led to the assertion of a purposeful Quebec nationalism, even to a separatist movement. The more
traditional form of French-Canadian protest, however, was resentment at Canadian entanglement abroad. Quebec reacted, not as a
partner in English-Canadian enterprises, but as a violent opponent.
Laurier's decision to send Canadian troops to the Boer War because
of the intense desire of English-Canadians that he should, was
countered by Henri Bourassa's vehement opposition; both on this
occasion and in the conscription crisis of World War I, Quebec
found its wishes cutting across those of the most imperially-minded
(and in these instances the most representative, at any rate the most
determined) of their fellow-Canadians. We can at this point appro-
priately introduce "imperialism" as a Canadian phenomenon.

In part, "imperial" thinking in Canada has been a matter of
simple reaction against the French-Canadian presence, an assertion
(some would think an over-assertion) of Britishness in the face of
an alien civilization. There is a sense in which the English-speaking

---

[*] Ramsay Cook, "Quebec: The Ideology of Survival", in A. Rotstein, *The
Prospect of Change* (Toronto, 1965), p. 44. This article provides a useful anti-
dote to much of the conventional treatment of French Canada.

people in South Africa, Kenya and Southern Rhodesia were all more English than the English before they received their mortal shocks of the 1960's; as minorities which had achieved temporary ascendancy over alien majorities through conquest or the reserve of power embodied in British overlordship, they used British symbols as badges and talismans to assert their identity and preserve themselves against harm from their temporarily subjugated neighbours. In a rather similar way, many English-Canadians, notably in Ontario, extended their British origins into politics to the point of claiming identity with Britain and superiority over their French neighbours. In the harsh times of Queen Victoria the matter might express itself most clearly in the thunderings of George Brown from the Toronto *Globe* and in the breaking of heads by Orange mobs in the street; in the Boer War, in World War I (and to some extent in World War II) it expressed itself in the idea of Empire unity and a conviction that Canada ought to fight on Britain's side whatever the quarrel. French-Canadian opposition, typified by Bourassa, only served to intensify this feeling.

One can say, then, that the presence of the French-Canadians has been one major source of motivation for English-Canadian imperial sentiment. But it is important also to recognize the United States as a further source. The United Empire Loyalists brought with them from the Revolutionary War the sense of an outraged British loyalty. The excesses of the U.S. troops in the war of 1812 left a considerable impression behind (in Quebec as well as in the English-speaking areas). The dangers of the American Civil War gave an impetus to Confederation. The determination of Theodore Roosevelt to get the most out of Canada, as in the Alaska Boundary question of 1903, made the United States unpopular with many emotional Canadians. Macdonald was able to win an election in 1891 with the slogan, "A British subject I was born, a British subject I shall die";* and Borden's party did the same in 1911 with "no truck nor trade with the Yankees". Whenever American politicians talked of Canada as an "adjunct" to the United States, they stirred the latent patriotism of English-speaking Canadians, to whom the British connection became simultaneously a symbol of

* Although Professor Underhill points out that Macdonald, dying soon after the election, was buried in a casket imported from West Meriden, Connecticut; it was an exact replica of that in which President Garfield had been buried not long before. North Americanism prevailed in the end. (Frank H. Underhill, *The Image of Confederation* (Toronto, 1964), p. 34.)

the past and an emblem of the difference which marked Canada off from the rest of North America.

It is now possible to see something of the internal circumstances which have made Canada separate from the United States, provided the basis of much of local politics, and given emotional significance to the tie with Britain. Even without the presence of the French-Canadians, the proximity of the United States would certainly have bred in Canada a political reaction, a sense of local difference, in spite (and to a great extent because) of Canada's economic dependence on the United States. The experiences of the past would have attained something of the same mythical quality as they did in fact achieve. But Canadian national sentiment on the English-speaking side might have been more diffuse, less British-centred, and more attached to local symbols—might have developed earlier, in fact, to something such as it is today. The presence of the French gave it a local habitation which was more Protestant and "racial" than it need have been; moreover, directly domestic differences such as those over religion became easily merged with a national image which, to be effective in international terms, would have needed to be more closely connected with the realities of the whole of Canada, not simply the prejudices of Ontario. Something like this has now occurred: those who are trying to establish a distinctive Canadian identity recognize the need to include the distinctiveness of French Canada and the diversity of New Canadian immigration if they are to have something to set against the dynamism of the United States.

However, in the formative periods of Canadian politics, two exclusive nationalisms were in fact produced. One was the protective provincialism of the *Canadiens*, the other the mixture of English, Scots and Northern Irish pugnacity which embodied itself in imperialism. Men of good will stood apart from the worst excesses of these two attitudes: Canada is fortunate that leaders such as Macdonald, Laurier, Borden and Mackenzie King pushed forward the notion of Canada as an entity composed of two traditions which must be reconciled. But we must recognize that much of the fire in Canadian politics, especially in time of war, has been kindled by the friction between the two traditions. Furthermore, much of the conventional feelings about Britain and the British connection has been forged in this fire. Britain has been a set-off to the United States in the often postulated "North Atlantic Triangle"; it has also been a lay figure which indignant English-Canadians could

use to extol their own virtues at the expense of their French neighbours. In the glare of these two images, the quieter but more permanent significance of Britain as a fount of customs and ideas has
often not been properly seen.

Let us now look at the relevant elements of Canadian-British
relations, as these shaped themselves in terms of the constitution,
the economy, and the problem of status.

The constitutional relationship between Britain and Canada is
closer than with any of the other Dominions, and is peculiar in its
own right. Whereas the constitutions of Australia, New Zealand
and South Africa contained all the necessary seeds of change within themselves, that of Canada, as embodied in the British North
America Act of 1867, did not. The need to entrench the rights of
the French-Canadians to language, school and church meant the
guarantee of rights to a permanent minority; any change in the constitution by means of majorities, however arrived at, might have
threatened this entrenchment. The need for some means of domestic
change in the constitution probably did not seem so important in
the 1860's as it became later, since the whole tendency of the discussion preceding Confederation was in the direction of a strong
federal government whose residuary powers would enable it to
take whatever steps might be necessary to deal with new problems.
In such circumstances it was not surprising that the task of amend-
ment should have been left to the British parliament, which had
shown itself amenable to Canadian wishes in the actual drafting of
the Act, and might be expected to be so again. In addition, it is
important to stress the symbolic aspects of the process of legislation by the British parliament to provide a constitution for the
whole of Canada. While the Speech from the Throne at the opening of the first new Canadian parliament in 1867 referred to
the British North America Act as having "laid the foundation of a
new nationality", that nationality was essentially monarchical in
character, and all articulate sections of opinion wanted it to be so.
The desire not to be identified with the United States had been
one of the motive forces behind the move for Confederation, which
was seen, not as a means of breaking away from Britain, but as a
way to greater opportunity for specifically Canadian development,
in close combination with Britain.

Constitutional difficulties have arisen, not from the power of
the British parliament to legislate for Canada (it has done so only
when asked, and Canadians have seldom asked it), but from the

power of review of the Judicial Committee of the Privy Council. At first this body took much the same view of the constitution's meaning as those who had drawn it up; but in the 1890's, through the agency of Lord Watson, in the 1920's through Lord Haldane, and again in 1937, it negated a great many efforts at federal legislation because these seemed to conflict with the obligation under Section 92 to preserve the provinces' right to legislate upon "property and civil rights in the Province".* The Judicial Committee gained a bad reputation in Canada as a collection of British judges who knew about neither federalism nor Canada; but it could be argued on their behalf that they had not asked to interpret the Canadian constitution, and that, if the Canadians could agree on someone else to supersede them, they would be glad to withdraw from the task. It became, on the contrary, all too clear, as the working shape of the constitution changed under the pressure of the Judicial Committee, that Canadian interests could not be harmonized so as to provide either amendments to the constitution or an agreed means of achieving amendments by domestic means. It is probable that Britain itself suffered little in Canadian esteem through the activities of the Privy Council. The root of the difficulty lay so clearly in Canada itself. Canada had been made a unit in 1867, but not a unity: the original provincial distinctions between the Maritime Provinces, Quebec and Ontario were reinforced in due course by the divergencies introduced through the entry of the prairie provinces and British Columbia. In political terms, the constitution became increasingly a means of preserving the autonomy of the provinces. The original aim of a strong federal government which would exercise surveillance over the provinces was thrust aside by new political forces. The constitution might have been intended to institute "a new nationality", but its effect was more to strengthen the differences between the widely separated areas of Canada. It is tempting to speculate that if social and economic affairs had been more the affair of the federal government, federal politics might have escaped some of the exhausting arguments over "status" which troubled it between the wars. However, the legacy of bitterness from the conscription issue in World War I would have been difficult to evade under any circumstances.

We may contrast the lack of resentment in Canada against

* It is a coincidence, but a confusing one for the student, that the section of the Australian constitution which has caused the most trouble is also Section 92.

Britain over the Privy Council decisions, with the storm of protest which arose over the Alaska boundary decision of 1903, where the decision of a single British nominee, widely believed to be under some influence from the British Government, secured a result which was detrimental to Canada. Here a direct political influence was held to be at work. Clearly, not all forms of connection between Britain and Canada have been equally important in setting the tone of relations between the two countries. The Alaska situation was directly influential in this sense; the Privy Council was supplementary. To a considerable extent, something of the same is true of economic relations between the two countries in the half-century or so after Confederation. There was no direct and purposeful attempt on Britain's part to push investment in Canada; the London money market was open to all who wished to come and bid in it, and Canada was not treated differently from others. "Jumbo, the big elephant bought by Barnum, is a matter of ten times more interest to London than twenty colonies," wrote George Stephen bitterly to Sir John Macdonald when he was trying to raise money for the Canadian Pacific Railway.* Similarly, when the Laurier Government enacted a system of preference for British goods in 1897, there was no response from Britain. The British Government might bestir itself when it saw an opportunity to get rid of some turbulent Irish paupers by paying the Canadian Government a million pounds; but this was hardly the kind of initiative which Canada could welcome without qualification.† It cannot be said that any British Government in the nineteenth century showed much desire to help or hinder Canada's economic development. To a great extent, this state of affairs must be credited to the generally *laissez-faire* approach to the colonies. It did, at any rate, prevent Canada from building up a significant tradition of dislike of British capital.

The British proposals which did cause difficulty were those associated with the name of Joseph Chamberlain, in his earlier period as Secretary of State for the Colonies, and in his later period out of office when he was trying to persuade Britain to adopt Tariff Reform. Chamberlain's schemes were for a combination of Empire trade, Empire defence, and some form of Empire Council. The resistance in Canada to these propositions was not primarily to their

* Donald G. Creighton, *Dominion of the North* (Boston, 1944), p. 349.
† The offer was made in 1883. Donald Creighton, *John A. Macdonald: The Old Chieftain* (Boston, 1956), pp. 350–51.

economic aspect. On its own, this might have proved acceptable to Sir Wilfrid Laurier and his supporters.* It was the possibility of tighter imperial control over Canada, of the participation of Canadians in war being a matter for decision in London, and of Canada's policies (such as those on immigration) being decided by forces outside North America, that deterred Laurier. There was no primacy to economics in this situation; Canadian nationalism was affronted by the apparent attempt to limit Canada's status.

In trying to understand the Canadian quest for "status" we come to the heart of the problem of relations between Britain and Canada in the period before World War II. Canadians were not keenly dissatified with the Monarchy, with the arrangements for their constitution, or with the economic relationship between the two countries. Those who were troubled were concerned about whether Canadian *policy* was being taken out of the hands of Canada's elected representatives and placed in those of the British Government. This was at the heart of Laurier's caution about schemes of "centralization"; it was what Borden objected to in World War I; and it was the fear that impelled Mackenzie King to be so awkward in imperial discussions when it was proposed to have a concerted Empire policy on almost anything. On King's visit to London as a young Deputy Minister in 1908 he wrote in his diary:

"There is in England a real *Governing* class, in the sense that it seeks to control and actually does control and guide the national interests both in England and in the Dominions beyond. The English mind has been so long trained in this way of looking at the world that I can see wherein it will be many years before it will ever come to actually appreciate what self-government means."†

On the same visit King attended a dinner of the Patriots Club, "including many of the leading Imperialists in England". There were some heady speeches about the need for the Empire to act as

* See the fascinating account in W. A. S. Hewins, *The Apologia of an Imperialist* (London, 1929), I, Ch. V, of Hewins's visit to Canada as Chamberlain's emissary in 1905, and of his long conversations with Laurier, who was then Prime Minister.

† Quoted in R. MacGregor Dawson, *William Lyon Mackenzie King: A Political Biography 1874–1923* (London, 1958), p. 168.

one. A certain speaker mentioned some of Laurier's actions as evidence of growing independence and disruption of the Empire. King boiled with rage, but silently; in his diary he wrote that he had been "little by little becoming more exasperated at the misunderstanding of Canadian motives by the imperialist group", and added :

"What was borne in on me particularly in listening to Lord Milner and the speeches of others was that it was not so much the welfare of human happiness irrespective of their race and creed, as the furtherance of the power and strength of the British race that constitutes the main purpose in their programme. Adam Smith, in his doctrine of *laissez faire* believed that man's self-love was God's providence—so the Englishman believes that in British rule the working out of God's will may come about . . .

Tonight's gathering has impressed me more than any event in connection with this present trip. I feel that it has added a permanent something to such political capital as I may possess."*

The final words were significant. King had learnt his main line from Laurier; but experience of the kind mentioned here confirmed what he had learnt, and gave him extra reason for suspecting the motives of the British Government when it suggested closer connection. The Dominion of Canada had been founded in the expectation of dignity and of near-equality with Britain; Sir John Macdonald had wanted it called a "Kingdom", and he had envisaged a situation in which

"England, instead of looking upon us as a merely dependent colony, will have in us a friendly nation—a subordinate but still a powerful people—to stand by her in North America in peace or war. The people of Australia will be such another subordinate nation. And England will have this advantage, if her colonies progress under the new colonial system, as I believe they will, that, though at war with all the rest of the world, she will be able to look to the subordinate nations in alliance with her, and owing allegiance to the same sovereign . . ."†

* Ibid., pp. 168–70
† Speech of February 6, 1865. See W. P. M. Kennedy (ed.), *Statutes, Treaties and Documents of the Canadian Constitution 1713–1929* (Toronto, 1930), p. 568.

The sense of "alliance" was strong in Macdonald's thinking, and he had rejected any notion that Canada was obliged to contribute soldiers to the British effort in the Sudan unless it was so inclined. Laurier, at the time of the Boer War, formulated the same idea, but felt constrained to contribute troops because of the force of feeling amongst English-Canadians. By the time King came to confide his thoughts to his diary, the notion of Canadian autonomy seemed to be under heavy fire: at Imperial Conferences Laurier had been pressed to accept a greater degree of centralization than he thought was in Canada's interests; Lionel Curtis and his Round Table groups seemed to be perpetually interfering in imperial affairs; a strong section of the Tory party in Britain wanted closer union, directed from above; and in Canada itself there was sympathy towards the idea of closer union on the part of those who stressed the "British" character of Canada, and were hostile to policies based upon the bi-racial and autonomous elements in the Canadian situation.

Arguments on this basis dragged themselves through the 1900's and 1910's in Canada, culminating in the bitter struggle over conscription, which split Laurier's Liberal Party, antagonized Quebec and led directly to its separatism in the period between the wars, and had such influence upon the formulation of Canadian attitudes and policy towards the League of Nations, rearmament, relations with the United States, imperial foreign policy, and the question of status. A letter from Laurier in 1917 conveys an emotional picture of the atmosphere of the time:

"Toryism has obtained an enormous influence in Ontario. In fact, Ontario is no longer Ontario: it is again the old small province of Upper Canada, and again governed from London. There is only one difference and the difference is only in the name. Upper Canada was governed from Downing Street with the instrumentality of the Family Compact sitting at York, now Toronto. Canada is now governed by a junta sitting at London, known as "The Round Table", with ramifications in Toronto, in Winnipeg, in Victoria, with Tories and Grits receiving their ideas from London, and insidiously forcing them on their respective parties. As to the Tories, I am not surprised, they are in their element, true to the instincts of their nature, to the traditions of their ancestors, but for the Grits, oh! for the old spirit of sturdy

Liberalism which still prevailed in my youth! Truly, I have lived too long."*

This letter draws attention to a point already made, that "imperialism" as a factor in Canadian-British relations cannot be regarded as simply a matter of a united Canada on the one hand and Britain itself on the other. It is true that, in both King's case in 1908 and Laurier's in 1917, influential groups in Britain were trying to bind Canada closer to British policy; true also that in Macdonald's case in the 1860's and 1880's no such group was actively at work, Macdonald thus being able to assert a degree of autonomy which no one of importance in Britain wished to rebut. But the point that matters most in Laurier's description is his recognition of imperialist ideas as a factor in Canadian domestic politics. Ontario was on its Protestant rampage; Quebec was condemned as unpatriotic because of its refusal to accept the Ontario interpretation of the obligation of a British subject. The primary division within Canada was the occasion for the assertion of British righteousness. It was easy for Laurier to incorporate Canadian Toryism into its British equivalent, and credit both with schemes for limitation of full Canadian autonomy.

At the same time as this febrile situation existed in Canada, Sir Robert Borden, the Conservative Prime Minister, was attempting to obtain in Britain itself what he regarded as a proper recognition of Canada's status. He wanted Canada to be fully consulted in the conduct of the war, to be a signatory of the Peace Treaty, and to be able to conduct its own foreign affairs (i.e. those which directly concerned itself) without interference. His position on "status" was not greatly different from Laurier's or King's.† In the heat of political fight he was no doubt at odds with them, but the difference was much more of emphasis in particular situations than of kind. He too was anxious to avoid a return to the days of "colonialism" when Canada was treated as an immature child. The fact that he had to deal with relations with Britain as part of the practical task of carrying on a war gave his treatment of "status" a particular twist: but in retrospect his approach seems very different from that of his most fervent English-Canadian supporters.

---

* Letter to Sir Allen Aylesworth of May 15, 1917, in O. D. Skelton, *Life and Letters of Sir Wilfrid Laurier* (New York, 1922), II, p. 510.

† See, e.g. his endorsement of the changes in imperial relations in the 1920's in R. L. Borden, *Canada in the Commonwealth* (Oxford, 1929), Ch. XIV.

I have given this extended treatment to "status" because of its great importance in Canadian politics in the thirty years before World War II, but I have tried to deal with attitudes of mind rather than the actual passage of events, since they seem to me to be much more important. Canada contained, as it were, a set of built-in social differences which expressed themselves, from time to time, in terms of the "status" Canada should enjoy as against Britain. The primary difference was between English-Canadians and French-Canadians. There was another between those who wished to stress the character of Canadians as essentially British and those who wished it to be recognized as Canadian. These two differences overlapped. There was also the indefinable influence of living so close to the United States. Sometimes this might stimulate Canadian consciousness, sometimes weaken it; the sense of connection with Britain might also be heightened or diminished. The presence of the United States did hasten demands for formal Canadian autonomy in treaty-making, because of the inconvenience and indignity of carrying on negotiations through the British; also, however, it strengthened monarchical sentiment and respect for certain British institutions (parliament, "law and order", etc.) in Canada. Canada would have been forced in any case to seek definition and enlargement of its status, in order to stand up to American pressure. It was unfortunate for Britain that this particular need became entangled with questions of "loyalty"; much might have been easier if Macdonald's original "Kingdom" concept had been steadily adhered to on both sides. But we must also put some of the blame for mutual misunderstanding and for Canadian reserve on imperialist sentiment in Britain, especially on the meddling Curtis and his associates. Intent on their own vision of what the Empire might become, they were inclined to move the Dominions around as pawns on their board. Their influence was not great, but unfortunately it *seemed* to be great at the very times when Canadian suspicions were most pronounced. Not all Englishmen, amongst the few who gave thought to such matters, reasoned as they did;* but their adverse influence on men like Laurier and King seems to have been out of all proportion to their influence at home.

---

* In *Richard Jebb and the Problem of Empire* (London, 1956), I have tried to show that there was another side to British imperialist thinking in the first decade of this century. Jebb's *Studies in Colonial Nationalism* (London, 1905) remains one of the best efforts by a contemporary Englishman at understanding the Laurier line.

Some blame also attaches to the endemic British inclination to treat Canadians as peculiar, if not disloyal, because they have so many connections with the United States and sound like Americans. It would be difficult to know less about a country than the man in the street in Britain knows about Canada. Only in wartime, when Canadians have come to help Britain fight, have they been given more than cursory attention. Perhaps this is because they play none of the sports that appeal to British people. British coolness and ignorance are still to be found in the upper reaches of society; they must have been even more frequent in the formative period (say, between 1880 and 1930) when Canada seemed peculiar because of its Frenchmen, suspect for its statements about autonomy, and potentially disloyal because of its closeness to the United States. The Canadian High Commissioner in London in the 1920's reported to his Prime Minister that he left British Ministers "with the conviction that in their hearts they have the same feeling towards me that they would have towards a child". He did not think much of their capacity :

". . . I would be sorry indeed if I did not think that Canadian affairs were not in more competent hands—men with, on the whole, more serious minds. We have, certainly, during the past few years, made some strides forward—the strides that a capable son should and must make if he is to obtain and keep the respect of his parents, but I will never be satisfied until they look upon Canada, if not with the deference they show our neighbours, at least with as much respect as they show to a South American Republic.

The statesmen here will find a hundred reasons, if necessary, to keep us in what they consider our proper position; reasons that obtained a hundred years ago. It accords better with their dignity that we should continue in the eyes of the world as dependents . . ."*

There was, of course, no active hostility towards Canada; it had done the right thing in the war, and its people were friendly if backward. The Canadians themselves, in imperial negotiations, were not always easy; the duchess embrace was suspected by many of their emissaries, while others succumbed to it with pleasure. Observing

* Letters from P. C. Larkin to Mackenzie King, 1922 and 1928, quoted in James Eayrs, *In Defence of Canada* (Toronto, 1964), pp. 14–15.

his fellow-Canadians in the throes of the 1926 Imperial Conference, a Canadian journalist wrote to his editor, "Maybe I am all wrong but it would be like a breath of fresh air to hear somebody get plain Canadian and call something a son of a bitch." None of the Canadian delegates obliged him. But, on leaving London, he was mollified by his final experiences amongst the English : "They're a queer lot over here, very laughable at times but at others revealing fine bits of character and conduct."* Perhaps this is a suitable commentary on the relationship.

* Extracts from letters from D. B. MacRae to J. W. Dafoe, quoted in Ramsay Cook, "A Canadian Account of the 1926 Imperial Conference", in *Journal of Commonwealth Political Studies,* Vol. III, No. 1 (March, 1965), pp. 58 and 62.

3

AUSTRALIA AND NEW ZEALAND

AUSTRALIA and New Zealand are the British "colonies" *par excellence*—peopled very largely by British stock, closely attached throughout many vicissitudes to Britain, and displaying in their social life qualities which foreigners immediately recognize as British. It is easy for the observer to think of them as carbon copies of Britain, especially when he compares them with countries such as India, to which British institutions were transplanted but in which the local soil was alien in so many respects. Yet Australians and New Zealanders, while admitting their close ties to Britain, have never thought of themselves as carbon copies of the British; even when describing themselves as "British", they have often added some qualifying phrase, such as "in a new land" or "under the Southern Cross". They have usually claimed the best aspects of Britain as their heritage, while rejecting those which they did not like or which did not seem appropriate to their southern surroundings. Conversely, much of the nationalism that has developed in Australia and New Zealand has done so largely in opposition, not so much to Britain itself, as to British symbols of royalty, nobility and privilege.

The situation of these two countries has always, in a sense, been simpler than that of Canada, since British settlement did not encounter another European group in possession when it began, there was no dominant neighbour near by in any way comparable to the United States, and the two countries were so far away from both Britain and Europe that whatever influences became localized were isolated from cross-currents which might complicate their social development. Yet it can be argued that, in the long run, their situation might prove more difficult than Canada's, in two ways. One is that the very absence of the factors which induced strong national feeling in Canada delayed its appearance in Australia and New Zealand; any assertion of a nationalistic point of view could long be attacked there on grounds of "disloyalty". The notion of a "British race" could be applied more plausibly in Australia and New Zealand than in Canada, because of the composition of

E

the population. Nationalism emerged more slowly, since it had less to grow on. When it did come, it came in response to catastrophe, such as the depression of the 1930's and the disasters at Singapore in 1942, and brought considerable disturbance with it.

The other way in which the growth of nationalism in Australia and New Zealand might prove more difficult than in Canada is that, while these countries have no strong immediate neighbour to react against, they have the harsher situation of being European outgrowths along a branch of Asia: as Asian strength increases, and as it becomes in some aspects more hostile towards the West, the position of Australia and New Zealand may look more anomalous and more dangerous. Nationalism can be expected to grow in such circumstances, but not with the same comforting concentration upon domestic differences as in Canada.

There are solid reasons why Australia and New Zealand should so often be regarded as the most British of the Commonwealth countries, whether one takes the Commonwealth in its emergent form of the 1920's or in its multiform of the 1960's. The main one, as everyone knows, is the composition of their population. Until after World War II, there had been no substantial immigration into either country from anywhere but the British Isles; even now, British immigration into Australia each year roughly equals continental European, and it still provides the bulk of immigration into New Zealand. It used to be said that these countries were "98 per cent British". There were aborigines in Australia, but these did not count.* The Maoris in New Zealand have fared much better, because of their greater numbers and adaptability, but their presence never lessened the Britishness of the *pakeha*.

Along with this reliance on Britain for population went the cluster of institutions already discussed in Chapter 1. These applied with special force to Australia and New Zealand. Public and private institutions were transplanted and immediately took root: the parliaments of the two countries are still very close to the Westminster model, their public services and systems of justice operate along much the same lines, their education systems have followed British models very closely, and their churches are the British churches unaltered except in regard to establishment. The great

---

* Even literally; the Australian Constitution contains a Section (127) stating "In reckoning the numbers of the people of the Commonwealth [of Australia], or of a State or other part of the Commonwealth, aboriginal natives shall not be counted".

exception which most Australians and New Zealanders would make to the statement that they had adopted British institutions lies in what they would call "social snobbery". The exception needs to be discounted: both countries still import British Governors and Governors-General, and preserve much the same conventions and atmosphere in the impact of these dignitaries upon local society as in colonial times. Moreover, both have found the knighthood a useful reward for public and political services. Undoubtedly, too, there has always been a great deal of social gradation, with comforts and rewards going to those with most money. The equivalents of English public schools flourish in both countries, and show no sign of lack of custom. But what is meant by the exception about social snobbery is that Australia and New Zealand still retain an awareness that they were places to which men could escape from the constricting power of aristocracy and privilege to prevent advancement from below in nineteenth-century Britain. The hunger for land was one example of this; the wish to start afresh with no advantages but one's immediate resources another. Folk-legend in both countries depicts Britain as traditionally a constricted country, in which people find it hard to get on without help from those with influence, especially the aristocracy. Again, religious memories have had something to do with the feeling: the abuses of establishment in England and Ireland helped to form the image of traditional Britain which many Australians and New Zealanders took in with their mothers' milk. A democratic tradition founded on the notion that "a man's a man for a' that" was established early in both countries.

Even more than Canada and South Africa, Australia and New Zealand depended in the nineteenth century upon British investment, and, to a lesser extent, on British trade. Their governmental systems, embodying roads, railways and communications, leant heavily on British loans. Their earlier staple exports of wool and gold found a world market, but their later movement into specialized meat and dairy products found a natural market in Britain. In the early twentieth century they attempted constantly to have this market safeguarded.* Such a situation did, of course, lead to

* It became a constant ploy for certain interests in the two countries, and often the Governments, to maintain that help in war merited preferential trade. Sir Earle Page, the Australian Minister for Commerce in 1936, managed to stop Britain concluding a favourable meat agreement with Argentina: "The matter, I said, was of such importance that I must have an immediate

recrimination as well as mutual advantage. The relations between borrower and lender, and buyer and seller, are not traditionally happy. But it meant that Australia and New Zealand were recognized adjuncts to the British economy, sharing the capital market and closely connected with the commodity markets. The establishment of British banks, insurance companies, pastoral companies and mercantile companies in the two countries made this connection closer.

Probably, however, the reasons for regarding Australia and New Zealand as the most "British" Commonwealth countries lie more in their actions in war than in their economic and social connections. Kipling made his Boer War English soldier say to his colonial brothers in arms:

> *You 'ad no special call to come, and so you doubled out,*
> *And learned us how to camp and cook an' steal a horse*
> *and scout.*
> *Whatever game we fancied most, you joyful played it too,*
> *And rather better on the whole. Good-bye—good luck*
> *to you!**

and similar sentiments were widespread in Britain in World War I and in the early years of World War II. The response of these two small countries in World War I was outstanding. While 22·11 per cent of the adult male population of the British Isles were recruited for service, and 13·48 per cent of comparable Canadians served overseas, the figures for Australia and New Zealand were 13·43 per cent and 19·35 per cent.† The Australian effort was achieved

---

* Rudyard Kipling, "The Parting of the Columns", in *Verse: Inclusive Edition 1885–1926* (London, 1927), p. 461.

† C. E. Carrington, "The Empire at War, 1914–1918", in *Cambridge History of the British Empire*, Vol. III (Cambridge, 1959), pp. 641–2. The South African figure, more difficult to arrive at because war was fought from bases in South Africa itself, is put at 11·12.

---

interview with the British Prime Minister. I indicated to Runciman that it would be politically impossible for his Government to treat Australia so shamefully when Australia had poured her men and her resources into the common fighting pool during the war, while the Argentine had stood on the sidelines and made hard bargains for her products. My arguments prevailed ..." (Sir Earle Page, *Truant Surgeon* (Sydney, 1963), pp. 243–4).

entirely by voluntary enlistment, the New Zealand one after 1916 by conscription. These figures require, perhaps, some correlation with the proportion of British-born people, which was roughly 13 per cent in Australia in 1914 and 22 per cent in New Zealand. Such a correlation, while it helps to explain some of the rush to the colours in 1914, does not help when we come to World War II, by which time the proportion of British-born had declined in both countries (to about 10 per cent in Australia and about 15 per cent in New Zealand).* Clearly, the sense of kinship was great, although the terms in which it has been expressed by orators were probably far simpler and less complicated than the actuality.

One can link with the heavy participation of these two countries in both world wars the fact that, in the inter-war period, they were the most vocal of the Dominions in demanding "Empire" policies in defence and foreign affairs, only to see their efforts break on the rocks of Canadian and South African resistance. Neither country showed much interest in the Statute of Westminster; the right-wing leaders of both were interested more in associating themselves with Britain than in demonstrating what they regarded as an empty independence. It was easy for them in this context to fall back upon that royalist and imperialist sentiment which still provokes surprise in visitors to Australia and New Zealand, as it did in the 1890's in Albert Métin:

"The Australasian worker has become a "gentleman" . . . Together with their manners, the worker is adopting the opinions of the British middle class on all matters except the Factory Acts and universal suffrage. He would not agree to a parliament elected by a franchise based on property qualification, like that of Great Britain, but he manifests a most unequivocal attachment to the monarchy, and the deepest reverence for the sovereign and the royal family. At trade union banquets the toast of the Queen or the King is proposed before all the others. In this connection, shortly before my visit, an English Socialist had disgraced himself by declaring that he respected the Queen as a woman, but could not discover in what way the workers were indebted to her . . .

Most Australasians are enthusiastic supporters of *Greater*

* Exact figures cannot be determined. The Australian figures are based on the censuses of 1911 and 1933, the New Zealand figures on censuses in 1911 and 1936.

Britain, of colonial expansion, even of conquest. In this connection I will quote a characteristic detail. In the large industrial city of Melbourne, there are two statues in front of Parliament House—one in honour of Gordon, the other in memory of the eight hours' day . . ."*

All of these aspects go to explain the "British" character of Australia and New Zealand. But it would be wrong to think that their British character has always made them sympathetic towards British ways or British policies. The individual Englishman has always had to run the risk of being called a "bloody Pommy" or its equivalent at the particular time and place.† He has been made to recognize that he is entering a new country in which established interests are not prepared to accommodate him at their expense, local ways are regarded as better than the ways he is accustomed to, and there is some suspicion that he may be trying to act the superior. These sentiments, largely unchanged since the earliest times, are to some extent the traditional reaction of the provincial to the city slicker: Australia and New Zealand have been cultural provinces of Britain, aware of their shortcomings and their lack of metropolitan suavity, and variously resentful and respectful in the face of British maturity. Irritation at the personal level has been paralleled by quarrels between governments; some details of these are given below, in the sections on Australia and New Zealand as individual countries. It will be noticed, however, that none of the quarrels with Britain has been serious, even though fiery colonists in the early and mid-nineteenth century might use the example of the Boston Tea Party to suggest that the American way was the best way. This lack of any serious rift between Britain and the southern countries needs explanation.

The sheer domestic preoccupation of Australia and New Zealand is one reason why they did not find themselves in serious disagreement with Britain. Their interest in the world at large is fairly recent. Their formative years were spent in isolation and hard work. The problems of local development were, in the case of

---

* From Métin's *Le Socialisme sans Doctrines* (1901), quoted in C. M. H. Clark (ed.), *Select Documents in Australian History, 1851–1900* (Sydney, 1955), pp. 676–7

† A friend of mine, who is an unmistakable Englishman, was once called a "kipper" in Australia. Inquiring about this variation on "Pommy" he was told it stood for "a two-faced bastard with no guts".

each colony (six in Australia and six provinces in New Zealand to start with), so pressing as to leave little room for argument about what the British Government should or should not do. By the 1850's the constitutional relationship had been settled in each case, and the colonies were in charge of their own affairs; the local Governor might sometimes be stiff-necked, and on rare occasions the British Government might impose some delay on legislation, but there was little or no reason to indict Britain as an anti-democratic force. Indeed, this forbearance and common sense, displayed by British Governments in the latter part of the nineteenth century, deserves more attention than historians have customarily given it; it is surely one of the reasons why there was so little friction between Britain and the colonies, and so much sense of connection. British Governments which would have been shocked at the idea of manhood suffrage and protective tariffs in Britain itself showed no significant resistance when these measures were put into effect in Australia and New Zealand. If there was a British yoke, it was light, and applied only in those spheres where some distinct effect upon the external relations of the Empire, or upon relations with other parts of it, was likely to result from ill-considered action by a colony. The British Governments of the 1880's and 90's which demurred at Australian and New Zealand efforts to annex Pacific islands and debar Indians from settlement considered that they were upholding general imperial interests in doing so; and their opposition had little effect in practice.

Thus, the colonies had little reason to quarrel with Britain in the late nineteenth and early twentieth century. Britain left them alone to do what they wished. But in addition there was a positive reason why family quarrels should not develop to any point of ferocity. It was that Britain provided for their defence. Hardly anyone questioned the proposition that the Royal Navy existed, not simply to protect the British Isles, but to defend every portion of the Empire against international conflict. As we have seen, the idea of British responsibility for immediate local defence disappeared as the colonies became stronger and more self-reliant; but the idea of the British Fleet as a guarantee of ultimate safety remained fixed in the minds of most Australians and New Zealanders until 1942.

It is no surprise, then, that Australia and New Zealand should have become and remained the most "British" of the Old

Dominions. It is desirable now to consider the distinctive character of each of these two countries.

AUSTRALIA

Australia began as a British gaol, and developed successively as a vast grazing ground, a source of minerals, a granary and larder, and a highly protected industrial machine. British investment and migration, along with Britain's capacity as a consumer of Australian products, had a great deal to do with this development. The consciousness of separate Australian identity came early, as men found new ways of doing things and recognized, if only dimly, that a new environment brought a different sort of life into being. Slow to develop in cultural terms (i.e. in the arts and expression at large), this consciousness showed itself first in politics : as the free settlers broke out of the early official boundaries, they demanded special advantages in the allocation of land; soon this involved an assertion of the right of self-government. Political action, once embarked on, quickly became a universal habit, so that localities began to demand special concession, churches asserted their claims to equality, gold-diggers banded together to improve their lot, intending farmers pressed for grants of land at the expense of the graziers who had preceded them, trade unions seized their opportunities for pressure on hours and wages; the Australian genius for combination and political pressure grew quickly, so as to make the governmental history of the country a matter of continual use of state machinery for sectional ends. It must be emphasized, however, that this consciousness of separate identity, while directed in the first instance against the image of the British Government as seen in the governors who had such power before responsible government began in the 1850's, thereafter became essentially sectional and local in character. There were six colonial governments to lobby with, and a vast range of local issues to argue about. There was no "Australia", except as a geographical expression and a place from which to send a cricket team, until federation was achieved in 1901. Before that date, each colony made its own arrangements with the British investor and the British Government; and the practice continued with scarcely diminished effect until the 1930's, although the federal government grew steadily in impact on Australians, and had the primary responsibility for external affairs.

It is important to recognize that the growth of an "Australian" approach towards Britain was essentially a social rather than a political matter. It was compounded, not of contacts between governments, but of the elements of social change involved in transplanting thousands of British people to a new soil and climate. Although Australia is vast, and the six colonies grew in relative isolation from one another, with little contact except that which arose from internal migration, the forms of society which appeared in each colony were remarkably similar, and attitudes to Britain were similar too. The two went together, because, as I have already suggested, Britain was widely thought of as the type of society on which people had turned their backs when they became Australians. The typical Australian picture of Britain became one of a little island tightly packed with humanity, carefully graded into social classes, run by aristocrats with Oxford accents, capable of developing worthy institutions, but also to be deplored for its treatment of the convicts and its heartless retention of the slums. Britain was the land of fog, rain, dirt, factories, slag-heaps, privilege; Australia was the land of sun, blue skies, outdoor living, cleanliness and opportunity. This double stereotype had enough plausibility to make it a handy weapon, which indeed it still remains.

Yet, while it can be called typical, it is too blunt an instrument to use in trying to discern the complex of Australian attitudes which developed towards Britain in the first century or so of Australian settlement; while keeping it in mind as an attitude which even the most imperially-minded Australian might display at certain times, we ought to look more closely at the considerable variety of pro- and anti-British feelings.

Both simple nationalism and simple imperialism developed as distinctive Australian attitudes: those who had reason to exalt Australianism and those who wanted to stress the ties with Britain, demanded full acquiescence in their extremist approaches, and in moments of heat would draw many into agreement. The extreme nationalist creed, expressed in the 1880's and 90's by the Sydney *Bulletin*, was simple. The nationalist asserted that Australia was being milked by British capitalists and fooled into acquiescing in British imperial adventures; Australians were bought off by the disposition of imperial honours, and the whole system of British control was epitomized in the symbol and influence of imported Governors.

"Their business was to foster grovel and give balls; encourage sport and the firing of blank cartridges; sympathize with poverty and suffering in a truly patrician manner; open church bazaars and grocery stores; flatter wealthy decrepitude, and erect a gorgeous popularity in the hearts of pugilistic loyalty generally . . . So the Imperialistic Governor speedily becomes a patron of rumbegotten wealth and a sort of grand panjandrum and lord high admiral of every species of vested interests in the colony over which he is sent to govern . . ."*

Radicals found it easy to identify the English governing classes with the vested interests of town and country in Australia, and republicanism or socialism with the removal of imperial symbols.

Sentiment of the opposite kind also existed, however. The decision of the New South Wales Government in 1885 to send a contingent to the Sudan was largely prompted by a letter in a Sydney newspaper from Sir Edward Strickland, a retired British army officer. Remarkable results followed the publication of words such as these:

"Sir: It was in the first moments of grief and indignation on hearing the news that "Gordon was dead" that the idea flashed across me that Australia should at once give expression to her great sorrow at the loss of this great commander and *preux chevalier* by following the example of a sister colony, Canada, and tendering to our Mother Country substantial aid in the time of need . . . A grand opportunity is now offered to Australia of proving, by performing a graceful, a loyal, a generous act, that she yields not to Canada or to any portion of the British Empire in loyalty and affection towards our Mother Country . . .

There is no sort of use in attempting to shut our eyes to the fact that England has now upon her hands two of the most bloody wars of the century, apart from possible contingencies with some European States. First, we have the warlike, brave Saracens, led by the Mahdi, and fighting under all the savage influences of fanaticism; we have attacked them on their own soil, and we can never retire from the field except as conquerors, unless we are content to have peace with dishonour. Secondly, we have the hardy Boer, a deadly shot and an excellent soldier. We

* *The Bulletin*, 2 July 1887; quoted in C. M. H. Clark, (ed.) *Select Documents in Australian History, 1851–1900* (Sydney, 1955), p. 801.

are on his soil, too, and there we must either assert the supremacy of English rule or yield the country to the Dutch . . .

Every Christian-born subject feels today that he has lost a friend in Gordon, therefore all Christendom will ring with praises of the gallantry of Australia in losing not a moment in tendering aid in the hour of need for the maintenance of the integrity of our nation and the ascendancy of Christianity . . ."*

Such statements were to prove common in the Boer War, in 1914–18 and in 1939–45; the simple assertion of imperial unity struck a responsive chord in Australia during each war. Of course, it is not necessary to assert that Australian opinion about Britain has ever been so widely polarized as in these extracts from *The Bulletin* and Strickland. Generally speaking, Australians became highly patriotic when war threatened, but were likely to grumble about Britain in times of peace. They might even take up both attitudes just illustrated. Henry Lawson, the poet of Australian nationalism, wrote in a lachrymose fashion about Britain after 1914. The difficulty with war, however, as it showed itself in the 1914–18 conflict, was that the concept of "loyalty", employed by the conservative forces in Australian society, might be pressed to the point where it admitted of no distinctive Australian interests at all. This in its turn would awaken latent suspicion and resentment of Britain, and set off charges and counter-charges between the two sides; the conflict in Canada over conscription in World War I had its counterpart in Australia, with similar charges on both sides.

Whereas in Canada the French-Canadians formed the hard core of anti-conscriptionism, with its accompanying hostility towards much that was British in the Canadian heritage, in Australia this part was played by the Catholic Irish. Constituting between a fourth and a fifth of the total population, they were clannish and much given to demonstrations for Home Rule in Ireland; Irish sentiment, religious fervour and an economic role as people with little property combined to make many of them emphasize the separateness of Australia and the perfidy of which the English were said to be capable. As in Canada, the simple-minded equation of patriotism with Protestantism by the local Orangemen made things worse.

* Sir Edward Strickland's letter, *Sydney Morning Herald*, February 12, 1885; reprinted in John Fairfax and Sons, *A Century of Journalism* (Sydney, 1931), p. 312.

The Irish provided a leaven of bitterness to the general Australian debate about Britain. In the main, however, that debate was worked out intermittently in terms of the adaptation British people were making, the tension between generations, the attempts to construct a colonial culture, and the condition of financial dependence. When times were bad, Australians were inclined to look on the British investor as a Shylock, although in better times they had laid every lure for his money. A British traveller in the 1890's found:

"Australians are inclined to complain, however unreasonably, that, had it not been for the temptations to which they were exposed by British capitalists, their Provinces could not have incurred the extravagant expenditure under which they are suffering and must continue to suffer. Australia, it has been said, owes to England merely the gratitude of the poor man towards his pawnbroker."[*]

The financial depressions of the 1890's and 1930's, with their catastrophic effects on employment in Australia, added fuel to whatever fire of anti-British feeling there might be.

Yet, when all this is said, it remains the case that most Australians, however ambivalent about this or that British aspect, thought of themselves as British and approved the link with Britain. One cannot provide precise evidence for this statement, except to say that the actions of Australians, especially in the Boer and World Wars, allow of no other explanation. Fortunately, the idea of being "British" allowed enough latitude to enable Australians to assert their individuality as a people while retaining the sense of general connection. They were British in their own way. The intense pride which they had for their troops in World War I existed alongside the refusal of a majority of Australians to allow those troops to be reinforced by conscription.

The disputes between Australian Governments and the British Government were relatively slight, as already suggested, but their substance was important in showing the development of distinctive Australian interests. Amongst the first was the determination of Victorians to establish protective tariffs, a policy which, while unacceptable to New South Wales and other colonies before federation, became the settled policy of the federal government. The

* Henry De R. Walker, *Australasian Democracy* (London, 1897), p. 296.

British Government never vetoed any protective tariff, but its displeasure was shown in the recall of a Governor of Victoria in 1866 because he supported a protectionist government to the annoyance of a free trade opposition and a free trade Colonial Secretary in London. Once federation was achieved, a general protective tariff was enacted, and has remained a feature of Australian policy. Predictions of disaster by English political economists from the 1860's onwards have not been fulfilled.

From the 1880's to the 1910's there was a series of differences of opinion between the British Government on the one hand and Australian Governments on the other about external matters, including immigration, the annexation of certain Pacific Islands, and the extent of Australian participation in naval defence. In sum, these help to illustrate the ambivalence of the more moderate Australian nationalism which was shaping itself. The immigration question was that of preventing coloured migrants from entering Australia; Australian radicalism, and later Australian opinion at large, became firm in its advocacy of a White Australia, with legislation to keep out Chinese, Pacific Islanders and others whose living standards were markedly different from the Australian. The British Government's approach was similar to its approach to like efforts in Canada and New Zealand: it did not want a blanket restriction on grounds of colour alone, because of its effect on foreign opinion, notably in Japan, and because it would mean the denial of rights to British subjects elsewhere in the Empire, notably in India. These doubts, expressed first about anti-Chinese legislation in individual colonies and later towards the consolidated White Australia legislation of the first federal parliament, had little effect. The upshot was that Australia consented to make a dictation test, similar to one in Natal, the legal test of an immigrant's capacity, but this was a subterfuge and recognized as such by everyone. White Australia became both an article of faith and a piece of effective law. Its basis was a conviction that Australia should develop in its own way, and not be a land in which Asians found opportunity; it was racist in utterance and intent, and it was to prove a source of intermittent embarrassment when Asian countries later gained their independence. Its importance in the context of relations with Britain was that dominant Australian opinion refused to recognize "imperial" interests, as defined by the British Government, as automatically Australian interests; moreover, in the sphere of immigration policy, it was prepared to challenge the whole conception of imperial interests. The parliament which legislated for White Australia also went on record in condemnation of Milner's "Chinese labour" policy in the Transvaal.

The matter of the Pacific Islands was similar in illustrating another aspect of the growth of specifically Australian interests, this time in the sphere of defence against European expansionism. Concern centred upon the New Hebrides and New Guinea, in which it was thought, in the 1880's, European powers would establish themselves and from which they might later threaten Australia. The colonial governments of Victoria and Queensland called upon Britain to annex these areas; the seriousness of their intent was shown by a Queensland *coup d'état* in what is now Papua in 1883. Australians had even less idea of what to do with the islands when they got them than the New Zealanders in the same period; nor were they prepared to do much about administering them, as when Britain asked for assistance with Fiji in the 1870's. It was simply that they wanted to deny them to other, stronger countries which might use them to Australia's disadvantage. In these cases Australians were not only refusing to accept the view of imperial interests formulated by the British Government; they were attempting to impose a quite different view of those interests. In essence, it was that the British Government must take positive steps to help the colonies achieve their own safety, but must not ask them to pay for its actions.

Something of the same attitude was manifest in Australian policies on defence up to the 1900's. "At the first Colonial Conference in 1887, Australian statesmen heard with undisguised amazement the opinion of the British Government that Australia ought to pay the expense of defending King George's Sound (Albany) and Thursday Island, and ought to contribute £126,000 a year towards the defence of Australian trade. Were not King George's Sound and Thursday Island stations important for *Imperial* defence and what had Australia to do with Imperial defence save to enjoy it?"* This policy of put and take towards the responsibilities of defence persisted until after federation, when a policy of self-reliance, in the form of compulsory military service and a Royal Australian Navy, was put into effect by a government

---

* G. Arnold Wood, "Australia and Imperial Politics", in Meredith Atkinson (ed.), *Australia: Economic and Political Studies* (Melbourne, 1920), p. 383. King George's Sound is in Western Australia and Thursday Island off the northern tip of Queensland.

under Alfred Deakin. Nevertheless, even after local responsibility for defence was established, the *sense* of put and take went on: Australia might be ultimately dependent on the Royal Navy for the destruction of a European power which threatened the Empire, but this would not mean that Australia paid for any part of it; payment was restricted to the defence of Australian shores.

These examples all show how Australia came to alternate between approval of the general system of empire and insistence that the interests of the Empire at large should be interpreted in an Australian way whenever Australia was involved. It is difficult to see how a sovereign state could have developed otherwise within the imperial bosom; but the working out of these Australian demands for special consideration sometimes caused heartburning in Britain and also in Australia, where simple-minded imperialists were liable to think that any divergence from the policy of the British Government foreshadowed revolution.

The experiences of World War I provided a further illustration of the tension between imperial and national sentiment. Commenting on the Australian decision in 1914 to offer a division of infantry instead of the four separable brigades which the Army Council wanted, the official Australian war historian observed that this was

"the first and greatest step towards settling the character which the expeditionary force was destined to assume—that of a national Australian army. The same question subsequently arose many times, in Gallipoli, France and Palestine, the British Staff having the greatest difficulty in understanding Australian nationalism or grasping the fact that it could be used for the benefit of the allies. He was a long-headed man who saw, though dimly, even at this early stage, the national interest in keeping Australia's force together."[*]

Uniformly, Australian politicians and military leaders demanded that their men fight as a distinctive force, with their own leaders and their own insignia. Intense resentment arose whenever it was proposed to split them up, whatever imperial or allied advantage might be said to result. The A.I.F. became the bearer of a national

* C. E. W. Bean, *The Story of Anzac,* Vol. I of *The Official History of Australia in the War of 1914–18* (12th edn., Sydney, 1941), p. 31.

tradition, subscribed to by all but those to whom the war itself was a mistake or a crime—a very small minority indeed. When the war ended, the A.I.F. formed the basis for an organization of ex-servicemen more influential than the British or American Legions. Australia acquired, not a national day* but a holy day from the war: April 25, the anniversary of the landing on Gallipoli in 1915, is still celebrated as a national holiday in which holiness, secularity, patriotism and good fellowship are inextricably mingled. The Gallipoli campaign, in which British troops outnumbered Australian and New Zealand, is remembered in Australia as a heavily Aust-ralian affair, the British role being confined to responsibility for putting the Australians ashore at the wrong place on the first day. The war encouraged a sort of returned soldier patriotism, in which, while tribute was paid to the military virtues and loyalty to the sovereign, the whole emphasis was laid on the valour, initiative, democracy, and informality of Australians as a people; it was conservative in its devotion to the symbols of monarchy, but radical in its rejection of formal titles and professionalism in war.

In spite of the frequently bitter clashes between them, this kind of Australian national sentiment was not entirely different from the other kind stimulated by the war, the isolationist nationalism which lay behind some of the resistance to conscription and was thereafter espoused by the Australian Labour Party, following its expulsion of W. M. Hughes and a number of its other leaders who had supported conscription. The child of the *Bulletin* nationalism of the 1880's, it was heavily overlaid with Irish suspiciousness and Catholic resentment, and partook of the generally isolationist senti-ment of the 1920's, as shown equally in Canada and the United States. But it too was shaped by a sense of what Australians were really like.

The existence of these two forms of national feeling, however, had less to do with relations with Britain than with divisions with-in Australia itself. The two attitudes were characteristic of the two main forces in Australian politics in the 1920's, the Nationalist and Country Parties on one side, and the Labour Party on the other. As in Canada with the division between Conservatives and Liberals,

---

* Officially, Australia's national day is January 26, the anniversary of the establishment of New South Wales as a penal colony in 1788. It has not proved a popular anniversary in other states, and is now an awkward date for Australian embassies abroad, since it is also India's national day.

the two emblems of the nation were used as sticks to beat one another. To change the metaphor, Britain might be the symbolic shuttlecock which these two battledores exchanged in their wordy encounters; but the quarrel was essentially between middle-class, business, professional and farming people on the one hand, with monarchy and loyalty as their highest symbols, and wage-earners on the other, with working-class solidarity and national exclusiveness as theirs. Britain might suffer in the process through excessive adulation and excessive denigration, but in practice the realities of origins and economic connections forced both groups into demanding favours from Britain while driving as hard a bargain as circumstances would permit.

So much for politics. In cultural terms, Australia went on making its own life, its idiom arising from the everyday work and converse of the people, its preoccupations in the southern sunshine crowding out many of the memories of Britain. An Australian poet in the 1950's pictured his grandfather breaking links with his native Ireland; the poem serves as an example of much that happened as Australia grew more self-conscious:

> *England, Ireland, Europe are clatter*
> *of tongues and hatreds none understands—*
> *among them voices we have heard, and matter*
> *touching us and the task in our hands.*
> *But direct memory breaks. We sever*
> *worn threads. It was more than a business affair:*
> *he bought my grandfather's house for ever*
> *did Donovan of the Square.*
> *The choice made and the new land entered,*
> *not for a day for days to be,*
> *what next but to grasp this life that centred*
> *in the south? The north had been sunk at sea.**

NEW ZEALAND

The most important single element in New Zealand's association with Britain is the close emotional identification with England and Scotland which was characteristic of New Zealand settlers once

* R. D. Fitzgerald, "Transaction", in John Thompson *et al.* (eds.), *The Penguin Book of Australian Verse* (Harmondsworth, 1958), p. 86.

F

systematic colonization began. Edward Gibbon Wakefield, the apostle of the New Zealand Company, wanted to establish colonies which would last because of the solidity of social structure which they embodied; having been dismayed at the hit-and-miss character of Australian settlement, whereby ragamuffins of various kinds obtained opportunities which they were not always able to use effectively, he was determined that New Zealand, in spite of the lack of respectability of the sealers and whalers who had established themselves in various quarters, would reproduce British social conditions at their best. New Zealand was to be a middle-class paradise; and this, in many ways, was how it developed. Through the system of group settlement, quite unlike the unco-ordinated colonization of most of the Australian colonies, direct links with England and Scotland were firmly established and strictly maintained. Two of the settlements, in Canterbury and Otago, were undertaken with the approval of the Churches of England and Scotland.

However, one must not go too far in attributing to the New Zealand settlements the ordered social patterns of closely-settled English counties. It was quickly found that New Zealand was best able to produce sheep for wool, not crops; before long, gold discoveries worked their inevitable way in disruption of social relations; as time went by, and refrigeration was perfected, New Zealand's rural areas turned themselves into small farmers' republics, without a counterpart of the upper classes to set standards and raise tone. The big house was missing.* To this extent New Zealand and Australia followed parallel courses. But the greater stability of the New Zealand settlements meant a closer identification with values and practices which the immigrants had brought from the British Isles; and these standards were consciously kept up. "To 'keep up' was the aim of those-who-mattered, even if it was only a matter of keeping up appearances. When two young men in the Canterbury settlement in 1852 were about to depart for the cold-mutton-and-damper life of a new sheep run, where they were in danger of becoming 'semi-barbarous', Charlotte Godley 'begged them to have a lay figure of a lady carefully draped, set up in their usual sitting-room, and always to behave before it as if it were their mother' ".† This carefully-draped lady, Britannia with the

---

* To some extent the big graziers – "squatters" – in Australia have supplied this element, but as working proprietors, not as landlords.

† Keith Sinclair, "Life in the Provinces", in Keith Sinclair (ed.), *Distance Looks Our Way* (Auckland, 1961), pp. 40–41.

face of Queen Victoria, has been an ever-present figure in New Zealand history. Social standards and habits have constantly deferred to her; politics has often, but not always, recognized her authority.

One of the most attractive yet only intermittently representative figures in New Zealand life, William Pember Reeves, wrote a poem called "a Colonist in his Garden"* which has long served as a text for New Zealand feelings about Britain. The colonist receives a letter from England, calling him home and saying with scorn of New Zealand:

> *Write not that you content can be,*
> *Pent by that drear and shipless sea*
> *Round lonely islands rolled,*
> *Isles nigh as empty as their deep,*
> *Where men but talk of gold and sheep*
> *And think of sheep and gold.*

> *A land without a past; a race*
> *Set in the rut of commonplace;*
> *Where Demos overfed*
> *Allows no gulf, respects no height;*
> *And grace and colour, music, light,*
> *From sturdy scorn are fled.*

The colonist muses over the letter, recalls with pleasure the sights and sounds of England, but says he will not return:

> *Here am I rooted. Firm and fast*
> *We men take root who face the blast,*
> *When, to the desert come,*
> *We stand where none before have stood*
> *And braving tempest, drought and flood,*
> *Fight Nature for a home.*

He has not turned his back on England, though; all around him are the English trees and flowers he has planted, and, amongst them, a local product epitomizing his union with the mother country:

* Conveniently available in Allen Curnow (ed.), *The Penguin Book of New Zealand Verse* (Harmondsworth, 1960), 98–101.

Yonder my poplars, burning gold,
Flare in tall rows of torches bold,
* Spire beyond kindling spire.*
Then raining gold round silver stem
Soft birches gleam. Out flaming them
* My oaks take ruddier fire.*

And with my flowers about her spread
(None brighter than her shining head),
* The lady of my close,*
My daughter, walks in girlhood fair.
Friend, could I rear in England's air
* A sweeter English rose?*

This we may regard as the Platonic form of New Zealand feeling. The actuality has often been more downright, more a matter of the emphasis of local interests and the conviction that it was Britain's duty to do what New Zealand considered right. But the sense of continuity and kinship has remained stronger in New Zealand than in any other of the old Dominions. In part this is due to the circumstances of colonization, in part also to New Zealand's continued isolation from other influences than British. Exports and imports, shipping lines, the movement of people back and forth: all of these operated on a bi-lateral exchange between Britain and New Zealand, with little interference from anywhere else, until quite recently. The hopes of some of the early colonists for a fruitful connection with the United States were not fulfilled. The only country to which New Zealanders were accustomed, apart from Britain, was Australia. The first British connections with New Zealand were through New South Wales, and the two countries, while clearly separate to those who live in them, have had certain experiences in common. New Zealand has had the advantage of being smaller, and more fertile and better watered; it has also had a quite different native people to accommodate. The traditions stemming from group settlement in New Zealand have often contrasted with the more raffish and haphazard background of Australia. But otherwise New Zealand has had similar economic experience in the development of its export industries, has preserved much the same standard of life as Australia, has taken in Australian migrants in good times and lost its own migrants to Australia in bad. The Australian colonies and the New Zealand Government cooperated in certain matters in the 1870's and 80's, and there was a possibility that New Zealand might enter the Australian federation. However, by the 1890's New Zealanders had acquired enough of their own distinctive institutions to fear the impact on these of the weight of population and political pressure of the six Australian colonies. Once it was clear that New Zealand would not be part of the Australian federation, more New Zealand self-consciousness began to appear. The term "Australasia", often used in the nineteenth century as a portmanteau word for Australia and New Zealand, began to be disliked by New Zealanders. While still intensely attached to their British connection, they began to appreciate their own special circumstances.

New Zealand started with forays by occasional white men against the Maoris; was Christianized from Australia; was reluctantly annexed by the British Government, in order that law and order might be maintained and justice done to the Maoris; was systematically colonized at several separate points in the two islands; gained responsible government with an atomized federal structure in the 1850's; and sloughed this off in the 1870's to emerge with a unified government that has since changed little in form. Population was small, distances were considerable in spite of the country's parvitude in comparison with Australia, and the separate settlements maintained a certain distance in their relations. Relations with Britain were much affected by the arguments over treatment of the Maoris, culminating in the Maori wars, which did not end until 1870. The first generation of New Zealand politicians were, in many ways, Boston Tea Party men: they continually complained about the British Government's undue solicitude for the Maoris, and then about its conduct of the wars. They did not actually demand a cutting of the painter, but their stock in trade was abuse of the Colonial Office. Similar reactions can be discerned in the history of New South Wales and Cape Colony; in each case it was easy for colonists to convince themselves that the British Government owed them protection but must always view its imperial trust as their interests dictated. Following the final settlement of the Maori wars, New Zealand politicians found a further stick with which to beat the British Government, in its failure to appreciate its imperial role in the Pacific islands. Throughout the 1870's and 80's, and on into the 90's, New Zealand leaders such as Sir Julius Vogel, Sir George Grey and Richard Seddon belaboured the British Government with schemes for the acquisition of Fiji, Samoa, even Hawaii.

The only concrete result, until World War I, was New Zealand's annexation of the Cook Islands and Niue in 1901. As with the similar demands from Australia, New Zealand motives were fear of expansionism by European powers, although there were also trading, missionary and other interests to satisfy.

Somewhere about 1887 a change took place in New Zealand thinking about the outside world. Before then the dominant note had been the nagging demands on Britain to satisfy this or that colonial need, as envisaged by the colonists themselves. Afterwards it was a more modest, indeed a self-effacing note. One New Zealand historian has seen the change embodied in two politicians, Sir Julius Vogel and Sir Harry Atkinson :

> "Thus in 1887 New Zealand spoke with two voices. That of Vogel was the voice of the past. It was confident and independent, willing if need be to face the world alone because in a sensible universe reason and not sentiment governed politics. But Atkinson spoke with the voice of the future : conscious that New Zealand was small and weak in a world full of potential menace, but conscious also that she was safe behind the shield of British power. In the years that followed, the spirit of Vogel was gradually ousted by the impulse towards uncritical loyalty which was fed by sentiment, by trade and finance, and by the slow decay of the sense of unshakeable security."*

From this time onwards, under leaders like Seddon and Sir Joseph Ward, New Zealand became known as the most loyal of the colonies and Dominions, the only one with an itch towards Imperial Federation (although this was more a matter of politicians' occasional speeches than sustained national policy), and one which could be depended on for opposition to such "separatist" policies as might come from Canada under Laurier or Australia when determined to have a navy of its own. The carefully-draped lady took charge of external relations; the English rose became the symbol of international action, as she had been, from earlier times, the symbol of social significance. From waging wordy war with the Colonial Office, New Zealand leaders turned their attention to social reform. Ballance and Seddon, the Prime Ministers who held office after the Liberal victory of 1890, provided the country with a variety of new institutions which caused Henry Demarest Lloyd to exclaim that :

* F. L. W. Wood, *New Zealand in the World* (Wellington, 1940), p. 77.

"The New Zealand idea is the opposite to that of some theoretical creators of society, that the rich are to become richer and the poor poorer . . . New Zealand leads in the actual movement now going on in the other direction—the aggrandisement of the middle class. The middle class is not to be exterminated, but is to absorb all the other classes."*

It can be argued that, whereas some of the founders of the New Zealand settlements were upper-middle class in the English sense, familiar with the practices of British government and capable of exchanging knocks on equal terms with the British governing classes, the New Zealanders of the 1890's and successive decades were lower-middle class and essentially provincial in their outlook; their acquaintance with Britain was less, their local preoccupations were greater, their sense of England's might was more romantic, their deference to the great men of the United Kingdom much more marked. "The colonial cringe", a phrase coined to describe certain aspects of Australian cultural response to English standards, is a harsh but effective description of an attitude which became noticeable in New Zealand reactions to British policy, just as it was evident in Australia in the 1920's and 30's. New Zealand's greater dependence in trade, and more heavily Protestant and less Irish population, encouraged a more single-minded devotion to British standards and policies than was found in Australia.

This attitude never characterized the whole population; it was simply the attitude of a majority which grew with time. The Labour movement in New Zealand, heavily spiced with I.L.P. attitudes from Britain and their equivalent from Australia, took up opposition to conscription in World War I; one of its leaders, Peter Fraser,† was gaoled for twelve months for sedition. But the contrast between the two anti-conscription campaigns in New Zealand and Australia is instructive. In Australia the issue of conscription split a Labour Party in power in the federal parliament, the acknowledged government of the country. The opposition to conscription was sufficient to prevail in two national referendums, and anti-conscriptionism remained a dogma of the Labour Party for at least a quarter of a century, affecting consideration of every major issue of foreign policy. Thus in Australia there was in World War I

* Henry Demarest Lloyd, *Newest England* (New York, 1900), p. 376.
† Mr. Fraser was later to be New Zealand's Prime Minister in World War II.

a strong sense of separate identity, nourished by Irish loyalties but sufficient in itself to inspire a substantial Labour movement with opposition to a policy which was presented as essentially imperial. In New Zealand the Labour forces gained less than a tenth of the votes cast at the national elections of 1914,* and the opposition to conscription had nothing like the force and drive which it maintained in Australia. As we have seen, the New Zealand contribution to the forces was proportionately greater than the Australian. Yet there was not the same revulsion against war, or the same undercurrent of anti-British feeling, in the New Zealand Labour movement as in the Australian. New Zealand loyalty remained unquestioned. The governments which New Zealand had between 1919 and 1935 were British to the core,† and the Labour Government which succeeded them, while concerned about the British investor's lack of confidence in New Zealand's first socialist government,‡ showed the warmest affection for Britain when war began in 1939.

The cosiness of reliance on Britain bred its own opposition, not that of dispossessed farmers or aspiring lower classes, but that of intellectuals, irritated at New Zealand's complacent part as: ". . . the destined race, rulers of conquered isles, sprouting like bulbs in warm darkness, putting out white shoots under the wet sack of Empire." New Zealand's very prosperity and social justice became an offence in itself:

> *This land is a lump without leaven,*
> *a body that has no nerves.*
> *Don't be content to live in*
> *a sort of second-rate heaven*
> *with first-rate butter, fresh air,*
> *and paper in every toilet . . .§*

Yet the New Zealand intellectuals' complaint, maturing in the 1930's and 40's, was not against Britain in itself, but against the provincial complacency which looked to the mother country for

* James Thorn, *Peter Fraser* (London, 1952), p. 44.
† They were shocked and ashamed at the pressure from South Africa, Canada and Ireland which led to the Statute of Westminster.
‡ There was a flight of capital from New Zealand in 1938 and 1939.
‡ These two quotations are from poems by A. R. D. Fairburn in Allen Curnow, *The Penguin Book of New Zealand Verse* (Harmondsworth, 1960), pp. 147 and 155.

all standards and advice, which dismissed foreign questions as matters for Britain to deal with as of right, and to which the posture of abasement was habitual. As in Australia and Canada, Britain readily became the symbol of conflicts within New Zealand society itself, clutched at in argument to provide either justification or complaint. The New Zealand debate, however, was slight in comparison with the vehemence of feeling in Canada and Australia.

4

SOUTH AFRICA

IN considering the background of South African relations with
Britain, it is difficult to avoid taking account of the fact that,
in this case alone amongst the Old Dominions, a terminus has
been reached. South Africa has become a republic and has left the
Commonwealth. These are two things which it would be difficult to imagine happening to Canada, Australia and New Zealand.
Since 1961, relations between Britain and South Africa have been
different from what they were before. Some have remained the
same: trade proceeds, investment continues, there is still a certain
amount of immigration into South Africa from Britain, and the
English language continues to be spoken in Capetown, Durban and
Johannesburg. But the monarchical element in South African
affairs, which English-speaking South Africans used to consider an
essential part of their heritage, has disappeared with very little
opposition, and South Africa is now, to Britain, a foreign country.
This major fact demands an explanation, part of which will come
when we consider the circumstances of the 1950's that led to
South Africa's unpopularity in the Commonwealth and the lack of
readiness of the British Government to support South Africa against
opposition. But a large part of the explanation must come from
the historical circumstances of South Africa; the events of 1961
were not caused simply by a constellation of forces of the immediate time. They were rather an outcome of nearly two centuries of
friction between forces in Britain and forces in South Africa, in
particular the nationalist traditions of the Afrikaners and their in-
flexible approach to native rights.

We must, then, attempt to trace some of the factors in South
Africa that prepared the way for the steps taken in 1961. However,
the rejection of monarchy and withdrawal from the Commonwealth
are not all that place South Africa apart from Britain and the
other Old Dominions in the 1960's. There is also the fact that
South Africa does not share that almost instinctive connection
with the Western powers, seen at its most obvious in alliance
with the United States, that seems natural and inevitable to

Canada, Australia, New Zealand and Britain. The American alliance, which is central to the foreign policies of these four, does not exist for South Africa. Here is a further difference which requires explanation. To some extent it can be explained in terms of post-World War II events; but it too needs to be seen in the context of South Africa's development as a special kind of Old Dominion.

Certain basic differences between South Africa and the others can readily be recognized. As we have seen, British emigration to South Africa was slight compared with the outpouring to Canada, Australia and New Zealand (and the massive movement to the United States). Except in the period of the gold rushes, in the 1890's, British emigration was never substantial. There were two reasons. The more important was that South Africa at no time offered wage-earning jobs for landless labourers and penniless city artisans, to the extent that Canada and Australia did. Unskilled work on the farms and in the towns was done by Africans. A black majority was always available for the jobs which in other Dominions would be done by immigrants, and these black men were paid a fraction of what white men would demand. It is true that South Africa did provide a certain opportunity for skilled men in the building trades, in the railways and in the mines, especially during the establishment of these industries or their rapid expansion. But jobs on these lines could be obtained only so long as black labour could be kept out of them, or "poor white" Afrikaners from the farms did not covet them. Once either of these conditions was fulfilled, there was little chance for the typical Irish, Scots or English emigrant in South Africa. The second reason why British emigration was never substantial was the existence in South Africa of a white group, non-British in origin, to which British immigration in any quantity spelt danger of dilution of the Afrikaner tradition and anglicization of Afrikaners at large. In consequence, there was always Afrikaner opposition to the kind of vigorous immigration programme which was commonplace in boom times in the other Old Dominions. The white South African population remained small, as it still is in comparison with those of Canada and Australia; and the British element in it remained a minority.

The "racial" conflict in South Africa (the term "racial" being used until very recent times to describe the tension between English-speaking and Afrikaans-speaking South Africans), has no counterpart elsewhere in the Old Dominions, even in Canada. The

Afrikaners* have a more militant and self-confident tradition than the French-Canadians. They can look back on their formation of two sovereign or near-sovereign states, in the Transvaal and the Orange Free State; they have the memories of a war fought within the past century against the British, on their own account and without any help from troops other than their own; they have made their own language out of the Dutch which originally signified their subordination to the Netherlands; they developed a nationalist movement, with the aim of taking power over the whole country and not simply a province, more than half a century ago; and they have always been the majority group amongst white South Africans, to such an extent that, for the first thirty-eight years of the Union of South Africa, every Prime Minister had been an Afrikaner General in the Boer War. No one but an Afrikaner has held that office since it began. The contrast with French Canada is obvious. There are also similarities, notably in the tension between a group with its own traditions and the set of traditions and customs which we have already distinguished as British. But French Canada has been an enclave in a predominantly English-speaking Canada, whereas Afrikanerdom, while exhibiting at times the same fortress mentality as French Canada, has had majority power in its grasp since South Africa was unified. This means that the "British" element in the South African population has had to play second fiddle in politics, even when it could obtain entry into cabinets, and has been able to exert influence only through Afrikaner politicians like Smuts, to whom the extreme forms of Afrikaner nationalism were repugnant. Although the British element was dominant in trade unionism and in business at crucial times, it had neither the cohesion nor the political skill to turn this sort of dominance to durable political advantage. While it is true that the Afrikaners were split politically for a considerable period in the Union's history, this did not necessarily mean a decline in Afrikaner political influence; if anything, it meant that both government and opposition had to take account of specific Afrikaner wishes, aims and susceptibilities.

A further point of difference between South Africa and the other Old Dominions relates to the degree of British interest in them.

---

* I shall use this term in preference to "Boers" or "Dutch", although these latter terms were, at various times, the most often used to describe the people in question. "Afrikaners" is what they call themselves now, and it has the further advantage of reminding us that we are dealing with happenings in Africa.

Paradoxically, although South Africa was, as we have seen, the Dominion to which the smallest number of British people migrated, it received the most concentrated attention from Britain. None of the other three countries has ever been the subject of so much British concern as South Africa between 1880 and 1910. The conjunction of the Boer Wars and the concentrated, heavy British investment in gold and diamonds made South Africa news in Britain, and a topic of British political interest, to an extent unparalleled elsewhere. The moving frontiers of South African settlement in this period caused far more concern than those of Canada; more was at stake, in terms of both foreign involvement and opportunities for British capital.

South Africa became, in fact, a source of myth in Britain. No other Dominion has achieved this. The myth was in two parts, thesis and antithesis, corresponding roughly to the positions taken up by the Conservative and Liberal parties at the turn of the century, but including other elements as well; South Africa became the perpetual bone of contention in the argument between Imperialists and anti-Imperialists. On the one side it was represented by the towering, mysterious figure of Cecil Rhodes, making new colonies in Bechuanaland and Rhodesia, and using wealth and politics to forward his conviction of a manifest destiny for Britain in Africa. Along with Rhodes went the cluster of business, military and other interests whose attention had been concentrated on South Africa, assisted by newspaper proprietors like Northcliffe and writers as good as Rudyard Kipling and as bad as Alfred Austin. Beginning with the rough-and-tumble adventures about which Rider Haggard constructed romances, this sort of mythical South Africa later appeared in more sophisticated guise as the playground of Lord Milner's "Kindergarten", from which one of its members drew the lesson which one of his characters expressed thus:

"I knew then the meaning of the white man's duty. He has to take all risks, recking nothing of his life or his fortunes, and well content to find his reward in the fulfilment of his task. That is the difference between white and black, the gift of responsibility, the power of being in a little way a king; and so long as we know this and practise it, we will rule not in Africa alone but wherever there are dark men who live only for the day and their own bellies."*

* John Buchan, *Prester John* (first published 1910), Ch. XXII.

As against this kind of *Chums Annual* thesis, the antithesis in the myth was a compound of Gladstonian liberalism, Cobdenite economy, nonconformist conscientiousness, and the kind of opposition to the activities of international big business that can best be represented by J. A. Hobson's *Imperialism*, in which South Africa bulked large as a source of examples. The Randlords, the Milner scheme of Chinese labour, and the wrongs of the Afrikaners were all elements in this antithetical picture of South Africa in the period of greatest British interest in the country; but it had deeper roots in British missionary opposition to the treatment of the natives by the Afrikaners, and, while it fastened for a time on the Boers as unjustly persecuted by imperialists, it was broad enough in scope to see South Africa as a prime example of vulgarity, cruelty, money-making and corrupt politics.

Whichever way the South African myth was taken, it was more exciting than anything concocted about the other Dominions, essentially humdrum in their development in spite of Australia's dramatic start as a convict colony, New Zealand's Maori Wars, and Canada's seizure from France. It was not only more exciting, but also different, because of the presence of two elements unknown elsewhere: the Afrikaners and the natives. The interplay between these two elements provides the basic reason for the ultimate detachment of South Africa from the distinctive formal connection with Britain that it previously shared with the other three.

The history of South Africa is unlike the history of those three. As we have seen, once Canada, Australia and New Zealand were established, their history was essentially domestic, with the British connection important mainly in terms of local issues or such domestically-based matters as trade. Britain did not play a prominent part in the affairs of these countries, although the British connection remained significant and was often a source of local argument. South African history, on the other hand, is very much a matter of constant tension, not only *about* Britain, but also *with* Britain. The divided nature of the white population fostered this state of affairs, and the existence of a massive black majority provided an unsolved problem to which neither white group could provide a final answer, and which intermittently became the subject of debate.

The original clash between Boers and British bears an uncanny resemblance to the argument between South Africa and Britain in the 1950's and 60's. An early South African historian, after analysing the correspondence with the Cape Government of those who trekked north in the 1830's, found the trekkers' grievances to be directed against both the British Government and British missionaries:

"The Imperial Government was charged with exposing the white inhabitants of the colony, without protection, to robbery and murder by the blacks; with giving credence in every dispute to statements made by interested persons in favour of savages, while refusing to credit the testimony, no matter how reliable, of colonists of European extraction; with liberating the slaves in an unjust manner; and generally with such undue partiality for persons with black skins and savage habits, as to make it preferable to seek a new home in the wilderness than remain under the English flag.

The missionaries of the London Society were charged with usurping authority that should properly belong to the civil magistrate; with misrepresenting facts; and with advocating schemes directly hostile to the progress of civilization, and to the observance of order. And it was asserted that the influence of these missionaries was all powerful at the Colonial Office in London, by which the colony, without a voice in the management of its affairs, was then ruled absolutely."[*]

The men who trekked from Cape Colony in the 1830's were attempting to escape not only from restriction of what they considered to be their rights and from interference in their treatment of the natives, but also from the imposition of English ways in the Cape, and the attempt to plant British settlers there. Lord Charles Somerset and his successors made English the official language and attempted to anglicize and render more efficient the administration of the Cape. The spread to the north, which resulted in the formation of the Orange Free State and the South African Republic (the Transvaal), was essentially a movement of protest as well as a search for wider opportunities. Long before Kruger or Rhodes were names of importance, the Afrikaner tradition had been established as one of resistance to British interference. It was equally grounded on resistance to black domination: the victory of Blood River in 1838, celebrated as Dingaan's Day in revenge for

[*] From George McCall Theal, *History of the Boers,* quoted in J. P. Fitzpatrick, *The Transvaal from Within* (London, 1899), p. 6.

Dingaan's treachery to Piet Retief, was central to Afrikaner pride and the Afrikaner sense of security.

On the basis of farming as the dominant economic pursuit, South Africa became temporarily stabilized in the 1870's with the two republics roughly balanced by the two British colonies of the Cape and Natal; this balance was disturbed politically by the continued assertion of British suzerainty over the republics, and then by the political consequences of the discovery of diamonds and gold at Kimberley and the Rand. Diamonds and gold turned South Africa into two countries, the people of which were intermingled. Aside from the formal boundaries, one of these countries was agricultural or pastoral, traditional, slow-moving, essentially pre-industrial; the other was dynamic, business-minded, increasingly urbanized and concerned with heavy risks and high profits. The Boer farmers were typical of the one, the Uitlanders in Johannesburg of the other. The British Government backed the second for a mixture of reasons: traditional mistrust of the trek-Boers, the search for wider boundaries, fear of German penetration, pressure from British firms and settlers, concern for British prestige, and the like. Tacit or actual British support of the Uitlanders in the Jameson Raid and the Boer War set many Afrikaners permanently against Britain, and the concentration camps provided a symbol of Afrikaner grievance for over half a century. Moreover, the adjustment between Boer and Briton in the Cape, which had shown itself during Rhodes's reign as Prime Minister there, came to an end. The two "countries" might have achieved an equilibrium if war had not occurred. Once it did occur, its effects were irremediable. They were compounded by Milner's abortive post-war effort to repeat the Somerset policy of anglicization on a wider scale. Perhaps he was right when he wrote in 1900: "If, ten years hence, there are three men of British race to two of Dutch, the country will be safe and prosperous. If there are three of Dutch to two of British we shall have perpetual difficulty . . ."* but his effort to encourage British migration failed, and the knowledge that his effort had been deliberate added a further element to Africaner resentment.

The equilibrium which Botha and Smuts achieved from 1910 to 1924, which was hailed at the time as a masterpiece of reconciliation after the miseries of the war, can now be seen as a temporary

* Quoted in W. K. Hancock, *Smuts: The Sanguine Years* (Cambridge, 1962), p. 174.

affair. The agricultural "country" in South Africa, largely Afrikaner, wanted peace and rest, and was prepared to fit in with
Botha's policies; the urban "country", largely British in origin,
concentrated upon the commercial advantages which Union provided, and was later upheld by the excitement of participation in
World War I. The equilibrium was threatened by the rebellion of
1914, but this was put down, not without adding its share to the
store of extreme Afrikaner resentment; the end came in 1924, when
Hertzog brought to power a Nationalist Government, leavened with
a few representatives of the South African Labour Party, representing a short-lived assertion of restrictionist privileges by white
labour of mainly British origin. Hertzog's dominance of the
Government was modified after 1933, when Smuts and his party
joined him, and the extreme Nationalists under Malan broke away.
But it was still government with the emphasis upon Afrikaner
rights and upon the achievement of the kind of symbolic independence for which Hertzog had campaigned since the Boer War:
flag, anthem, language, access to jobs, restriction of the Cape franchise, clarification of the link with Britain, and the establishment of
independent South African diplomacy.

The eclipse of Hertzog by Smuts in 1939, on the issue of wartime neutrality, began a short period of nine years in which interests
dependent upon the British connection gained the upper hand; but
Afrikaner dominance was restored in its extreme form under Malan
in 1948, and has continued ever since. Once again, the symbols of
the British connection became a matter of prime consideration; but
this time it was the native question that occasioned most dispute.
Having smouldered on throughout the years of uneasy alliance between Smuts and Hertzog, and made itself felt only occasionally
under Smuts's wartime rule, it became in the 1950's both an international issue and a source of acute disagreement with Britain. For
the first time, forces outside the British–South African relationship
exerted pressure on Britain to break, or not to attempt too strongly
to preserve, the formal link with South Africa. In 1961, the combination of international obloquy, denunciation from liberals in
Britain, and the intransigence of the Afrikaner Nationalist Government, forced South Africa and Britain apart.

The attempt to assert British values and solutions in South
African policies has thus rebounded upon those who tried it,
whether in the early efforts at anglicization or the later commitments to the British side in two world wars. Such difficulties for

G

British political interests have proved compatible with opportunities for British economic interests in both trade and investment. While it is true that British economic influence has fed Afrikaner discontent, it has added to, rather than created, the stock of Afrikaner feeling against Britain. Basically, the drive against British symbols and influence has remained what it was in the 1830s—or the extreme nationalists have preferred to think of it so.

It will be seen that, just as South Africa has been a source of myth in Britain to an extent beyond that of any other Old Dominion, so Britain has been, in South Africa, a more potent source of myth than elsewhere. To those who were striving to build the Afrikaner tradition Britain was easily represented as the embodiment of "soulless goldkings acting in the name and under the protection of an unjust and hated government 7,000 miles away" (Smuts in his Boer War document, *A Century of Wrong*).* English newspapers could be charged with a deliberate policy of representing the Boers as

> "the embodiment of all that is low and worthless. They are at once the enemies of England and murderers and unscrupulous robbers who exterminate and rob the innocent natives. It is in this light they are presented to the British public who are only too ready to see their own righteousness and humanity shining like a light in the darkness of African barbarity and Boer godlessness . . ." (Hertzog in a university essay.)†

Such strains run right through the history of South Africa. Their counterparts exist, but not of the same strength. Against the ox-wagon sentinels and the Broederbond on the Afrikaner side, we have to pit the Sons of England and the defiance of Stallard's Dominion Party. In both cases Britain became a symbol of a magnitude beyond the reality of its prosaic self; a symbol of hate on one side, of love on the other. We have seen how this same process operated in Canada and to a lesser extent in Australia : Britain became the shuttlecock of local political groups, tossed backwards and forwards as a symbol of their animosity. But in South Africa, while the two main groups would belabour the symbol to express their dislike of one another, especially in debates over flag, anthem or language, a greater animosity towards Britain itself was cultivated

* Hancock, op. cit., p. 109.

† Oswald Pirow, *James Barry Munnik Hertzog* (London, n.d.), p. 19, quoting a condensation by C. M. van den Heever.

over the years. This direct animosity had reasons stronger than any which the experience of the other Dominions, devoid of Jameson Raids or Boer Wars, could produce. Indeed, it is important to recognize that throughout South African history it was often possible to unite some of the Afrikaans- and English-speaking political forces behind a policy of opposition to the "the Imperial factor", whether it was Rhodes and the Bond berating the British Government for its boundary treaty with Germany in 1890, or the South African fusion government calling for the cession to South Africa of the High Commission Territories in the 1930's. The impression that Britain, for its own purposes, pursued policies in Africa divergent from those which suited South African interests was common to both groups in South Africa. The English-speaking did not, of course, cultivate the excesses of anti-British feeling that characterized the extreme Afrikaner nationalists; but they were sufficiently akin to the Afrikaners in ultimate local interests to succumb eventually to the final pressure to conform to Afrikaner nationalist conceptions of their interests.

Only in South Africa did Britain meet a constant, dedicated and effective nationalist movement, supported in its basic tenets by interests derived from local conditions (i.e. the native question), and embodying a local tradition strong enough to resist and eventually master the British tradition which proved so powerful in the other Dominions. The force of this fact becomes apparent when we look at the forms of political activity carried on by the two "races" in South Africa. The most furious political arguments, from the inception of the Union, took place amongst the Afrikaners, not between the two groups or amongst the English-speaking. In part this is because of the inveterately political spirit of the Afrikaners:

"No sooner have they set up a leader or a government but they start undermining their own handiwork and all our history has been one of hiving off into bickering factions and of internal quarrels among ourselves.

Even during the Great Trek, the *épopée* of our race, there were petty divisions and sordid jealousies, and under the two republics there was constant civil strife, with opposing commandos chasing each other about the countryside. We are like the Irish; when we have no external enemy we turn upon ourselves."[*]

* Deneys Reitz, *No Outspan* (London, 1943), p. 73.

The main reason, however, is that only amongst the Afrikaners has distinctively South African political argument been able to bite. The English-speaking South Africans have never, since Union, achieved their own distinctly South African frame of reference. They either asserted Imperial propositions which outraged their extreme Afrikaner opponents, or rode into office on the coat-tails of Smuts. Once his masterly presence was removed, their political poverty was revealed. Smuts himself gained his eminence through a combination of support from the English-speaking sections and business groups with an appeal to the sentiment which many Afrikaners felt for him and Botha. As this sentiment died, or turned against him, his position worsened.

There are two underlying, durable reasons why the English-speaking South Africans had to take second place in their country's politics. One was their minority position. The other, and ultimately more important, was that they could never formulate a distinctive position on the colour question. It was impossible, in the light of the privileged status which white men of both races enjoyed, to put forward or even to formulate a policy markedly different from that of the Afrikaners of either wing. When Creswell, the leader of the South African Labour Party, made his pact with Hertzog's Nationalist Party in 1923, in order to oust Smuts, he attempted to put before a meeting of Platteland farmers, staunch Nationalist supporters, an explanation of his party's views on socialism and trade unionism. He spoke in English, which many of his hearers did not understand. But one of his followers rose afterwards to translate: "The Leader of the Labour Party has just explained that his policy is to put the nigger in his place and to repatriate all Asiatics." Colonel Creswell was then cheered to the echo and carried shoulder-high to his car.* He was not in all things a typical English-speaking South African, but he was typical enough in this: he could not formulate a constructive native policy, and did not wish to. The same was true of the ally of the English-speaking South Africans, Smuts, who confessed his bankruptcy in a letter in 1906; he wrote of the natives:

". . . I don't believe in politics for them. Perhaps at bottom I do not believe in politics at all as a means for the attainment of the highest ends; but certainly so far as the natives are concerned politics will to my mind only have an unsettling influence . . .

* Pirow, op. cit., p. 96.

When I consider the political future of the natives in S.A. I
must say that I look into shadows and darkness; and then I feel
inclined to shift the intolerable burden of solving that sphinx
problem to the ampler shoulders and stronger brains of the
future."*

Without any means of thinking out a policy to deal with the
pressure from the native population as it grew more urbanized,
more educated, and more aware of changes elsewhere in Africa,
the English-speaking South Africans and their allies had no ultimate defence against the demands of the Afrikaner extremists that
they acquiesce in Afrikaner standards for the sake of preserving a
white front against black encroachments. It is easy to trace the
melancholy movement of South African politics towards a white
consensus on *apartheid*.

To say this is to run rather ahead of the juncture which this and
the preceding two chapters were intended to preserve. As general
introductions, they were supposed to deal with matters up to the
period of World War II. But in this case we are concerned with
something of a complete story, rather than a continuing narrative;
and the questions posed at the start of this chapter impel some consideration of tendencies which have now reached completion. South
African politics is, and has been, composed in different ways from
those of the other Old Dominions. The differences come in regard
to economic interests, and also over the connection with Britain.
In South Africa the kind of broad difference now represented by
the Nationalists and the United Party was economically a country-
city difference, which in its turn corresponded to an Afrikaans-
English speaking difference. (There are notable exceptions, but this
broad variation applied until comparatively recently.) The connection with Britain was viewed traditionally by the Afrikaans
group as undesirable, by the English-speaking group as a worthy
one. As the Afrikaans-speaking population has increased, as the
force of the nationalist myth has grown, as the threat of black
domination has increased, and as Afrikaners have increasingly
found jobs and money in the cities, the Afrikaner nationalist power
has become dominant. This has meant, in practice, an increase of
pressure against British symbols and the British connection. The
English-speakers have been able to offer little but a token resistance
in the form of delaying action of various kinds. The pattern is very

* Quoted in Hancock, op. cit., p. 221.

different from either Australia and New Zealand, with their politics still grounded on differences in economic status, and Canada, in which, while "racial" considerations are important, they apply to a minority which is firmly located in a particular part of Canada, and takes its place amongst the primarily regional (and also economic) bases of Canadian politics. The 1931 statement by Winston Churchill, about sections in each Dominion which put the Imperial connection at either its highest or at the minimum, was a true statement, but of much greater importance in regard to South Africa than the other three with which we are concerned. Only in South Africa did this aspect become and remain decisive in settling political lines of force. The hope of Smuts and Merriman before Union that in politics their country would "conform— federalism apart—to a Canadian pattern of growth"* was a vain one in the end, although it seemed for a time to be fulfilled.

Another way of putting the difference between South Africa and the other Old Dominions is that, whereas for all four the connection with Britain was partly a bread-and-butter affair and partly a matter of emotion, in the other three cases the weight was on the bread-and-butter side, while for South Africa it was on the emotional side, which in this case was hostile emotion. This may seem a strange way to put it, in view of the vast British investment in South African mines. My meaning is that emotionalism, in the sense of symbolism (including the adoption of a national posture) went further and lasted longer in South Africa. British–South African relations, over all, have not shared the same "family" atmosphere as relations between Britain and the other three; there has been more of the air of genuine diplomacy about them, in spite of Smuts's incorporation into the British political machine in both world wars. The major issues between Britain and South Africa— the disposition of the High Commission territories, British policy towards native advance in near-by territories, the status of Indians in Natal, and the question of neutrality—have been more formidable, more the kinds of things that constitute traditional diplomacy, than the arguments over trade which have been for so long the stuff of negotiation with the other Dominions. It is true that the South African dislike of "Hoggenheimer" the Randlord can be paralleled by dislike of British capitalists elsewhere, and that Britain has had trade arguments with South Africa too; the conscription issues in Canada and Australia in World War I carried

* Hancock, op. cit., p. 268.

many of the overtones of South African disputes about Britain. But, in general, South Africa has stood apart since before Union, and stands farther away now than ever.

It is thus not surprising that in the 1960's South Africa should stand by itself in regard to monarchy and membership of the Commonwealth. Its isolation from the general Western alliance, especially from the United States, is no more difficult to account for. Whereas in both world wars South Africa was an acceptable ally (though contributing little outside Africa), it is not so now. The change is not in South Africa but in the rest of the world. South African policy towards its black population was previously respectable; it is no longer so, especially in the United States, where strenuous efforts have been made for many years to impress on Afro-Asian countries that American policy is neither "racist" nor "colonialist". Here, as elsewhere, the pervading issue of colour in South Africa gives it a uniqueness which no other country shares, preventing it from being accepted as an equal partner by others, in spite of its non-socialist economy, its cultural affinities with Britain and Western Europe, its essentially western political system, and its past efforts as an ally.

5

BRITAIN AND THE FOUR 1918–1945

THE period from 1918 to 1945, from the end of one war to the end of another, can aptly be called that of the "Statute of Westminster Commonwealth", or of "Dominion status". The autonomy of the four countries we are discussing was made manifest, and the expression "British Commonwealth of Nations" was appropriated to deal specifically with their situation (and that of the Irish Free State). The period is something of a natural epoch in their relations with Britain, so much so that certain people still regard it as a time in which were set standards to which events ought to conform. Frequently, in the succeeding two decades from 1945 to 1965, there were disconsolate and rueful references to the time when, it was felt, the Dominions achieved their full status, and yet the British Empire remained a reality. In a sense, the British Commonwealth of Nations achieved its apotheosis in those days in World War II when

> "the four High Commissioners in London gathered together at the Dominions Office most afternoons at three o'clock under the chairmanship of the Secretary of State . . . These meetings might last two hours or more. They were always very pleasant affairs, though occupied by very serious matters. In the early days Cranborne dispensed tea and cakes while his Secretary read out the reports . . ."*

Such a cosy situation, while brought about primarily by the war, was also the product of the constitutional changes which had occurred since the previous war; it was not static, and contained within itself the seeds of further change which were to make the Commonwealth relationship a different one in later years.

The period is naturally separable into two sections, those of peace and war. The peace section, from 1918 to 1939, is important because of the efforts made to deal with three major issues of relations

---

* G. Heaton Nicholls, *South Africa in My Time* (London, 1961), p. 382. Nicholls was South African High Commissioner from 1944 to 1948.

between Britain and the four, the issues of status, foreign policy, and economics. In this chapter I shall deal with these in turn, then describe briefly the political changes which took place in each of the Dominions and their experiences in World War II, and shall finally ask how matters stood with regard to the general relationship when World War II ended.

THE STATUS ISSUE

Some reference has already been made in Chapter 1 to the status issue. It needs to be considered in two related aspects, those of constitutional nicety and of politics. Contemporary discussion did not succeed in separating these two, and it would be surprising if anyone could finally do so; nevertheless, both need to be recognized. The question of constitutional nicety was important. A great many thinking people in Britain and the Dominions had grown up to believe that a single Crown meant that all the King's men were subject to the King's authority, and that this authority was exercised ultimately through the parliament at Westminster. The idea of colonies cutting themselves off from this authority or attempting to appropriate it entirely to themselves smacked of "separatism". Yet it was clear that the growth of the Dominions as self-contained states, managing their own affairs in the domestic sphere, meant that sooner or later a major clash of policy between Britain and a Dominion might arise, and that the King might be placed in an impossible position. At the same time, it was clear that Britain would hardly be in a position to coerce a Dominion against its will.*

This background of constitutional oddity pursued Britain and the Four throughout the period, whether in terms of flags and anthems, the formation of foreign policy, the naming of envoys, or the nomination of Governors-General. Gradually, a solution was found in practice, even while resisted in the abstract. Commonwealth affairs remained wrapped in a cocoon of theory, from which would emerge from time to time the formidable voice of Professor Berriedale Keith. One must not over-emphasize the importance of constitutional nicety as a political fact: both Britain

---

* This extreme situation never actually occurred between Britain and one of the Four, although something like it arose between Britain and the Irish Free State in the 1930's.

and the Dominions were moved by forces within and beyond themselves, which were not to be overborne by theoretical considerations. Yet it is clear that these were of some consequence to the
principal actors in the drama (they worried King George V and
King George VI, for example), and they were capable of being
used for political purposes.

The main political aspects have already been foreshadowed.
Briefly, they were that Canada and South Africa sought a clearer
definition of the status of the Dominions, while Australia and
New Zealand did not. The delphic utterance of the 1926 Imperial
Conference on the status of the Dominions was occasioned by the
need to placate General Hertzog, and took its actual form from
arguments in which he was a prominent participant, but its substance had been gained through the efforts of Canada at previous
conferences, and from the increased stature which the Dominions
had achieved by their actions in World War I. The conservative
governments of Australia and New Zealand resisted these efforts to
clarify and define status; they were permeated by returned soldier
sentiment, they were reluctant to accept any independent role in
the world, and they looked to Britain as guide and provider. In
Britain itself there was, as we have seen, some concern about the
possible consequences of clarification, but a much greater sense of
the need to satisfy Dominion sentiment in order to preserve some
kind of British front in the world at large.

It would be tedious to re-trace the course of the definition of
Dominion status, when this has been done in so many books.* The
essence of it was the assertion of Dominion autonomy, by means
of equality with Britain, freedom from technical British control
over law-making, freedom to undertake treaties, and the assumption
of a right of independent diplomacy. Canada was in the forefront
in some of these spheres, South Africa in others; the Irish Free
State, in its brief period as a Dominion, accelerated the process,
especially in regard to the Judicial Committee of the Privy Council
and the assertion that treaties between Dominions were diplomatic instruments of the same quality as treaties between ordinary

---

* See, e.g. W. K. Hancock, *Survey of British Commonwealth Affairs*, Vol. I
(London, 1937); K. C. Wheare, *The Statute of Westminster and Dominion
Status* (London, 1938 and subsequent editions); R. McG. Dawson (ed.), *The
Development of Dominion Status, 1900–1936* (London, 1937); A. Berriedale
Keith, *The Dominions as Sovereign States* (London, 1938); Heather J. Harvey,
Consultation and Co-operation in the Commonwealth (London, 1952).

sovereign states. Australia and New Zealand provided little but disapproval, except when J. H. Scullin, a Labour Party Prime Minister of Australia for a brief period, claimed and gained the right to nominate the Australian Governor-General in spite of the unwillingness of King George V to appoint a particular Australian to the post. For much of the 1920's and 30's, arguments over status were conducted at the level of generalities, intended to apply to the Dominions as a whole; in South Africa, however, questions of the local flag and anthem became matters of the keenest controversy. It was from South Africa, too, that the most important question of all was raised: that of the right of Dominions to be neutral in a war in which Britain was involved.

Such a right of neutrality was basic to extremist Afrikaner Nationalist opinion. Britain's wars were seen as wars of conquest, from which the Afrikaners had already suffered; although resistance to World War I had been crushed by Botha and Smuts in 1914, the men who led the rebellion had been canonized by a later generation of Nationalists. Neutrality and the eventual right to set up a republic were symbols of power. This particular claim had not been made before by any political group of consequence. Laurier, who had postulated the right of a Dominion to decide the extent to which it would exercise belligerency in a war in which Britain was engaged, had not questioned the technical right of Britain to involve the Dominions in war as a matter of law. The claim to neutrality was, in effect, a claim to disown the Crown: how could the King be at war and not at war at the same time?

The lengths to which exponents of the Commonwealth would go in attempting to evade the dilemma of neutrality in the 1930's are shown by the report of the Sub-Commission on War and Neutrality of the first British Commonwealth Relations Conference, held in Toronto in 1933.* Having pointed out that the members of the Commonwealth were all members of the League of Nations, and that this, together with their adherence to the Kellogg Pact, obliged them to act against aggressors, it went on:

> "This survey, based on the realities of the modern world, makes it clear that old conceptions as to declaration of war and as to neutrality can have little if any place in the policies of the law-

---

* Arnold J. Toynbee, *British Commonwealth Relations* (London, 1934), pp. 179–81. The sub-commission's rapporteur was H. V. Hodson.

abiding nations. It seems clear to us that in perhaps every case that can be imagined the machinery of the League or the obligations assumed under the Kellogg Pact will make clear to the nations of the Commonwealth the course that they should all pursue.

It seems to us academic and unprofitable to consider legal constitutional difficulties which might arise if there were no Covenant and no Kellogg Pact . . . it would serve no useful purpose to try and foresee problems in one field, that of war, which we are entitled to hope are never likely to arise, and to seek to apply to them legal conceptions as to war and neutrality appropriate to the pre-League world."

In fact, of course, the post-League world proved very much like the pre-League world, in that neutrality could and did become a live issue in South Africa in 1938 and 1939, while Eire was able to practise it between 1939 and 1945. The point for our purpose, however, is that neutrality postulated the British Empire as no longer a single entity with a single sovereign, but as a multiple entity in which, while the person of a single sovereign remained, it did so by virtue of recognition that the Crown was divisible and was, in fact, a number of crowns worn by the same person.

Curiously enough, the demonstration of this fact came, not in 1939, but in 1936, when, because of differential legislation in the various Dominions consequent upon the abdication of King Edward VIII,

"the accession of King George VI to the throne of his various Kingdoms took place on three different days. He became King of South Africa on 10 December. He became King of Great Britain and Northern Ireland, of Australia, Canada, New Zealand, and the rest of the Empire, except India, of which he became Emperor, on 11 December. He became King of the Irish Free State on 12 December."*

The spacing out of the Canadian and South African declarations of war in 1939 showed the same state of affairs: Dominion status meant that the Crown was divisible, and that the King had more than one Kingdom.

* B. K. Long, "Crown and Commonwealth", in E. Thomas Cook (ed.), *The Empire in the World* (London, 1937), pp. 132–3.

I have stressed the importance of the royal position because it was the legal key to the status of the Dominions. The Statute of Westminster, passed by the British Parliament in 1931, was a self-denying ordinance in which that parliament forewent its right to legislate for the Dominions without their request and consent. But this still left in reserve the royal prerogative, which, while it had been confined and domesticated in the Dominions in a variety of ways, might still be said to encompass the ancient right of declaration of war and obligation upon the King's subjects to serve in his wars. The events of 1936 and 1939 showed that the King was made in the first instance by his Dominion parliaments and was governed in his decision on peace or war by their domestic requirements. This was a change indeed from earlier times and wars.

It was customary in the 1930's to say, when recognizing that the Dominions had acquired equal "status" with Britain, that they had still not acquired equal "stature". The point was valid; more will be made of it below in considering the foreign policy issue. Its practical consequences in the conduct of day-to-day affairs can be seen in the operation of what came to be known later as the "Commonwealth system", i.e. the business of communication between Britain and the Dominions, in which the British part was paramount.

In order to show appreciation of the increased importance of the Dominions after World War I, a separate Dominions Office was created in 1925 to conduct business between Britain and the Dominions. There had been a Dominions section in the Colonial Office since 1907, and, even after the creation of the Dominions Office, staff continued to be shared between the two departments. A single Minister held both portfolios until 1930. Such an arrangement looked like a distinction without a difference, but it gained significance in the 1930's, when the Governors-General of the Dominions ceased to be the local representatives of the British Government, and were replaced by resident British High Commissioners, who took their orders from the Dominions Office. The Dominions' High Commissioners in London, who had previously been representatives of no clear status, were given closer access to British departments. They approximated more nearly to the position of ambassadors, although the title Ambassador was withheld because it was considered that the King could hardly appoint an ambassador to himself, and because a more intimate association than the ambassadorial was intended. The High Commissioners came to be channels of high-level communication between their countries and Britain. However, while this was widely accepted as a sensible method of doing business, especially in regard to foreign affairs (on which Britain had almost a monopoly of information), it awakened morbid fears of "commitment" in Mackenzie King as Prime Minister of Canada. He instructed his High Commissioner, Vincent Massey, in 1936 that, while he could see a British Minister alone, he could not see him in "consultation" with the other High Commissioners; this meant that on occasion the other High Commissioners met the unhappy Massey sitting in the Dominions Secretary's ante-room when they came out from discussions with him.* It was not until 1938 that Mackenzie King felt sufficiently safe from entanglement to allow Massey to attend with the others. Such an example shows that, while the Dominions were gaining "status" in one respect, that of continuous consultation, the lack of equal "stature" between themselves and Britain was still evident and could convince Dominion nationalists that they might be drawn into commitments which they would find unwelcome.

The Commonwealth system, operating continuously by the end of the 1930's through the High Commissioner in London and in the Dominion capitals, and through the growing Departments of External Affairs of the Dominions, was formalized by the Imperial Conference, which continued to meet with some regularity until its last meeting before the war, in 1937. The actual progress of the status issue is to be traced through the deliberations of the meetings in 1923, 1926, 1930 and 1937. The Conference was very much as it had always been, an opportunity for British Ministers to display themselves before their Dominion counterparts, and vice versa. In the eyes of the world, however, its main function was to demonstrate the cohesive quality of the British Empire, a term which remained in use in spite of the attractions of the new term "British Commonwealth of Nations". The latter was, in any case, unduly technical. The official explanation of the position, as stated by the 1926 Imperial Conference, was that an outer circle (the British Empire) contained three constituent sections: the British Commonwealth of Nations (Britain and the Dominions); the Indian Empire; and the Colonial Empire. While this explanation suited everybody for different reasons, it was not very exciting; no great political theme pervaded such a three-ring circus.

* Vincent Massey, *What's Past is Prologue* (Toronto, 1963), p. 240. The whole of Chapter 8 is of great interest in this connection.

THE FOREIGN POLICY ISSUE

The foreign policy issue between the wars was a simple one in essence, although it led to much tortuous reasoning. It was that Britain did not wish to involve the Dominions in war without their consent; the Dominions did not want to be dragged into a war at Britain's coat-tails; the Dominions were vaguely supposed to have a kind of suspensive veto over British actions which might lead to war; yet no machinery was devised to provide a common foreign policy for the Empire, since South Africa and Canada shrank from any ties which might lead to responsibility for British policy, while Australia and New Zealand were so primitive in their knowledge of foreign affairs, and so preoccupied with their own domestic problems, that their good intentions about 'an Empire policy' could not begin to be translated into anything effective.* The Dominions showed, by their different approaches to the Chanak crisis of 1922, and by their common opposition to the Geneva Protocol in 1924, that they could not be expected to follow automatically any policy which Britain put forward. But they also showed, by their mulishness and isolationism of later years, that they were not prepared to devote the necessary energies to working out the implications of Dominion status in the foreign field. Some minority groups, such as the Nationalists in South Africa and sections of the Labour Party in Australia, wished to demonstrate Dominion status by contracting out of international disputes altogether, and remaining neutral in a war. This was a logical enough position in the abstract, however doubtful it might be as a remedy for the particular circumstances of the 1930's. But most Dominion opinion was not prepared to go as far as this. Most people who thought about foreign affairs seemed to wish for involvement, yet not to will the means by which it could be made effective. Some took refuge in the League of Nations as a means of resolving difficulties; others thought "consultation" would be sufficient to straighten out the kinks in the British countries' approach to foreign affairs. But mostly they seemed to hope for the best without preparing for the worst. This set of uncertainties led to the consequence that

* The reader's attention is directed to the magisterial treatment of these matters in Nicholas Mansergh, *Survey of British Commonwealth Affairs: Problems of External Policy 1931–1939* (London, 1952).

"Great Britain in 1938 had to face the responsibilities of a World Power in the knowledge that her ability to participate in a world war depended on the support of a number of distant States, bound to her by intangible ties which, however powerful in an emergency, were not strong enough to make a consistent Commonwealth policy easy to formulate. The point where Britain was immediately threatened, i.e. in Europe, was of less obvious importance to the Dominions, and Britain's instinct of national self-preservation was constantly checked by the far slower reactions of other members of the Commonwealth."*

To put the matter in this way is to blame the Dominions for the consequences of a state of mind which was, in any case, endemic in Britain itself at the time; such attitudes as refusal to face unpleasant facts and a disposition to think the best of the European dictators, because of the unpleasant implications of thinking the worst, were not confined to the Dominions. What was distinctive about them, however, was their sense of isolation and insulation, of keeping themselves apart from the problems of a Europe which had plunged them into war in 1914. This attitude was most noticeable in Canada, but it was also plainly evident in Australia, South Africa and New Zealand. There was considerable similarity between their feeling and that of the revulsion from war of the Middle West of the United States: a suspicion of Europe, an inclination to believe that war was made by militarists or arms manufacturers or devils of some other sort, a conviction that new countries should not make the mistakes of old ones, a disinclination to indulge in international action because this might lead to responsibility for other people's affairs. Canada under Mackenzie King showed a lead to other Dominions which they were not loath to follow, except that, by the end of the 1930's, Australia and New Zealand were rather more inclined to consider possible involvement.† After the triumph of "status" in 1926, discussion of foreign affairs largely faded out of the agenda of Imperial Conferences. The Dominions retreated into their own shells; the economic depression of the

* *The History of The Times*, Vol. IV, Part II (London, 1952), p. 1021.
† It is significant that, according to Paul Hasluck, an official historian with full access to Australian confidential files, "the Australian Government appears to have been the only Dominion to propose a close examination of the major issues of foreign policy and defence and at the same time a consideration of the means and methods of defence" at the Imperial Conference of 1937. (*The Government and the People 1939–1941*, Canberra, 1952, p. 56.)

1930's forced them into domestic preoccupations, except with trade, and thus aided the natural inclination towards isolationism which had been evident in the 1920's. There was, however, considerable military liaison through the Committee of Imperial Defence and its offshoots.*

When the Munich crisis broke on the world in 1938, the Dominions were among the forces pressing upon the British Government to appease Hitler. Not a great deal of pressure was required; Neville Chamberlain and his colleagues were exercising the "instinct of self-preservation" in a way which dictated pacification, not belligerency, and which was fully acceptable to the Dominions. There is, indeed, something instructive in the fact that, in spite of the divergent approaches which they showed to certain international questions, the Dominions were united in deploring the idea of a morganatic marriage for King Edward VIII in 1936, were united in urging "appeasement" in the final report of the Imperial Conference of 1937, and were united in support of Chamberlain in 1938. In all these matters the four Old Dominions were joined by the Irish Free State. Their leaders combined a miasmic respectability in upholding the principle that the King could not marry a divorced woman, with a considerable unreadiness to face the facts of international life. Baldwin and Chamberlain, worthy men of blameless personal conduct and a comprehensive lack of experience and interest in the complexities of European politics, were suitable counterparts for them. It is easy to agree with Lord Vansittart's verdict on the policies of the Dominions: "One could not blame them, one could not admire them, one could not admire anybody."†

The problem of how to co-ordinate or combine the attitudes of the Dominions with that of Britain was not solved before 1939. Yet it is instructive that the Old Dominions were united in support of Britain in the 1939 declaration of war, although this required a change of government in South Africa. The "foreign policy issue" disappeared under the stress of Hitler's absorption of Austria and clear intention to bring all Europe under his control. What influences caused the Four to take Britain's part in September 1939?‡

* See D. C. Watt, *Personalities and Policies* (London, 1965), Essay 7.

† Lord Vansittart, *The Mist Procession* (London, 1958), p. 529.

‡ All four countries were, of course, heavily dependent on Britain for advice on foreign affairs, since they lacked diplomatic posts of their own. To this extent they were likely to reflect any change in the official British position.

The Australian and New Zealand cases were, as might have been expected, simple. These countries were British in background, were accustomed to regard Britain as indispensable to their defence, were heavily dependent on Britain for trade and for the protection of the seaways, and were apprehensive about the connections between Hitler, Mussolini and the Japanese, the last of whom they were accustomed to regard as their natural enemies. The alternative to involvement was isolation, with no sort of assurance or even indication that the United States would be interested in their defence. Attitudes in Canada and South Africa were more complicated. In both cases it is clear that simple "Empire" sentiment was a strong impelling force amongst those elements which had traditionally supported the British connection. There was hesitancy in Quebec and downright opposition from the Nationalists in South Africa. But in both countries there was also the sense of habitual association with Britain, coupled with a strongly-developed distaste for Hitler's actions. This latter point, applicable also to Britain, helps to explain why the British countries swung from enthusiasm for appeasement in 1938 to agreement on war in 1939. In 1938 they grasped at the last straw of peace, doing so with excessive zeal in order to overcome the doubts and fears which Hitler's previous actions had aroused. In 1939 the last straw had gone, and was widely seen to be gone; it was with something of a sigh of relief that leaders turned to resistance in place of appeasement, Hitler having demonstrated that the stifled doubts of the year before were only too true. This change of mind, obvious in Britain, was slower and more piecemeal in some of the Dominions, because of their earlier isolationism and their greater distance from events; but it took place there all the same.

In the end, then, the foreign policy issue was solved by events. Each country came to the same conclusion in 1939, some more readily than others; the Irish did not come to it at all, and thereby parted finally from any close official relationship with the Four.

THE ECONOMIC ISSUE

There was, of course, no single economic issue in the relations between Britain and the Old Dominions between the wars, any more than at other times. Each country had a complex economy involving a variety of interests, Britain's being very much the most complex of all. Whenever an attempt was made to treat such a constellation of issues as a single problem, the effort soon proved insufficient. But this was the period in which the problems seemed to be converging into a single issue, or a few issues which could be handled together; in consequence, we are able to look at the situation in terms of "men, money and markets", in a way which would be more difficult at other periods.*

Broadly speaking, the influences of World War I caused the Dominions to accentuate the demands which they had made before the war for a privileged position in the British market. Not only had they provided food and fibres which Britain needed in vast quantities to carry on the war; they had also enlarged their capacity to produce these goods, and had made commitments which would keep production at high levels. Their returned servicemen wanted better treatment than before the war; in countries which still thought of themselves as mainly food producers, in spite of growing industrialization which the war had fostered, politicians naturally promised farms to the men back from the front. It was easy to maintain that Britain should favour those countries which had stood by her in the war, rather than those, like Russia, which had fallen out of the fight, or those, like Argentina or Denmark, which had not been in it at all. Moreover, wartime experience seemed to many in the Dominions to point the way to a closer organization of Imperial resources: if the British countries could ship hundreds of thousands of men around the globe, equip them and feed them, and at the same time control the marketing of such normally intractable products as metals, wool and wheat, why should they not organize themselves for mutual benefit in peace? Why should there not be a redistribution of people which would strengthen the younger countries while removing from Britain much of the population which it could not support? Money and laws seemed all that were needed to make the Empire a reality.

As against this Dominion demand for special consideration, there stood the British interest in free trade, based upon the need for cheap food and raw materials. Pre-war trade, as we have seen, had not been primarily with the Dominions; their share had been quite small. The great sources of British imports lay rather in the Americas and in Europe. Moreover, the great markets for British

* Readers of W. K. Hancock, *Survey of British Commonwealth Affairs*, Vol. II, Part 1 (London, 1940), will recognize my indebtedness to Chapter III, in which these matters are treated with great authority.

goods lay in those same places, not in the Dominions. Along with the desire to keep down the British import bill went a widespread conviction that, if Britain erected barriers to other countries' goods in favour of Dominion goods, those other countries would retaliate. To the charge that it was unfair to treat "foreigners" on the same plane as kith and kin, the British reply was that a world in which trade barriers were raised against Britain would bring benefits to nobody. The schemes for organization of whole commodity markets under government supervision or government guarantee met black looks from the City of London, to which the idea of multi-lateral trade was as natural as breathing.[*]

The Dominion effort to enmesh Britain in guarantees had met some success in 1917, when the Imperial War Cabinet and Conference decided that the time had arrived to make the Empire "independent of other countries in respect of food supplies, raw materials, and essential industries", to which end they supported:

> "(1) The principle that each part of the Empire, having due regard to the interests of the Allies, shall give specially favourable treatment and facilities to the produce and manufactures of other parts of the Empire.
> (2) Arrangements by which intending emigrants from the United Kingdom may be induced to settle in countries under the British flag."[†]

This declaration, which embodied the general Dominion aim, was given some force by the British budget of 1919, which, while it did not provide adequate preferences from a Dominion point of view, did give the Dominions some advantage in the case of goods which were already subject to duty. The nearest the Dominions got to what they wanted was the promise of the British Conservative Government of 1923 to provide significant preferences for goods which saw competition between Empire and foreign producers, but which were not produced in Britain, or of which the

---

[*] This is a condensed account of British opinion. It is necessary to remember that in the 1920's and 30's the British political parties were sharply divided on Free Trade, Labour and the Liberals being for it, the Conservatives against. But the course of politics in the 1920's, especially the 1923 General Election, ensured that Free Trade policies would remain in operation throughout the decade.

[†] Cd. 8566 of 1917, quoted in W. K. Hancock, *Survey of British Commonwealth Affairs*, Vol II, Part I (London, 1940), pp. 126–7.

British producers were few, such as tobacco, dried fruits, canned salmon and honey. That government's defeat at an election in which protection and preference were live issues, meant an end to any effective move in this direction until the Depression and the Ottawa conference of 1932.

Meanwhile, the Dominions, having failed to get what they wanted in the field of "markets", had done something in regard to "men". Britain agreed to assist settlement in the Dominions, not only through assisted passages for migrants, but also by contributions towards substantial schemes of economic development which would establish the migrants in productive work. The 1920's were, in fact, a period of heavy emigration from Britain. But a great deal of this was self-impelled rather than the result of government policy; and the development schemes, of which only a few were put into effect, were a sad disappointment. It became clear that the Dominions, especially Australia and Canada, were over-reaching themselves in migrant settlement as they had done in soldier settlement, and in much the same ways : inadequate preparation of settlement areas, failure to find people who would stick at the work, cultivation of crops which became drugs on the market, misplaced credit, and bad luck with international trade. Successful migration was to the cities, not the country. Demands for increased protection for the manufacturing industries into which migrants and local people had been absorbed grew inexorably; and this meant, in practice in most cases, protection against British imports.

Assisted migration might have produced some of the results hoped for it in the 1920's if it had been remorselessly carried out in the spirit of Foggartism;* but no one was prepared to deal with it in this way. The Dominions themselves were not unanimous in their enthusiasm for immigrants. South Africa and Canada were careful to take no more migrants than their capacity for employment seemed to dictate; New Zealand and Australian trade unions watched immigration figures with a sceptical eye, and correlated them whenever possible with unemployment. The basic difficulty, however, was that the vision of migration to the wide open spaces

---

* Foggartism, the invention of Sir James Foggart, a character in John Galsworthy's *The Silver Spoon* (Book II of *A Modern Comedy*), was a scheme for establishing agricultural colonies in the Dominions to take people from the British slums. It was adopted as a policy to push in parliament by Michael Mont, Soames Forsyte's son-in-law. Galsworthy's treatment of the matter casts a useful contemporary sidelight on English views of the Dominions in the 1920's.

of the Dominions was out of date. The population of most rural areas in those countries was falling off as more advanced methods of agriculture freed people for work in the cities; substantial extension of rural production was hardly practicable at a time when markets were proving harder to find, and competitors in the Americas and Europe were striving to capture what markets there were.

A combination of hopes blighted, heavy competition and falling or stagnant prices caused Dominion leaders to look even harder at the British market, and to rage with even greater fury about the British persistence with free trade, especially with the slogan of a free breakfast-table. Their exports of meat and dairy products, in particular, could be expanded if the British would give up their addiction to Argentine beef, Danish bacon and everybody else's butter. But, as the inter-war period wore on, it became clear that, even if Dominion pressure could dislodge some of these competitors from the British market, there was another formidable figure to take into account: the British farmer himself. Milk, meat and wheat, the three staples of British farming, were all directly competitive with Dominion products. While British farmers had natural advantages in some fields, such as fresh milk, they were aware that Canadian cheese or New Zealand butter and lamb constituted just as much a barrier to higher prices for British products as anything coming from Europe. If Britain could be brought round to agricultural protectionism, the local farmer could get first cut at his own market. He might not mind Dominion producers getting second cut, and the foreigners coming nowhere; but he wanted first cut for himself. Successive National governments showed more and more courage in advancing the claims of the British farmer. The more this happened, the more the hopes of Dominion farmers for big new markets filched from foreigners faded; the most they could hope for was to hold something like their existing quotas.

Agricultural protectionism in Britain did not show its full possibilities until after the Ottawa conference of 1932, but its shadow was one of those cast over this, the only "Empire" conference that has ever attempted substantial economic change. It met to try to temper the effects of the "economic blizzard", the Great Depression which had hit the Dominions so hard through their dependence on exports of primary products, the prices of which had fallen catastrophically from 1929 onwards. Unemployment and loss of markets caused the British Government to think again about mutual preference; for once, the prospect of a *quid pro quo*, in the shape of sheltered markets in the Dominions for British manufactures, seemed worthwhile for its own sake. Britain and the Empire could talk business at last, since Britain had something more to gain than the rather vague consolidation of imperial ties which had been all that schemes of preference offered before.

It was not the best of conferences. "The British ministers are all mediocre men," wrote Heaton Nicholls,* who was there to watch the interests of Natal sugar producers. "This gathering of Empire statesmen has really been a gathering of ordinary men, very ordinary men, some of them with a slight vein of eloquence and able to manufacture platitudes easily, but most of them knowing precious little about the trade and industry with which they were called upon to deal." "One must not take Ottawa and its output too seriously", wrote an Australian economist who was present.† "After all the pomp and public expectation, mutual irritation, more than once, went near to wrecking the negotiations of delegations who had sworn to advance the sacred cause of Empire trade." The British delegation found Bennett, the Canadian Prime Minister, especially trying. "Instead of guiding the conference in his capacity as chairman," wrote Neville Chamberlain of Bennett in his diary, "he has acted merely as the leader of the Canadian delegation. In that capacity he has strained our patience to the limit."‡ When the British delegation returned home, Ramsay Macdonald, as Prime Minister of the National Government so recently established, received an acid letter from Lord Snowden, who had accompanied him out of the Labour Party but was not prepared to go with him as far as Protection :

"The Delegation went to Ottawa with the declared intention of increasing inter-Imperial trade, and securing a general lowering of world tariffs. We had their assurance that nothing would be agreed to which hampered our freedom to negotiate with foreign countries for the lowering of tariffs. They have come back after

* G. Heaton Nicholls, *South Africa in my Time* (London, 1961), p. 245 (from Nicholls's diary). Sir Keith Feiling hardly convinces a sceptical eye in writing: "Our delegation was strong: Baldwin, Chamberlain, Hailsham, Runciman, Thomas, Gilmour and Cunliffe Lister, reinforced by industrial advisers like Weir and civil servants like Horace Wilson . . ." (*The Life of Neville Chamberlain*, London, 1947, p. 211).
† E. O. G. Shann, *Quotas or Stable Money?* (Sydney, 1933), p. 5.
‡ Feiling, op. cit., p. 215.

weeks of acrimonious disputes and sordid struggles with vested interests, with agreements wrenched from them to avert a collapse, and an exposure to the world of the hollowness of the talk of Imperial sentiment in economic affairs."*

The Ottawa agreements precipitated the resignation from the National Government of Snowden and the Samuelite Liberals, and the isolation alongside the Conservatives of Macdonald and Simon. It was not, however, the sole cause of these resignations. The determination of the Conservatives to press on with forms of protection had estranged the Free Traders in the Government before Ottawa convened.

What was achieved at Ottawa? It is still difficult to say. There was certainly some change in the direction of British trade after the agreements were signed. "The proportion of British imports coming from the Empire rose from 29 per cent in 1930 to 35 per cent in 1932 and 38 per cent in 1935. In 1938 it was 40 per cent ... The change in the direction of British exports was somewhat less striking. The proportion going to the Empire rose from 43·5 per cent in 1930 to 48 per cent in 1935 and 50 per cent in 1938."† There was, then, some shift in trade. The difficulty was that there was no substantial increase in trade. Baldwin, in making the opening speech for Britain, had spoken of the conference's task as "clearing out the channels of trade", and this had had the sort of response which the Dominions wanted at the time, that of clearing some foreigners out of the British import trade. But it had not evoked the response which, on the whole, the British had wanted, that of encouraging world trade to increase. The immediate gains from the switch in trade were valuable for those interests which benefited from them, but they did not suffice to improve the overall position of either Britain or each of the Four. Britain had not given a great deal away; soon, however, the pressure of the British farmer edged the British government towards withdrawing some of what it seemed to have given.

On the Dominions' side there was soon dissatisfaction, in two main forms. One was concerned about the future of local protected industries, which might suffer from the obligations accepted by Canada and Australia at Ottawa to submit future schemes of

---

* Quoted in G. M. Young, *Stanley Baldwin* (London, 1952), p. 169.

† Frederic Benham, *Great Britain under Protection* (New York, 1941), pp. 102, 104.

protection to independent tariff commissions or boards, in order not to prejudice unduly the opportunities of British exporters. In Australia the Tariff Board did its job effectively and (if the word can be used in this connection) scientifically, in spite of cries of despair from the local Labour movement; in Canada the Tariff Commission, under the eye of a much more heavily protectionist government than the Lyons government in Australia, wasted its time in academic inquiry, and put no effective brake on tariff policy. The other form of Dominion dissatisfaction was of rather more importance. It was the discovery that, no matter how the Ottawa agreements might be interpreted, they did not suffice to satisfy the export demands of Dominion producers.

"Australia was taught this lesson by a threat to her basic industry, wool growing. Even New Zealand, the Dominion whose economy was most closely fitted to the sheltering British market, learnt during the anxieties and conflicts which followed Ottawa that the British market was ceasing to be a sufficient outlet for her productive energies."*

In the case of Canada, the Ottawa agreements were something of a make-weight against the United States, which had been pursuing a fiercely protectionist policy throughout the 1920's. "If American policy had been less hostile in the three years after 1929, it is unlikely that Canada would have pursued so energetically her policy of British preference . . . a catastrophic crisis coupled with unneighbourly treatment was sufficient inducement for the Dominion to look for refuge in the British Empire. Recovery in the United States and the adoption of a more liberal commercial policy by that country gave Canada the opportunity, which she lost no time in seizing, of interpreting the principle of Imperial preference in a less violent and offensive manner."† In South Africa there was little disposition in the Hertzog governments to enlarge concessions to Britain at the expense of European countries.

Regarded as a temporary effort to relieve depression difficulties, Ottawa was a modified success; it certainly improved matters for a number of politically sensitive industries in the Dominions, and

* Hancock, *Survey of British Commonwealth Affairs*, Vol. II, Part I (London, 1940). p. 266.

† D. R. Annett, *British Preference in Canadian Commercial Policy* (Toronto, 1948), p. 92.

did not noticeably increase Britain's import bill. It gave British industries a talking-point in their effort to achieve fair competition with protected Dominion industries. Some of its long-term effects were not so praiseworthy. It may well have prolonged the life of certain uneconomic rural activities in the Dominions, especially in Australia, although it is likely that local political pressure would have sustained these somehow or other. It was something of a drag on Britain's attempt in the early 1960's to enter the European Economic Community, since much of the Commonwealth complaint with which Britain had to deal was based upon the likely impact on industries which Britain had, in effect, guaranteed in 1932 and continued to guarantee in later agreements. The biggest drawback of Ottawa, however, seems in retrospect to have been its effect on opinion in the United States. During World War II and in the years immediately after it, Britain and the Dominions were faced with an American orthodoxy which resisted many of their efforts to overcome it. It was based upon the idea that at Ottawa an attempt had been made to set up a closed economic system, the main aim of which was to make life difficult for the United States by keeping its primary products out of Britain and its manufactures out of the Dominions. The trouble was, in part, that American opinion had taken the contemporary protestations about Ottawa at face value. British and Dominion leaders had united in misrepresenting the importance of their agreements at Ottawa, if in nothing else. Instead of saying that they had made a number of bi-lateral agreements in which no special interest got all it wanted, but all got some of what they wanted, and that the greater part of British and Dominion trade was not affected by what had been decided, they kept saying that history had reached a turning-point. The Americans can be blamed for continuing to believe this in the face of the evidence of later years, but they cannot be blamed for having believed it at the time. Post-war difficulties gained much from the persistence of the idea that British Empire had done something radical to itself at Ottawa.*

So much for "men" and "markets". "Money" is a shorter story. Britain continued to be the main source of capital for the Dominions in the 1920's and 30's, and the position of Dominion Government

---

* I have not attempted to go into the agreements in any detail. There is ample material in Hancock, op. cit., and a good brief summary of the agreements from the British side in Frederick Benham, *Great Britain Under Protection* (New York, 1941), Ch. IV.

stocks as trustee securities gave them a certain advantage in London. But access to money was necessarily limited by prospects of return and repayment. The depression caused a considerable decline in Dominion public borrowing in London; in fact, this almost ceased in the 1930's. Private financing (especially in the establishment of branches of British firms behind the Dominions' tariff walls) increased as the 1930's went on, but there was no resumption of the massive government borrowing which had been such a feature of the years immediately before World War I and of the 1920's. The Dominions had provided themselves with much of the expensive public capital equipment which they needed for development, notably in railways, and their governments had been sobered by the interest burden which had proved so hard to bear in the acutest depression years.

In spite of this increased caution in government borrowing, the southern Dominions grew relatively more important in British external finance in the inter-war period. The United States dropped out of British investors' calculations, Canada turned to the United States or financed itself, and Latin America no longer attracted the British investor as it had; these tendencies, plus the fact that a large quantity of British investment in the United States had been sold during World War I, meant that British overseas investments were concentrated more in the areas linked directly with sterling. Britain remained a large overseas investor, but the investment was increasingly concentrated in the Empire, with Australia, South Africa and New Zealand outdistancing Canada.

Such a concentration, together with the stringencies of the depression, helped to create the climate of opinion in which the "sterling bloc" was born. Before 1931, Australia, New Zealand and South Africa used sterling as the basis for their currencies (indeed, had currencies identical in name and value with sterling) because this was traditional, accorded with the realities of their trade and investment, was most suitable in terms of the payments they had to make for invisibles such as shipping and insurance, and offered the readiest connection between their currencies and gold, which was the basis of the system of international exchange. When the economic blizzard struck, and Britain went off gold in September 1931, it was necessary for the overseas countries to decide whether to follow sterling or gold. Australia and New Zealand had already been forced off gold. They adopted sterling straightaway; their currencies were unable to maintain parity, however, because of the catastrophic drop in their export incomes, and they had to devalue in terms of sterling in 1933 to rates which have remained constant ever since in Australia's case but been restored in New Zealand's. For South Africa the question was complicated by the fact that the country was the world's biggest gold producer, and also by General Hertzog's desire not to seem to be following slavishly in Britain's wake. In the last few days of 1932, however, South Africa also went off gold, under pressure from the political intrigues of Tielman Roos and the flow of capital out of the country; thereafter the currency was kept in strict relation to sterling, like those of Australia and New Zealand. Canada remained aloof from these changes, as was only to be expected in view of its trade and investment relations with the United States.

The "sterling bloc" which resulted from these manœuvres (and similar ones by such diverse countries as Portugal, Iraq, Greece and the Scandinavian states) had no clear definition, except through the fact that the members kept their currencies in line with sterling as a monetary standard. There was no organization of the bloc in any formal sense, but the countries in question all wished to pursue stable commodity prices, and were likely to be favoured by the British Government as outlets for investment, in case any stringency arose in this respect.

The sterling bloc (to be transformed into the formal "sterling area" in 1939) was another source of American suspicion. Like imperial preference, it was to cause untold argument and arouse illimitable confusion when Britain and the United States began to discuss post-war economic arrangements. Yet, like the Ottawa agreements, it was in essence a simple act of self-preservation which carried with it no assurance of a closed economic system.

DOMINION POLITICS, 1918–1939

There is a certain similarity in the politics of the Four between the wars. The major event in such case was the depression. This thunderbolt from the outer world was the main cause of the Dominions being aware of that world's existence. Otherwise, they were concerned with their own development and social conflicts.

In Canada the dominant figure was Mackenzie King, of all successful politicians the most peculiar and far-fetched. Canada's lack of obvious national identity, and its inability to define its national politics clearly in terms of issues, were personified in the man of whom a Canadian has written :

He blunted us.

We had no shape
Because he never took sides,
And no sides
Because he never allowed them to take shape.

He skilfully avoided what was wrong
Without saying what was right,
And never let his on the one hand
Know what his on the other hand was doing . . .

He seemed to be in the centre,
Because we had no centre,
No vision
To pierce the smoke-screen of his politics.

Truly he will be remembered
Wherever men honour ingenuity,
Ambiguity, inactivity, and political longevity.[*]

King became Prime Minister first in 1921, when he took office with a minority in parliament but the support of the Progressives, a temporarily strong group of members representing the anti-city sentiment of the prairies. King had succeeded Laurier as leader of a Liberal Party still smarting from the division over conscription in the war; his main opponent was Arthur Meighen, who had replaced Borden as leader of the Conservatives, but was to make consistently wrong political choices throughout his life, being unable to emulate his predecessor's combination of bluff honesty and political shrewdness. Meighen had a brief run in 1925, but King won again on the issue of his treatment at the hands of the Governor-General, Lord Byng, and remained in office until 1930. The Progressives disintegrated, and King's Liberal Party reaped much of the benefit. From 1930 to 1935 a Conservative Government under R. B. Bennett had the task of facing the depression. Its traditional remedies of high tariffs were not of much use. In his final

* F. R. Scott, "W. L. M. K.", quoted in Frank H. Underhill, "The Revival of Conservatism in North America", *Transactions of the Royal Society of Canada,* June, 1958.

months in office, Bennett tried to switch to an imitation of Roosevelt's New Deal, but was defeated, in a tidal wave of support for King, at the general election of 1935. The depression gave a lease of life to Social Credit and the Commonwealth Co-operative Federation (C.C.F.) in the prairie provinces, but the great centres of population remained divided between Liberals and Conservatives. Thereafter, King operated a perpetual government until his death in 1948. It was hard to know what he stood for, except that he was the Government. His Conservative opponents became increasingly disheartened; Bennett left Canadian politics, Meighen remained unpopular, and no leader of consequence was found in King's lifetime. Meanwhile, Canada climbed out of the depression and deepened its ties with the United States.

In Australia the Prime Minister of World War I, W. M. Hughes, whose insistence on conscription had split the Labour Party and who had then coalesced with his Liberal opponents to form a National Party, was replaced as Prime Minister in 1921 by S. M. Bruce. Bruce was more acceptable to the newly successful Country Party, whose votes in parliament were needed to keep the Nationalists in office. Thereafter Australia was governed by coalitions of the National (later renamed United Australia) Party and the Country Party, except from 1929 to 1932, when a distracted Labour Government held office without an Upper House Majority. The coalition forces were strengthened by the break-up of this Government, one of its ministers, J. A. Lyons, joining the anti-Labour forces and soon after becoming their leader. He was succeeded in 1939 by R. G. Menzies. The situation remained unchanged until 1941, when, the coalition having been greatly weakened by disagreements about place, position and policy, a Labour Government took office under John Curtin, to remain until 1949. The depression was alleviated by attempts to curtail overseas spending, by high tariffs and prohibitions, by cuts in incomes, and, later, by schemes of public works and debt conversion; however, it was the recovery of overseas prices that provided the impetus to the reviving prosperity of the late 1930's. As already indicated, the unbridled optimism of the 1920's had evaporated, and efforts were directed towards an attempt to live without the constant stimulus of government loans from abroad.

In New Zealand, as in Canada and Australia, the men who held office during the worst part of the depression were then beaten and remained out of office for a number of years. In New Zealand's case the anti-Labour parties, which had shared the government since early in the century, were finally driven out in 1935, and Labour took office for the first time under Michael Savage. Health, welfare and housing schemes were started with great zeal; for a time New Zealand Labour was a source of direct inspiration to its fellow Labour Parties in Britain and Australia. Moreover, the left-wing fervour which got these schemes moving was also evident in foreign policy, so far as adherence to the League of Nations was concerned. For a time New Zealand was the lonely apostle of collective security amongst the Dominions. But this enthusiasm did not survive the bleak experiences of 1938, and the New Zealand Government, while perhaps a shade less lyrical than the governments of the other three Dominions under scrutiny, was in accord with the efforts of Neville Chamberlain. Also, in 1938 and 1939 New Zealand was preoccupied with an acute balance of payments problem, expressing itself in a flight of capital which the Government attempted to stem by emergency measures which were to become commonplace everywhere as part of wartime financial policy, but greatly disturbed the City of London at the time. Savage was succeeded by Peter Fraser soon after the war began. The tone of New Zealand Labour Governments remained much the same (hopeful, energetic, idealistic but unimaginative in the ceaseless preoccupation with bread-and-butter issues) until Labour finally gave way to its opponents in 1949. The opponents were, by then, largely indistinguishable from the Labour Party to the outside observer, except for the expected difference in clichés.

We have already seen something of the changes in South Africa. Smuts was beaten by Hertzog in 1924, following an accumulation of wartime and post-war grievances amongst the Afrikaner population; Hertzog remained Prime Minister for fifteen years. From 1933 onwards, he ruled in combination with Smuts, following a Fusion of the Nationalist and South African parties in the United Party. Hertzog's ultras detached themselves to become the Purified Nationalists under Dr. Malan. They seemed to be making little headway in the 1930's, but benefited ultimately from Hertzog's personal defeat on the issue of participation in the war in 1939. Hertzog's replacement then by Smuts meant a further lease of life for the United Party, but its hold on Afrikaner voters weakened when the war was over. Malan won the elections of 1948, since when his party has gone from strength to strength. Meanwhile, South Africa had developed greatly as an industrial country, with more discoveries of gold and other minerals, the consolidation of its cities, and the use of Africans for more complex jobs. The Fusion Government took Africans, Indians and Coloured people further from the full franchise than they had been before; this work was to be completed after 1948.

It would be wrong to find too many common features in these four stories, but certain features contrast with the situation in Britain. One is the much greater importance of rural interests in the Dominions, affecting their party systems and legislation in a number of important ways. Another is the concentration upon economic issues in Australia and New Zealand, with its background of parties formed along lines of fairly clear economic interest. A third is the ethnic basis of politics in South Africa, paralleled in part by the situation in Canada; much of the explanation of Mackenzie King's quietism was his wish not to disturb Quebec. A further point is the great dependence of all four countries upon a small range of exports, making issues of trade policy, especially tariffs and marketing schemes, matters of great moment in the period between the wars. Finally, there is the fact that, while issues of "status" were important in Canada in the 1920's, they had faded out in the 1930's; they remained issues in South Africa for the whole time, but did not matter in Australia and New Zealand, except as reflections of the dependent economic position in which these countries stood to Britain. Foreign policy was little discussed or understood in any of the four, except where the issue of status could be twisted into a shape like that of foreign policy; thus, the events of 1938 and 1939 were doubly shocking and unwelcome.

WARTIME EXPERIENCES

The four Dominions declared war within a short time of Britain's doing so, and remained belligerents to the end. It is true that the Dominions, being far off, took their participation at first rather more lightly than Britain did, but they were effective allies in the dispatch of fighting troops to the Middle East and to Britain itself, in their assistance with air training and their stationing of squadrons in Britain, and, above all, in their special arrangements for the supply of food, raw materials and arms.

Canada stationed troops in Britain early in the war, bore the brunt of the Dieppe raid in 1942, and provided substantial forces for the invasion of Europe. It was also the venue for the Empire Air Training Scheme, established late in 1939 by agreement between Britain, Canada, Australia and New Zealand. Canada's own security was guaranteed by the Ogdensburg agreement of 1940 with the United States; a scheme of joint military planning was established, with institutions which have become permanent. Canada's domestic politics remained fairly serene throughout the war, except for a clash over conscription within the Government which led to the resignation of the Minister for Defence, Colonel Ralston. Conscription was not enforced, in spite of heavy pressure. Mackenzie King considered that its effect in Quebec would be disastrous. He was determined to avoid the experience of the previous war.

South Africa's war, like Canada's, was mainly a quiet affair, confined again to the African continent. Alone amongst the Four, South Africa had active dissension at home to worry about. There was no repetition of the armed rebellion of World War I, but Afrikaner Nationalists showed little enthusiasm for the war effort, and there were numerous accusations against extremist Afrikaner organizations, on the ground of sympathy with Germany. The official Nationalist party was confirmed in its wish for a republic, arguing that it was South Africa's constitutional connection with Britain that had embroiled it in war.

Australia and New Zealand, in contrast, had a highly eventful war. They were soon in the field with expeditionary forces, giving Britain effective support in North Africa; their parts in the disastrous campaigns in Greece and Crete were out of all proportion to their populations in comparison with Britain's. Both were concerned about the prospect of Japan's entering the war, and tried hard to ensure the presence of substantial British forces in the Pacific, based on Singapore, to which an Australian division was sent. After the Pacific war began they still had troops in North Africa (the New Zealanders playing a notable part in the Italian campaign), but their main effort was necessarily directed towards self-preservation. For the remainder of the war they formed part of the U.S. sphere of influence, not the British: Australian forces were under an American general and New Zealand under an American admiral. Since the Japanese were able to occupy New Guinea and bombard Australian ports, it is not surprising that these two countries should have turned to the United States for help, although their doing so caused some heart-searching in Britain and some discontent amongst their own traditionalists.

I

Two problems, one old, one new, emerged to complicate the relations of Britain and the Dominions during the war. The first was that of the control of the forces which the Dominions committed to the fight; the second was how the Dominions were to influence decisions made about the war by Britain and the United States. Both matters were bound up with the unique character of Winston Churchill's leadership.

The first problem mainly affected Australia and New Zealand, although it also involved Canada at times.* In the first two years of war in the Middle East the Australians, under General Blamey, and New Zealanders, under General Freyberg, were led by men with more experience of command in war than the British generals under whom they were set to fight. Moreover, both had been given "charters" by their governments, enabling them to make representations to their home authorities if they thought that their troops were being unduly split up or committed to enterprises with no chance of success.† It took a long time for British military authorities to appreciate the special character of the Dominion forces. British generals and Mr. Churchill were inclined to treat them as simply parts of the British army. Yet this was emphatically what the Dominion governments did not want: their combination of national pride and concern for their troops' safety (especially after the harrowing experiences of Greece and Crete) led them to insist on their troops being ultimately subject to their own supervision and that of their designated commanders. After Pearl Harbor the matter took a more serious turn. In spite of requests from Churchill and Roosevelt that certain Australian troops should be diverted from the Middle East to Burma, the Australian Government insisted that they return home, for use in due course in New Guinea. It is evident that, from Churchill's standpoint, this was a denial to the British cause of forces which he had a right to commit as he thought fit; from the Australian standpoint it was the legitimate use of national forces for a national end. Churchill did not take easily to the idea of forces which he could not control,

* See Vincent Massey, *What's Past is Prologue* (Toronto, 1963), p. 323, for a case in which the British War Cabinet took a decision involving the welfare of 2,000 Canadian prisoners-of-war after the Dieppe raid "without the opportunity of Canada expressing her views, although two Canadian Ministers were in London in addition to the High Commissioner".

† See W. F. Murphy, "Blamey's and Freyberg's 'Charters'", in *Political Science* (Wellington), Vol. 16, No. 2 (September 1964) for comparative treatment of the four Dominions' experience in this respect.

and he seemed to prefer to think of the Commonwealth as an entity possessing resources to be marshalled for British ends: he saw no contradiction between these and the ends of particular Commonwealth countries.

This latter point helps to define the Dominions' problem in trying to influence decisions made about the war by Churchill and Roosevelt in partnership. Massey noted in his diary in July 1943:

> "The real difficulty lies in the exclusive control of the direction of the war in London and Washington and the failure to recognize a smaller participant like Canada as not only producing men and material but having a voice in the major decisions. It is quite clear, however, that this war will finish without any change in the machinery of direction and one can only do one's best in the circumstances to attempt to reconcile Canadian pride with existing practice."*

This problem, while irritating for Canada, was regarded as vital by the Australian Government after Pearl Harbor. It had had its difficulties beforehand in coping with British–American bilateralism: the secret agreements between British and American military staffs early in 1941 about a concentration of American effort on Atlantic rather than Pacific operations had come as a *fait accompli* to Mr. Menzies,† and there had been general dissatisfaction with the British effort at Singapore. Once the Pacific war began, it was the direct interest of the Australian and New Zealand Governments to see that men and materials were diverted to the Pacific from Europe. The setting up of a Pacific War Council in Washington was a direct result of pressure from Australia's Minister for External Affairs, Dr. Evatt, but it cannot be said that this, or any of his other spectacular efforts, effectively changed American policy. Any diversion of resources to the Pacific probably occurred because of domestic political pressure in the United States itself. So far as the allocation of supplies was concerned, the Dominions were specifically excluded from the Anglo-American Combined Boards which made decisions about shipping, munitions, raw materials and food. Canada gained entry to some of these boards, but not Australia,

* Massey, op. cit., p. 353.
† See Nicholas Mansergh, *Survey of British Commonwealth Affairs: Problems of Wartime Co-operation and Post-War Change 1939–1952* (London, 1958), pp. 108–9. The book is relevant to every aspect of wartime experience.

New Zealand or South Africa, in spite of protests. It suited the U.S. Government to deal directly with the British Government on behalf of the Commonwealth, because this meant dealing with a single authority instead of a number; and it suited the British Government, which needed all the strength it could muster if it was to wield any influence over the U.S.A. Britain welcomed the opportunity to act for the Commonwealth as a whole and demonstrate its own leadership.*

It was inevitable that Britain, in such desperate straits after 1940 and with such a variety of wartime problems to solve, should have wished to assume the leadership of the Commonwealth effort, especially when its Prime Minister was such a dominant man. It was also inevitable that the Dominions, concerned about their own difficulties, should want to be heard on matters that affected them. As indicated at the start of this chapter, there was constant contact between the Dominions Secretary and the High Commissioners in London, but this was mainly a matter of reporting decisions, not of making them. The system suited South Africa and Canada, but not Australia. The New Zealand response was muffled, varying between support for the Australians and loyalty to the British Government. Mr. Attlee's recollection was:

"There was difficulty with the Australians for a time. They wanted a greater share in the direction of the war and that their representative over here should sit in on everything. That was

* See Mansergh, ibid., pp. 128–30 for the facts of the matter. Mr. Churchill's approach to the Australian Government's wishes was consistently hostile, though his language varied in rigour, depending on the circumstances. In January 1942 he put his position frankly to the King: "Your Majesty will see that in spite of all the arguments we have used, the Commonwealth Government, which has a majority of two, is determined to have recourse to the United States. They have the idea that they can get better service and more support from the United States than they can from us. It would be foolish and vain to obstruct their wishes. From what I know, I fear they will have a very awkward reception in Washington. Access to the supreme power is extremely difficult. It is only granted to few and then in abundant measure. The lengthy telegrams they send will be addressed to subordinate officials and officers. It may be that, having knocked at this door, they will come back again to ours. If so, they will be very welcome . . . It is always good to let people do what they like and then see whether they like what they do. I do not think they will succeed in displacing the effective centre of gravity from London." (Quoted from royal archives in John W. Wheeler-Bennett, *King George VI*, London, 1958, pp. 681–2.)

Bruce. It wasn't received awfully well by Winston. I used to bring Bruce in where I could, but what they were really after was someone permanently in the War Cabinet, which you couldn't have done without bringing in everybody else. Winston was against having a sort of Commonwealth Cabinet. I agreed with him. It would have been a very difficult thing to arrange and it would have meant having their own Prime Ministers, or someone with equal authority, there all the time."[*]

This comment helps to explain why the Commonwealth system of consultation achieved no new form in World War II. There were suggestions at the start of the need for an Imperial War Cabinet, but these came to nothing. Prime Ministers like Menzies and Smuts were welcome to sit with the War Cabinet when in London, but British official opinion was opposed to anything more formal; in this it had Mackenzie King's support. Nevertheless, the Australian Government was convinced of the need to have someone at the centre of the British war effort. In 1941 Mr. Menzies wished to travel to London to carry out this function, but was stopped by local political opposition. Instead, one of his ministerial colleagues, Sir Earle Page, was sent, but he did not manage to achieve anything more in constant influence on the direction of the war than the High Commissioner, Mr. Bruce. The Australian feeling survived the change of government to a Labour Ministry under Mr. Curtin, who attempted without success at a meeting of Commonwealth Prime Ministers in 1944 to have a Commonwealth Secretariat established, in order that information and decision might be made more immediate and widespread. He had no success; both Smuts and King were adamant that existing arrangements were sufficient. Curtin was not convinced. Flourishing the Yalta conference agenda at an English visitor in 1945, he explained that there were several items which vitally affected Australia, but he was not to be consulted in advance. "The time will come when someone sitting in this chair will say : 'I won't put up with it' ", he said.[†]

It could well be argued from the British side that Curtin's Government had not gone out of its way to tell the British what it proposed to do with the Americans : Dr. Evatt had been a highly nationalistic foreign minister, and his attitude towards Britain and the Commonwealth had been very much that of picking the eyes

[*] Francis Williams, *A Prime Minister Remembers* (London, 1961), p. 54.
[†] J. C. W. Reith, *Into the Wind* (London, 1949), pp. 505–6.

out of the opportunities offered, but accepting no responsibility for anything that might go wrong. The Australian Government was, in fact, anxious to prevent decisions that might go against its interests, and desirous of using Commonwealth resources when these might directly increase its stature in Pacific matters; but it had no wish for a common Empire policy for affairs at large, and its general inclination was to avoid connection with those British policies that might cause it trouble.

Considerations such as these prevented any progress with vague schemes for imperial unity after the war, as propounded, for example, by Lord Halifax at Toronto in January 1944. He went no further than to say that

> "In all the common fields—Foreign Policy, Defence, Economic Affairs, Colonial Questions, and Communications—we should leave nothing undone to bring our people into closer unity of thought and action . . . Not Great Britain only, but the British Commonwealth and Empire must be the fourth power in that group upon which, under Providence, the peace of the world will henceforth depend . . ."*

but this was sufficient to throw Mackenzie King into what Massey called "paranoiac fury". To King, it was

> "like a conspiracy on the part of Imperialists to win their own victory in the middle of the war. I could not but feel that Halifax's work was all part of a plan which had been worked out with Churchill to take advantage of the war to try and bring about this development of centralization, of makings of policies in London, etc. . . . If Hitler himself wanted to divide the Empire he could not have chosen a more effective way."†

It would be hard to find a more nonsensical reaction to what was at the most an intimation, much less a plan; but King was King, and his reaction was faithfully reproduced by much Canadian opinion.

A judgement on the value of these wartime opinions is difficult, since it cannot avoid hindsight. It is plain now that both Halifax and King were wrong: there was no prospect of the Dominions

---

* *The American Speeches of the Earl of Halifax* (London, 1947), pp. 281–2

† From King's diary; quoted in Vincent Massey, *What's Past is Prologue* (Toronto, 1963), p. 393.

pulling together with Britain in common responsibility for the range of issues which Halifax envisaged, partly because they saw disadvantages for themselves, partly because their preoccupations lay elsewhere, partly because their sense of national pride demanded autonomy; at the same time, there was no British "conspiracy" to ensnare the Dominions, although there was an understandable desire to have the support of these countries in the attempt to retain Great Power status for Britain in post-war conditions which, while they could not be clearly foreseen, were bound to prove difficult.

THE SITUATION IN 1945

When the war ended in 1945 the Dominions were all on the winning side; relations with the United States, whilst complex, had been sorted out satisfactorily; the formal organization of the Empire remained as it had been, monarchical, flexible, consultative, adaptable. Each Dominion had been able to take its own line in the war. Two had even signed a solemn agreement about what they wanted the world—or at any rate the Pacific—to be like after the war (the Australia–New Zealand agreement of 1944). In spite of Mackenzie King's intermittent frenzy, even Canadians were now inclined to believe that they were truly independent; the chairman of the Canadian delegation to the third unofficial conference on British Commonwealth Relations stated firmly: "Let us now with great solemnity and all respect duly embalm and tuck away in some forgotten crypt beyond the possibility of resurrection, the word 'status' in so far as it is used in an intra-Commonwealth sense."[*]

When the nations assembled at San Francisco to consider the draft for the charter of the United Nations, Australia and New Zealand proved to be stubbornly opposed to British support for the principle of the veto which the United States and the Soviet Union would not give up. On colonial questions too these two countries had been a thorn in the side of the British, arguing for a conception of "trusteeship" which seemed for a time to cut directly across British wishes about the post-war development of colonial territories.[†] But they remained dependable allies and countries on which Britain had learned to rely for help in matters of supply.

[*] Edgar J. Tarr in Richard Frost (ed.). *The British Commonwealth and World Society* (London, 1947), p. 149. The conference was in 1945.

[†] On these matters, see F. L. W. Wood, *The New Zealand People at War* (Wellington, 1958), Chs. 22–6.

The effects of the war upon the general relationship between Britain and the Old Dominions can be stated in broad terms. It is clear that the overseas countries, especially Australia and New Zealand, had a more independent position in foreign policy than in 1939, and were more confident of their ability to negotiate and be listened to. At the same time, there was a much greater sense of solidarity and practical co-operation with Britain than in 1939. Whereas at the outbreak of war the common experience of Britain and the Dominions had been that of dwindling international trade and intercourse, uncertain foreign policies and arguments about status, in 1945 the various governments had become accustomed to practical co-operation in such fields as production, finance and military training, had been involved in numerous enterprises which, whatever their immediate results, had had a happy ending, and were members of a victorious coalition. Despite disagreements, they had achieved a great deal. They were now accustomed to co-operate whenever the opportunity occurred.

Moreover, there was the association with the United States to add to the fund of common experience. This had its drawbacks in plenty. The United States had been a generous but wayward ally, unpredictable in many of its reactions; its official approach to the British Empire was one of suspicion, President Roosevelt echoing many of its less informed politicians' shibboleths about the evils of imperialism. Cordell Hull had shown an implacable determination to destroy the system of imperial preference which represented, for certain interests in the Dominions, a charter of economic guarantee, the difference between prosperity and depression for particular industries. The United States was suspicious of the workings of the Sterling Area. Its own international economic policies were sufficiently unpredictable to lead a New Zealand writer to say, "It is the United States rather than Russia which is now the great enigma."* Yet, against these drawbacks, there was the great gain that the United States had turned away from isolationism to involvement in world affairs, and seemed likely to remain involved. The rejection of Wilson in 1919, which many British observers regarded as setting the pattern for American aversion from international action, seemed to have been itself rejected. Soon the Truman Doctrine and the Marshall Plan were to show that isolationism was dead as a practical policy. From now on, each of the

* From a New Zealand preliminary paper for the 1945 unofficial Commonwealth Relations conference; Frost, op. cit., p. 11.

Dominions, and Britain itself, would have to make the best terms it could with an America which was an active participant in world politics. On the whole, the change was welcome to Britain and the Dominions. But the problems of how to retain the 'special relationship' so carefully cultivated by Churchill, and to make the British Empire acceptable to dominant American opinion, were genuine ones.

As already indicated, the formal constitutional relations between Britain and the Dominions had not been affected by the war, although the divisibility of the Crown had been effectively demonstrated through the separate declarations of war by Canada and South Africa. Strictly speaking, relations were as they had been in 1939. In practice, however, certain elements had been added, especially on the economic side. The Sterling Area had become, on the outbreak of war, a formal association with strict rules. The gold and dollar resources of the Empire (except for Canada) had been pooled under British direction; there was strict control of imports; British dollar securities had been sold to provide the sinews of war; the initiation of lease-lend by the United States had not altered the need to husband scarce resources of foreign currency. For both financial and logistic reasons, trade within the Commonwealth had been preferred to trade outside it. The Commonwealth was, in fact, in 1945 much more of an economic unit than it had ever been before. What deliberate intent had failed to do in the 1910's and 1930's, the stress of circumstances had done in the 1940's. Schemes of bulk purchase could not be dismantled overnight; in any case, no one wanted them dismantled immediately. Dominant economic opinion in all the Commonwealth countries was that the future was uncertain, that unemployment might grip the peacetime economies once more, and that any means of ensuring stability in production and distribution ought to be retained. The conclusions of the unofficial British Commonwealth Relations conference in 1945 are especially representative here:

"Practically all members of the Conference agreed that from a long-run standpoint it is a primary British interest to re-establish a world economic system in which the United Kingdom could again, as in the past, enjoy the substantial benefits likely to accrue from multilateral trade exchanges. But everybody was also agreed that for a period, the limits of which cannot at the moment easily be forecast, a substantial part of the control machinery set up during the war, and in particular the foreign exchange control machinery, must be maintained. Formal approval of a multi-lateral system does not therefore necessarily mean very much, for some people who would like to maintain controls indefinitely are quite happy to pay lip service to a multilateral system to be established in a remote future if by so doing they could allay the suspicions of some of their critics. Especially in view of the many uncertainties ahead, the value to Great Britain of the sterling *bloc* connection was at least no less than it had been before the war, and drawing attention to the risks of instability inherent in a close association with the dollar, one U.K. dele-gate asked his Dominion colleagues whether they might not take a similar view, regarding the advantages to be gained from a more permanent link with a probably more stable sterling cur-rency as sufficiently solid to induce them to maintain the sterling *bloc* connection."*

Such suppositions in the economic field had their counterparts in other fields of possible co-operation. There was, for example, a widespread assumption that joint defence planning would con-tinue. But the main centre of discussion was "regionalism", a word of power which meant different things to different men. In wartime discussions it had begun as one of Churchill's ideas for post-war international organization. He had been in favour of regional arrangements whereby the countries immediately concerned with a dispute would have the task of settling it, but had abandoned this when the American Government veered towards a world-wide security organization guaranteed by the Great Powers.† Another of its forms was widely propagated by Australia and New Zealand: the view that their own security would be enhanced if they were in charge of Commonwealth responsibilities in the Pacific. Dr Evatt told the New Zealand High Commissioner in 1943 that "Australia and New Zealand in co-operation should be the foundation of the British sphere of influence in the South West and South Pacific.

---

* Frost, op. cit., p. 105. In reply the Canadians entered a caveat symptomatic of their uneasy relationship with the sterling area in the next ten years or so.

† For an elaboration of Churchill's idea in Commonwealth terms, see Sir Edward Grigg, *The British Commonwealth* (London, 1943), Chs. XIII and XIV. Grigg's scheme did not involve the sort of responsibility for the Do-minions that Evatt (see below) had in mind; but it had similarities to Smuts's scheme (see below also).

The future safety and prosperity of these two Dominions depended on their having a decisive voice in these areas." He was also "inclined to suggest that it would be wise for Great Britain to transfer all British colonies in these areas to Australia and New Zealand, Australia gradually to take over the Solomons area and New Zealand to take Fiji, etc."* A somewhat similar scheme was put forward in 1943 in London by Smuts, who was clearly anxious that British colonies in Africa should not proceed with divergent native policies from those of South Africa. Proposing that there should be some grouping of British colonies into larger entities, he went on :

". . . you will find that it is quite possible to bring these new groups closer to a neighbouring Dominion and thereby interest the Dominion in the colonial group. In this way, instead of the Dominions being a show apart, so to say, having little or nothing to do with the Empire, and taking very little interest in it, these regional Dominions will become sharers and partners in the Empire . . . you will bring to bear on the problems of these colonial groups the experience and resources and leadership of the local Dominions, too."†

In the broader sense advocated by Evatt and Peter Fraser of New Zealand, and the narrower sense advanced by Smuts, the regional idea seemed to promise everything for the Dominions concerned and little or nothing for Britain. Neither made much headway, except that Australia was able, by having them dubbed British Commonwealth representatives, to place its nominees on the War Crimes Tribunal and the Allied Control Council in Japan after 1945. There was no British response to the idea that British colonies might be taken over or supervised by neighbouring Dominions.

Nevertheless, there was significance in the regional idea as applied to security, both because it was rejected at the time by Canada and advanced with such determination by Australia and New Zealand. Canada, being already part of the American regional defence system, could afford to deprecate the idea of regional pacts or arrangements as a substitute for a world-wide security system;

* F. L. W. Wood, *The New Zealand People at War* (Wellington, 1958), p. 312.
† J. C. Smuts, *Jan Christian Smuts* (London, 1952), p. 447.

Australia and New Zealand, having had the benefits of American protection in war, naturally wished to retain these in peace, so long as they were not subject to American fiat but were able to make their wishes known more directly than under the wartime system of grand strategy. These were the realities behind the "regionalism" arguments of the time. They foreshadowed the constant post-war quest of Australia and New Zealand for American involvement in their and Asia's affairs.

At the close of the war Britain and the Four stood at the edge of a new epoch in their relations. Behind, shaping many of their approaches to contemporary affairs, lay the arguments over status, the attempts at mutual economic assistance, the experiences of migration of people and capital, the broadening institutions of monarchy, the assumptions of unity in foreign policy and defence; ahead, discernible in some measure but to a great extent hidden, lay the problems of emergent nationalism in Asia and Africa, the Cold War, the tension between dollar shortage and multilateralism in trade, the complexities of Britain's relations with Europe, and the difficulties of adjustment to a situation in which the United States would play, for some of the Dominions, the role allotted in the past to Britain.

6

COMMONWEALTH STRUCTURE AND
IDEAS 1945–1965

I N turning to the events of the post-war period, a useful intro-
duction seems to be the changes in the structure of the
Commonwealth of Nations, since these measure, in some
degree, changes in the relationship between Britain and the Four.
Some of them, such as the acceptance of republics within the
Commonwealth, can be described with fair accuracy; they involve
stated changes in formal practice. Others are more difficult to
describe, because they are concerned with slow alterations in custom.
So are the changes that have occurred in ideas about what the
Commonwealth is and how it ought to operate.

The changes in structure include the acceptance of republics,
with consequent changes in the position of the Monarch, and what
has been described as "the end of Dominion status"; the disappearance of the Imperial Conference, which from 1907 to 1937
was the hallmark of imperial consultation; and changes in the
machinery of Commonwealth relations, especially in Britain.

THE REPUBLICAN ISSUE

The acceptance of republics in the Commonwealth was a direct
consequence of the appearance of three new Dominions, India,
Pakistan and Ceylon, in 1947. The Congress Party had long since
rejected the idea of "Dominion status", as that had been foreshadowed by Edwin Montagu and promised by Lord Irwin; it had
opted for a republic as part of a general rejection of the Crown and
all that it stood for in the Indian Empire. Although Lord Mount-
batten had been accepted as the first Governor-General of independent India, Mr. Nehru made it known in 1948 that, while
India wished to stay in the Commonwealth, it would have to be as
a republic.* A British Cabinet committee was already at work,
looking for a formula which would "enable the greatest number

---

* Except where otherwise indicated, the source for much of what follows
is J. W. Wheeler-Bennett, *King George VI* (London, 1958), Part III, Ch. XI.

of independent units to adhere to the Commonwealth without
excessive uniformity in their internal constitutions", but it found
great difficulty in bringing forward anything which did not involve
a link with the Crown. The most promising solution seemed to be
something modelled on the Irish External Relations Act of 1936,
which had retained the monarch in Eire's external relations without giving him any function within Eire itself. It looked as if the
only solution might be some arrangement of "inner" and "outer"
membership, which could conceivably bring Burma and Eire back
into the fold, but at some cost. (Mr. Costello, the Prime Minister of
Eire, had announced his intention of making Eire a republic while
these deliberations were going on.) Preliminary talks by Sir Norman
Brook, the Secretary to the Cabinet, in visits to Canada, Australia
and New Zealand had indicated that the Governments of those
countries were determined that their own position in regard to
the monarch should not be put in question. However, all were
prepared to help in finding a formula that would suit India's
needs; the attitude of Mr. J. B. Chifley, the Australian Prime
Minister, in a letter to the Canadian Prime Minister, Mr. St.
Laurent, was typical of their approaches:

> "I feel the question to be decided is of very great importance
> and I think that we should do all that is possible to retain India
> as a friendly power. Although I recognize there would be very
> great difficulties in retaining India within the Commonwealth
> should it become a republic, I am not so much concerned with
> formalities as with the need to maintain friendly relations. I
> feel that India must certainly be the leader of the Asian peoples
> and provide a bulwark against any onward rush of Communism
> through that area."[*]

The final solution was enunciated by a meeting of Commonwealth
Prime Ministers in April 1949, but was evidently found only a
short time before that. To the last minute, bogus solutions kept
appearing in public: the King would be a "Fountain of Honour",
he would be the president of a Commonwealth Conference, he
would be the President of India, there would be a treaty relationship between Commonwealth members; but the actual solution was
a well-kept secret up to the time of its announcement in the Prime
Ministers' declaration, which stated:

* L. F. Crisp, *Ben Chifley* (London, n.d. – 1961?), pp. 284–5

"The Governments of the United Kingdom, Canada, Australia, New Zealand, South Africa, India, Pakistan and Ceylon, whose countries are united as Members of the British Commonwealth of Nations and owe a common allegiance to the Crown, which is also the symbol of their free association, have considered the impending constitutional changes in India.

The Government of India have informed the other Governments of the Commonwealth of the intention of the Indian people that under the new constitution which is about to be adopted India shall become a sovereign independent Republic. The Government of India have, however, declared and affirmed India's desire to continue her full membership of the Commonwealth of Nations and her acceptance of the King as the symbol of the free association of its independent member nations and as such the Head of the Commonwealth.

The Governments of the other countries of the Commonwealth, the basis of whose membership of the Commonwealth is not hereby changed, accept and recognize India's continuing membership in accordance with the terms of the declaration.

Accordingly the United Kingdom, Canada, Australia, New Zealand, South Africa, India, Pakistan and Ceylon hereby declare that they remain united as free and equal members of the Commonwealth of Nations, freely co-operating in the pursuit of peace, liberty and progress."

What was the solution which took so long to arrive at? It was that, whereas in pre-war days "allegiance to the Crown" had been regarded as an absolute pre-condition of membership of the Commonwealth, it was now considered that to recognize the King as symbol of the free association between the members of the Commonwealth was sufficient: allegiance was not necessary. So long as India contined to recognize the King as a symbol, it need not recognize him as King. The reasoning was based on an ingenious interpretation of the Preamble to the Statute of Westminster, said to have been suggested by Professor K. C. Wheare of Oxford.* It left entirely intact the monarchical position in Britain and in the countries which wished to retain monarchical institutions; it gave the King a

---

* The relationship of the new formula to the Preamble is explained with customary lucidity in K. C. Wheare, *The Statute of Westminster and Dominion Status*, 5th edn. (London, 1953), Ch. XII.

continued status as a Commonwealth institution; it freed India from "the Crown", with all its associations of coercion and control; and it provided the perfect formula for saving face in Britain and in India.

The new arrangement was received wtih reactions varying from composure to delight in the Old Dominions. The interests of none of them were vitally affected by what had happened; their own positions had been maintained. It is possible, however, that the ease with which the final solution was reached had been affected by the composition of the Governments with which Britain had to deal. No Canadian Liberal government was likely to put difficulties in the way, especially since Mr. Lester Pearson, the Secretary of State for External Affairs, was a firm believer in close relations with India. As Canadian representative, he was able to point out that the new situation was possible because, in the past, the Commonwealth had resisted the temptation "to organize its activities in a fixed, formal and centralized manner".* Dr. Malan, the Nationalist Prime Minister of South Africa, had even more reason for welcoming the move, since it opened the way to that combination of republicanism with Commonwealth membership which might enable his party to achieve its own ends without violating the susceptibilities of English-speaking South Africans. His great opponent, Smuts, was, for obvious reasons, "very anxious that the exception which has been made in the case of India should not become a precedent for other cases";† but to many in South Africa it seemed clear that it would.

The crucial countries with which to obtain agreement might well have been Australia and New Zealand, where, it was widely believed, feeling for the monarchy was stronger than elsewhere. Here the Attlee Government in Britain was fortunate in that the two Prime Ministers, J. B. Chifley and Peter Fraser, were both anxious to accommodate India if this could be done without endangering the position of the King in their own constitutions, and were, moreover, both Labour men whose sense of connection with the British Labour Government was strong.‡ Mr. Attlee later stated more than

* Quoted in Robert A. Spencer, *Canada in World Affairs,* Vol. V, *1946–1949* (Toronto, 1959), p. 402.

† Malan's and Smuts's speeches in parliament on the new formula are in Mansergh, *Documents,* Vol. II, pp. 859–74.

‡ "Well, when does the executive of the Empire Labour Party wish to resume?" said Ernest Bevin with a grin to the Australian and New Zealand leaders at a discussion before the 1946 Prime Ministers' meeting. (L. F Crisp, *Ben Chifley* (London, n.d.), p. 280.)

once that he got on just as well with non-Labour Prime Ministers from other parts of the Commonwealth as with Labour ones. Even so, it is quite possible that he would have encountered more difficulty if Mr. Menzies, then in opposition in Australia, had been Prime Minister in April 1949. It is unlikely that a different New Zealand Prime Minister would have taken a different attitude from Mr. Fraser's, but the tone of his agreement might have been less understanding. However, these are perhaps unworthy suppositions; the new arrangement with India was welcomed in Britain by Mr. Churchill, and comparable politicians in Australia and New Zealand were likely to follow his lead.

The recognition that a republic could be a member of the Commonwealth, and that allegiance to the Crown was not a necessary aspect of Commonwealth membership, was the last great formal step in defining the nature of the Commonwealth. The other changes in structure to which attention is directed in this chapter have all been consequential. The acceptance of republics has, in fact, made no difference to the relations between Britain on the one hand and Canada, Australia and New Zealand on the other; but it proved the stumbling-block that eventually precipitated South Africa's departure from the Commonwealth. The matter is dealt with at some length below (Chapter 9); its relevance here is that the convention arose that a Commonwealth member wishing to become a republic should give *notice* of its intention and should invite the agreement of the other members to its continuing Commonwealth status.* When the South African Government eventually decided to make South Africa a republic and simultaneously retain its Commonwealth membership, it had to ask for this formal permission, which in other cases, following India's, had been granted without discussion. South Africa's Afro-Asian opponents proceeded to discuss the formal request in terms of South Africa's *apartheid* policy. The South African Government withdrew the request and left the Commonwealth, having realized that the request would not, in fact, be granted. Thus, an arrangement which in 1949 was widely regarded as a concession by the Old Dominions to a new Commonwealth member, became in 1961

* I examined this oddity in the Sir Thomas Holland Memorial Lecture for 1961: see *Journal of the Royal Society of Arts*, Vol. CIX, No. 5061, August 1961, p. 715, especially Professor Mansergh's letter quoted there. The practice was still current in 1965, when the Gambia applied for permission.

the occasion for the ignominious withdrawal by one of those Old Dominions from the association of which it was a member of long standing.

This is perhaps an appropriate point at which to mention another republican matter in which Canada, Australia and New Zealand were involved: the departure of Eire from the Commonwealth and its assumption of republican status. Since 1922, Eire (first as the Irish Free State) had been a Dominion with a difference. The term "Dominion" had not been used about it; it attended no Imperial Conference after 1932; its trade and other disputes with Britain in the 1930's had been accompanied by the passing of an External Relations Act in 1936 which, in effect, confined the King's authority to the issue of letters of credence for Irish envoys, and by the proclamation of a new constitution in 1937 which made Eire a republic in all but name. It had remained neutral in the war. In 1948 its status was shadowy, but British and Commonwealth ministers had not felt inclined to try to push the matter into the light of day; they had stated in 1937 that the new Irish constitution did not, in their view, alter Eire's position as a member of the British Commonwealth, and had not felt impelled to go further. However, as already indicated, Mr. Costello in 1948 declared his intention of repealing the External Relations Act and proclaiming a republic. The issue was treated as a Commonwealth one, not simply as one involving Britain and Ireland; the Prime Ministers of Australia, New Zealand and Canada took part in discussions at Chequers with British and Irish representatives, and the special arrangements later made by Britain (that Eire would not be treated as a foreign country, though not as a Commonwealth country either) were reproduced in the laws of these Dominions also. This was a case in which Dominion pressure was decisive. People of Irish origin in Canada, Australia and New Zealand might have felt an affront if Eire had been summarily refused the privileges which its citizens enjoyed in Britain, simply because of a constitutional adjustment; Ireland, as a Mother-Country in her own right, deserved special treatment. "It was the original intention of the United Kingdom Government to insist that secession meant the ending of trade preferences and alien status for Irish citizens in the United Kingdom. It was deflected from its course by pressure from the overseas Dominions. 'If we had taken a different line from the one we decided to take,' admitted the Lord Chancellor, 'we should have acted in the teeth of the advice of the representatives of Canada, Australia and New Zealand.' "*

There is a sense in which this marked a settling of the Irish account for those three countries. As recently as thirty years before, Ireland had still been a factor in their politics; the Easter Rebellion had awakened feelings of loyalty and repulsion; Irish clannishness, Irish oppositionism were still manifested in directly Irish ways. Since then, social cleavages over the Catholic issue had remained significant in many localities,† but, once the Irish Free State was established, the Irish issue lost its force. Irish-Canadians and Irish-Australians kept their fervour for local quarrels. The failure of Eire to enter the war represented a real parting of the ways. There was little attempt to justify this amongst the hyphenated Irish in the British countries abroad; apart from other considerations, they no longer thought it their business. The 1948 arrangements put paid to the whole score, with good will on all sides. Except for some mild scuffling between Mr. Menzies's Government in Australia and the Irish Government about how the Australian Ambassador to Eire should be designated, later relations between Eire and the Old Dominions have little to offer the historian.

The Monarchy

To write about the Monarchy is always difficult, especially in the context of Commonwealth relations. Consider statements such as these:

"The Commonwealth possesses, in its Constitutional Monarchy, one of the finest devices that modern democracy has for the conduct of public affairs. To it, the Commonwealth probably owes its life, and certainly much of its strength."‡

"The Crown stands for all that is best in us. Its aura transcends

* Nicholas Mansergh, *Survey of British Commonwealth Affairs: Problems of Wartime Co-operation and Post-War Change 1939–1952* (London, 1958), p. 288. The whole of Ch. VI is of great interest in this connection.

† King William still rides in procession on his white horse through the streets of Sydney on the anniversary of the Battle of the Boyne. The horse has nothing else to do but this one yearly task. It is not a long procession.

‡ H. V. Hodson, "The Crown in the Commonwealth", in Sydney D. Bailey (ed.), *Parliamentary Government in the Commonwealth* (London, 1951), p. 21.

even the boundaries of the Commonwealth itself. The world is aware of it. There exists today no human institution whose influence for good surpasses that of the Monarchy we cherish."*

Can these statements, which could be paralleled from many other public men, be true? It is hard to believe that they contain more than a vestige of truth. When South Africa ceased to be a monarchy, and left the Commonwealth, there is no evidence that the conduct of public affairs changed in any respect, or that any influence for good had been withdrawn. The same social mores prevailed. The same Government went on acting as it had acted before. If there were standards before the event, they were still there after it. Would there be any difference if Canada, Australia or New Zealand became a republic and left the Commonwealth? It can be argued that they are not likely to do so, since republican tendencies in each of them are slight compared with those that existed in South Africa; this is a true and important point. But, if we take the English-speaking South Africans, amongst whom republicanism was neither a tradition nor a policy, is there any evidence that their conduct, attitudes, emotions and aims were any different after South Africa abandoned the influence of the Monarchy?

One argument which can be put against the drift of these questions is that the Monarchy was, in South Africa as in the other Old Dominions, an indispensable accompaniment to that complex of political and legal institutions which we recognize as part of the common heritage of the British nations, and which most of us value, whatever views we may take about Monarchy as such. It can be argued that, if Britain had not had Monarchy to sustain and crown the free institutions which it developed and exported, those institutions would not have had their particular character; moreover, their export would have been less complete, and less easy, if they had not been tied together and sealed with a crown. Since we have no example in which the royal seal was not present, the argument cannot be proved or disproved. But there seems to be a good deal in it. Up to a certain point, British institutions may well require Monarchy to make them stick. Beyond that point, Monarchy may be as irrelevant to the continuance of those institutions as it has been in South Africa.

Considerations such as these need to be brought to mind if one

* Vincent Massey, *Canadians and their Commonwealth* (Romanes Lecture, Oxford, 1961), p. 20.

is to account for the continuation of monarchical sentiment in Canada, Australia and New Zealand. The changed Style and Titles which came into effect after Queen Elizabeth ascended the throne in 1952 seem to have had little effect in either Britain or the Dominions.* They were in fact very similar, the only difference being that, whereas South Africa simply said that Her Majesty was "Queen of South Africa and of Her other Realms and Territories", the others made it "by the Grace of God of the United Kingdom, X and Her other Realms and Territories Queen", X being the name of the country in question. The term "Head of the Commonwealth", which reveals some interesting constitutional tangles if one looks at it closely, has not troubled the Old Dominions. Thus, if one is looking for changes in the significance of Monarchy to relations between them and Britain since 1949 or 1952, one must look for alterations in the actual functions performed by the Sovereign and her family, and in opinion about them, rather than in legal forms.

There has undoubtedly been some increase in the personal impact of the Queen and her family upon the overseas Realms. No previous sovereign has travelled so widely and assiduously as Queen Elizabeth; her consort and her sister have travelled widely too; her aunts, uncles and niece have done work of the same kind; it will not be long before her children are embarking on similar journeys. The Old Dominions have benefited greatly from this process. The Duke of Edinburgh is now almost as familiar a figure in Australia and Canada as in Britain. The pattern of these tours, which seems to owe much to the Royal Family's tour of South Africa in 1947† has now become fairly settled.‡ As with a royal visit in the British provinces, every effort is made to enable as many people as possible to see the Queen, and to ensure that people who have a notable record of public service are able to meet her. There is a different style of tour, sometimes undertaken by the Duke or Princess Margaret, in which objectives are more limited and the time involved shorter, but similar aims are in view. On the whole, these

* Though it would be interesting to know what official reaction there was to King George VI's observation that "if the title Head of the Commonwealth as opposed to head of the British Commonwealth is going to be used then Australia I feel must alter her name." (J. W. Wheeler-Bennett, *King George VI* (London, 1958), p. 727.)

† See ibid., pp. 689 ff.

‡ There is a useful and sympathetic account of the planning of royal tours in Dorothy Laird, *How the Queen Reigns* (London, 1961), Ch. 11.

tours have been great successes, although at times the Royal visitor
has been subjected to more hand-shaking and travel in the heat
than flesh and blood can be expected to enjoy.

The possible dangers of extended royal contact with the Old
Dominions were demonstrated during Her Majesty's tour of Canada
in 1964, when separatists in French-Canadian centres turned their
backs on her. Their protest was presumably against the lack of
opportunities for French-Canadians in Canada itself, and thus
formed part of the general revival of French-Canadian nationalist
feeling; in this sense no rebuff to Britain was intended, and the
discourtesy was to the Queen of Canada because she symbolized
the system of government which, according to militant French-
Canadians, favoured others at their expense. But it was a rebuff
to her personally, was accepted as such by royalist Canadians, and
disliked as such by some people in Britain; above all, it cannot have
been palatable to her. It is hardly fair to a Queen to subject her to
discourtesies intended for a government which she rarely sees
and over which she does not have even the vestigial influence which
she has in Britain.

Allied with this problem of implicating the Queen in the internal
quarrels of a country with which she has little to do, is that of how
to share her between her Realms. Whether the Queen is an indispensable link in the Commonwealth chain or not, she has to
look like one. The changes made in the Coronation Service in 1953,
and the prominence of Commonwealth leaders in the procession
through the streets, were signs of this; and subsequent events have
confirmed it. But the Queen cannot be everywhere. Moreover, she is
paid for by Britain. When there is a royal tour of a Commonwealth
country, the actual expenses are paid by that country, except for
transport to and from it; but the general establishment of Monarchy
is essentially a British cost. The Queen's home is in Britain; her
family is there; her associations are essentially British; her active
constitutional functions are overwhelmingly British. She could not
be effectively removed from Britain and made to lead a peripatetic
life, with a change every few months from one realm to another.
This is why schemes for local homes for the Queen have fallen
down, in spite of persistent suggestions that she should have the
equivalent of Buckingham Palace in each of the countries of which
she is Queen.* Somehow, it has been necessary to preserve the

* In Canberra, which still has a number of vacant spaces, one hillock was
reserved by an ambitious town planner for the royal residence.

delicate balance between the Queen as monarch of each of her realms, and the Queen as monarch in Britain. Experience seems to suggest that this is best done if her local role is not over-emphasized in Canada, Australia and New Zealand.

What then remains of the questions asked at the beginning of this section? The opinions of Mr. Hodson and Mr. Massey do seem to go too far; neither the sense of social connection of the overseas countries with Britain, nor their association with Britain in world politics, depends upon having a common sovereign. Yet there is undoubtedly considerable warmth and affection towards the Queen in the three overseas realms. Perhaps Mr Dermot Morrah is right:

> "A Governor-General can be a perfectly efficient head of the state; but as head of society he is inadequate for peoples who have grown up in the British Empire and breathed the atmosphere of monarchy as a way of life. Their sense of kinship with one another, and with their fellow-subjects of the same allegiance in other lands, requires an object of personal devotion, such as they cannot find in the temporary holder of political office, but only in affectionate loyalty to a person exalted above all partisan politics."*

This is the case for Monarchy on general grounds. It is a strong case, especially in Britain. At the time of a Royal tour, it is a strong case in Australia and New Zealand, where nothing comparable with the 1964 events in Canada has occurred. One's real difficulty is in deciding whether the sentiment which is satisfied by monarchy will continue to be satisfied in those countries by a British monarch. As I suggest below, the growing nationalism of those countries expresses itself more in function than in emotion; it may be rendering the monarchy unnecessary. Even if rendered unnecessary, the monarchy might well continue as a picturesque survival, an occasional visitation of colour and splendour and remoteness, valued precisely because these qualities are not indigenous to Canada, Australia or New Zealand. To what extent it will remain a source of inspiration, in the sense in which inspiration has been postulated in the quotations in this section, is an open question. My impression is that, in all three countries, sentiments such as I have quoted are expressed by old men rather than young men, by people of British

* Dermot Morrah, *The Work of the Queen* (London, 1958), pp. 181–2.

birth rather than those of local birth, by conservatives rather than their opposites, and by those with a stake in ceremonial, military and public offices rather than those without it. Republicanism is an occasional but highly eccentric phenomenon. It cannot be said that monarchy has any strong opposition. Its dangers lie, not in opposition, but in apathy.

DOMINION STATUS

Since the war there has been less and less talk of "Dominion status": new countries seeking membership of the Commonwealth look first for "independence" and then knock at the Commonwealth door, being received with acclamation by the existing members. Whereas Dominion status was a single, unified business of being self-governing and belonging to the British Commonwealth of Nations, there are now two separate processes. It is possible to imagine a British colony gaining its independence and not being accepted as a member of the Commonwealth. Southern Rhodesia is the most likely candidate for this experience. What change, if any, took place in the status of the Four when the emphasis shifted from Dominion status? South Africa now possesses neither Dominion status nor membership of the Commonwealth; but has there been any change in the position of Canada, Australia and New Zealand?

It is worth noting some of the attributes of the phrase "Dominion status". It was a description of the condition of the self-governing colonies after 1907. Any precision which it had was given to it by the Balfour statement of the Imperial Conference of 1926, and by the Statute of Westminster of 1931. It was talked about more in Canada and South Africa than in Australia and New Zealand. Its final appearance in documents of importance was in 1947, when India and Pakistan were made Dominions; dependencies gaining independence after that were not described as Dominions. "Quite soon after World War II the term began to go out of favour."* Professor Wheare encountered five objections to the term. One was that it suggested domination by Britain; another that it was not applied to Britain itself, and so implied some lack of equality with

---

* K. C. Wheare, *The Constitutional Structure of the Commonwealth* (Oxford, 1960), p. 13. The objections to the term "Dominion status" which follow are taken from pp. 14–17.

the other Dominions; a third that it had been used to describe so many degrees of self-government since 1907 that it was now ambiguous; a fourth, that it did not apply to Ireland, which was a Mother Country in its own right; and fifth, that it had about it the sense of a mother–daughter relationship which was no longer appropriate. No doubt it was the exceptional person who held all these objections at once, and they were not common in Australia or New Zealand; but they were real enough to cause the Canadian Government to omit "Dominion of" from Canada's name after 1947,* and for the Dominions office to be renamed the Commonwealth Relations Office in the same year. Mr. Attlee explained that the old name was "liable to convey a misleading impression of the relations between the United Kingdom and the other members of the Commonwealth."†

It seems clear that the change in usage is a distinction without a difference, except in terms of the speed and tone of political change. Nothing happened to the Old Dominions when people stopped using the term "Dominion": their constitutions were unaltered, their position as sovereign states was unchanged, their membership of the Commonwealth was as undisputed as it had been before. What marked them off from the later possessors of Commonwealth status was that, whereas the new countries acquired their independence by a distinct Act of the British parliament which marked a sharp division between dependence and independence, the Four had gone through no such experience. Their independence had come to them by stealth. The Statute of Westminster had been an *ex post facto* acknowledgement of an existing condition, and had been so hedged about with local qualifications that its total effect was small, especially in Australia and New Zealand. Dominion status had been less a matter of conferment than of occurrence. Independence, as later conferred, was a decisive step. But Dominion status and independence meant the same in the end. It is perhaps symptomatic that this book should bear the name it does. In spite of the objections to the word "Dominion", it still lingers in the mind as a term that suits the countries with which this book is concerned: "old Commonwealth states" is clumsy and "white Dominions" potentially insulting; "Old Dominions" seems to have the right

* R. A. Spencer, *Canada in World Affairs 1946–1949* (Toronto, 1959), p. 369.
† House of Commons, July 2, 1947; quoted in Heather J. Harvey, *Consultation and Co-operation in the Commonwealth* (London, 1952), p. 171.

touch of past and present. The end of Dominion status is not quite yet, if only in literary terms.

THE IMPERIAL CONFERENCE

Just as "Dominion" ceased to hold whatever magic it might have had before, so the Imperial Conference could not survive the war and the changes which followed it. According to Mr. Hodson,

> "It was surely not on the initiative of the United Kingdom Government, but on that of the Dominion Governments, or some of them, that the Imperial Conference was quietly smothered in its bed after World War II—put down like an old dog which had become feeble and smelly, and which must not now be mentioned before the children, lest they embarrass by asking what became of him."*

The last Imperial Conference was held in 1937. There was a special wartime meeting of Prime Ministers in 1944; the first post-war meeting took place in London in April and May, 1946. In form it was obviously more a continuation of piecemeal wartime meetings than of the Imperial Conference: at no stage were all the Prime Ministers together at once. The first week was confined to Britain, Australia and New Zealand; Smuts attended from the second week; and Mackenzie King did not arrive till the third week, by which time Mr. Chifley had gone home, leaving Dr. Evatt behind to act for him. The word "conference" was not used in the final communique. It did not make an appearance again for many years, the word "meeting" taking its place.† The same applied to the 1948 meeting of Prime Ministers. When that was announced, Mr. Mackenzie King stated that

> "the meeting in London is not, as some have assumed, in the nature of an Imperial Conference at which several Ministers and their advisers will be present and where a decision upon

---

* H. V. Hodson, *Twentieth-Century Empire* (London, 1948), p. 131.
† The 1965 meeting was firmly described by the British Information Service as "the Commonwealth Prime Ministers' Conference" in heading the communique; but by then the significance of the change had disappeared. (G116-a-SUB, July 1, 1965.)

policy will be made. It is a meeting between the Prime Ministers of Britain and of certain other nations of the Commonwealth to discuss matters of common interest in a manner which will permit of the freest possible exchange of views for reference back to their respective governments."*

It is fairly clear that King had something to do with the failure to resume the Imperial Conference, and that, if there was any "smothering in its bed", this was due to influences from Canada and South Africa, rather than from the Asian Commonwealth countries, as later myths might suggest. There was certainly some indignation in Britain, expressed by Conservative newspapers such as the *Daily Mail, Daily Express, Sunday Times* and *Daily Telegraph*, at the fact that meetings of Prime Ministers no longer produced "great Empire declarations". But we must not put the whole blame (if it is blame) on Mackenzie King. No doubt the British Government was pleased that it did not have to go through the ceremonial motions with which the Imperial Conference had become encrusted, and no doubt the other Commonwealth leaders were glad that they were brought together for specific business, rather than to demonstrate solidarity. The numerous inter-governmental conferences of the war years had accustomed everybody to this kind of practical discussion. There was a very real sense in which the spirit of the age was against continued Imperial Conferences—partly because "Imperial" was not the word it had been; partly because of the increased tempo of governmental activity in each of the countries concerned, with the consequent difficulty for Prime Ministers of spending long periods in London; above all, because the assumptions which had lain behind the Imperial Conference could no longer be sustained.

There has not, in fact, been much difference between the things discussed or the practical procedures at pre-war Imperial Conferences and post-war meetings of Prime Ministers. The main difference has been in the assumptions. Always behind an Imperial Conference lay the feeling that the countries of the Empire ought to present a united front to the world, and that this unity ought to be expressed in common approaches to defence, foreign policy, economic development and loyalty to the throne. Much of the activity of Imperial Conferences in the 1920's and 30's consisted of papering over the cracks in imperial unity, in order to present

* *The Times* August 26, 1948.

this kind of united front: it was assumed that Britain and the Dominions would lose face if their divergent interests were revealed to public gaze. It was an uncomfortable situation, but thought to be necessary. After the war it was no longer thought to be necessary. There were still statements about "unity" in the communiques, but the actions of the Commonwealth members in taking diverse stands in foreign policy and sometimes quarrelling publicly with one another showed that this unity, if it existed, was of a Pickwickian kind. Gradually the Prime Ministers became accustomed to disagreeing, and found that it did them no harm after all. They could get along quite well without great Empire declarations.

The actual differences in procedure from the Imperial Conference reflect these differences in assumptions. No resolutions are passed at meetings of Prime Ministers, although the communiques reveal a good deal of common agreement on matters of concern. There is no White Paper afterwards (the Imperial Conference used to issue a summary of proceedings). While Britain has sent the invitations, this was apparently by courtesy, not by right, as was British chairmanship; it is quite possible that meetings will take place elsewhere than in London, although London has great advantages for busy Prime Ministers who want to get some business done on the side. From the beginning arrangements about the agenda, etc., had been made by the Commonwealth Relations Office in London, in communication with the Cabinet secretariats and kindred bodies of the overseas members; the Commonwealth secretariat, agreed on in 1965, has now taken over this task.

For Canada, Australia and New Zealand, the frequent Prime Ministers' meetings have provided opportunities of summing up the new members, especially those from Africa, whose relations before independence had been entirely with Britain. Prime Ministers with long memories, like Sir Robert Menzies (who attended the last Imperial Conference, in 1937), may sigh for the glitter of pre-war gatherings and the intimate atmosphere of meetings immediately after the war, when there were only a few faces round the table. It is natural that the Old Dominions should feel like this; natural, also, that they should feel some slight apprehension in the presence of so many black faces, since neither Canada, Australia, or New Zealand is noted for militancy in the anti-colonial cause. But it is widely considered (especially in Canada and New Zealand) that diplomacy with the rising Afro-Asian forces is better carried on in the relaxed atmosphere of Prime Ministers' meetings, and the discussions that go with them, than solely in the corridors of the United Nations. The three surviving Old Dominions have recognized all along that Britain's problem of decolonization is made less difficult by the prospect of Commonwealth membership for colonies approaching independence; and they have not complained about the increase in numbers. South Africa did make a half-hearted attempt to stop African membership when it became clear that Ghana was to be advanced to independence, but the British Government would have none of this, and South Africa got no support elsewhere. Now that South Africa has gone, thus removing the worst source of friction between white and black representatives, the meetings of Prime Ministers are a useful means of testing opinion, floating schemes for co-operation, and getting to know other people.

CHANGES IN NATIONALISM AND COMMONWEALTH IDEAS

Nationalism has been a constant theme in the history of the Old Dominions, as we have already seen, although its growth has been unequal as between one and another of them. It is possible, however, to discern certain changes in the form and expression of nationalism amongst them in the post-war period. The change is part of the general shift from a position in which following Britain was regarded as orthodox and natural, to one in which co-operation with Britain is embarked on when it is considered to be worth while.

First, there has been a decline in what might be called emotional nationalism. It is true that the Nationalist Government in South Africa has striven, with much success, to keep militant nationalism alive, and that separatism in Quebec has reached at times a height of emotion unequalled for many years. These have, however, been the main manifestations of emotional nationalism; and even they suggest a movement away from the cruder kinds of emotion. In South Africa the Nationalists have consciously attempted to broaden their appeal to take in all white South Africans. Since 1948, when Dr. Malan's Government took office, there has been a clear trend away from attacks on the British and the past, to attacks on India, the Communist countries, militant African states, and the U.N., as sources of international criticism of South Africa and saboteurs of its racial policy. At the same time, the Nationalist appeal has became more sophisticated. It is now capable of appealing to far more white South Africans than in the 1930's, because it is based on what they conceive to be their interests; it is no longer the narrow orthodoxy of a sect.

The Quebec example has certain similarities, although, as the expression of a permanent minority, it differs from the negotiation from strength of the Afrikaner nationalists. It is expressed with greater depth and awareness of contemporary circumstances than Quebec ever mustered before. The age of M. Maurice Duplessis is over. Furthermore, it is noticeable in Canada that English-Canadians show more understanding of Quebec than they used to. There was a revival of traditional British feeling when the Queen was insulted in 1964, but it did not last long; it is more significant that English-Canadian scholars have set themselves to understand the reasons for Quebec resentment, that the sacred books of the separatist move-ment are sold in university bookshops as far afield as Vancouver, and that solid efforts are being made by the Federal and Quebec Governments to improve Quebec's economic position. In Canada at large, old-style nationalism is disappearing.*

The same is true elsewhere. While emotions remain significant, they are not being canalized in the simple pro-British, anti-British form of earlier years: the kind of dichotomy which Mr. Churchill saw in each of the Dominions in 1931 is largely a thing of the past. Nationalism is now more likely to express itself in the active pursuit of particular interests in the international field. These are sometimes material and economic, sometimes directly political, sometimes a matter of prestige abroad. They are pursued, not with-in the narrow range of relations with Britain alone, but over a vast international field through the network of negotiation between states that has been such a notable feature of post-war diplomacy.

---

* The fact that the Canadian parliament spent many weary hours in 1964 debating a new national flag might suggest otherwise, But the flag was agreed to in the end, and the controversy "also revealed, to the consternation of Mr. John Diefenbaker, the Opposition leader, the weakness of dwindling royal-ist sentiment in Canada. French-Canadians were surprised by evidences of a distinctive national spirit in English Canada, particularly among younger people, which had little to do with anti-British or anti-American opinion . . . Crucial support for the flag came from English-speaking Canadians who re-fused to adopt the Diefenbaker contention that it was a rejection of Canada's British heritage". (Peter Desbarats, "The Problem of Unity", *The Times Supplement on Canada*, February 27, 1965.)

The smooth professionalism which Canadian or Australian representatives show at meetings of GATT or the U.N. is in marked contrast with their fumblings at the League of Nations. Now that the Old Dominions have diplomatic posts in so many countries, they are able to carry on independent negotiations for their own ends without the need to worry about the protocol of working through Britain; their consultation with Britain is a mixture of courtesy and a nice calculation of national interest, not the deference of a junior to a senior.

This self-reliance, which is now the most obvious manifestation of national self-assertion amongst the Old Dominions, is not confined to diplomatic activity. It is also a feature of their international economic ventures, and of the organization of their contacts with other countries in a variety of non-official spheres. At the risk of extreme generalization, one can say that, for the Old Dominions, nationalism is now a matter of taking on the world; it is no longer a matter of keeping one's end up with Britain. Whereas in the 1920's and 30's the Dominions seemed so frequently to be looking for a British answer to their problems, in unfamiliar undertakings such as broadcasting or airlines, or in difficult spheres such as the equipment and maintenance of their armed forces, now they look much more widely for help, and are, to a considerable extent, able to give help themselves. The extent of technical aid from Australia, Canada and New Zealand to Asian countries under the Colombo Plan is a measure of the extra stature which these countries now have.

However, it is important to recognize that self-reliance does not mean self-sufficiency in any exclusive sense. As the Old Dominions have become less emotionally involved with the idea of status, and as their economies and machinery of government have improved in range and quality, they have shown a readiness to co-operate with Britain on questions in which it seems they have something to gain. The next two chapters will give a number of examples of this sort of fruitful co-operation. Now that Britain is no longer a protector but is an ally in such bodies as NATO, SEATO and ANZAM, the idea of equality is more realistic than before the war. Stature has caught up with status. Besides, it is true of Britain, as of Canada, Australia and New Zealand, that each is ultimately a dependent of the United States; in such circumstances a natural harmony of interests will often show itself. Co-operation has been significant in defence arrangements (including defence science, a sphere of wartime co-operation which has continued unabated, especially be-tween Britain and Australia), in the operation of the sterling area (though here Canada has necessarily been outside the range of activity, while privy to what was being done), in certain forms of trade, and in a number of aspects of foreign policy. It is now rare for Britain, Canada, Australia and New Zealand to differ markedly in their assessment of American policies, or to come to widely different conclusions about what happens in the Communist world or in Africa. South Africa is in a different category, as the next chapter will show.

In the field specifically considered in this chapter, that of changes in the structure and operation of the Commonwealth, Britain has found Canada, Australia and New Zealand willing partners. There have been some backward looks, especially from Australia,* but, in the main, it has been clear to the governments of these three countries that there was no alternative to the widening of the Commonwealth to include the Afro-Asian members. Not only their governments, but also most of their commentators on world affairs, have supported the idea. It would have meant a sharp clash with Britain to do otherwise; and the will to attempt that clash simply did not exist in Canada, Australia or New Zealand, though it did in South Africa. In any case, the way had been paved in the 1920's. The Commonwealth was already flexible enough to contain the new countries which Britain was setting free and over which the British Government wished to retain the kind of influence which common membership of the Commonwealth implied.

The whole swing of thought in Commonwealth matters has been similar in Britain and the other three surviving Old Dominions, although the speed of the swing has varied. It has been away from single policy to multiple policy, away from unity to diversity, away from dependence to co-operation. The knowledge that the Commonwealth could not be a closed system, either politic-ally or economically, has spread slowly but without significant re-sistance. On the surface, certain attitudes have remained as they were. The ritual screamings of the *Daily Express* kept alive in Britain in the post-war period the out-of-date ideas of the 1920's and 30's. Mr. Diefenbaker sonorously intoned imperial platitudes for which he could find no corresponding policy in practice. It has been the custom for new Australian High Commissioners in

---

* For details of some of these backward looks, see J. D. B. Miller, *The Commonwealth in the World* (London, 1960), pp. 278–81.

London to mourn a vanished imperial unity. But none of these had any obvious effect. The ideas which gained ground were either those which rejected the Commonwealth as a fake or those which attempted to find some constructive role for the new form which the Commonwealth assumed as the number of member-states grew. The second of these positions has been the more important. Such active thinking about the Commonwealth is more common in Britain than in Canada and more common there than in Australia or New Zealand, but its effect has been noticeable in all of those countries.

If one were to take books about the Commonwealth as some guide to the movement of ideas, there is a fairly clear line of change. The representative book twenty years ago was one like Sir Edward Grigg's *The British Commonwealth* (London, 1943) or H. V. Hodson's *Twentieth Century Empire* (London, 1948) or John Coatman's *The British Family of Nations* (London, 1950)—a book written by someone with active experience of the Empire, with a keen appreciation of its importance and of the role of the Crown, and with a wish to find new ways of preserving its former characteristics while retaining unity amongst its members. The representative book now is either one like Guy Arnold's *Towards Peace and a Multiracial Commonwealth* (London, 1964), with its thorough rejection of the former trappings of the British Commonwealth and its conviction that the new members provide the motive force for an effective Commonwealth in the future, or an uncertain piece of neo-imperialist public relations such as Derek Ingram's *Partners in Adventure* (London, 1960) in which something of the same goal is pursued without the attempt to recognize the drawbacks of a traditionalist approach.* Whether one takes directly political books from the British Labour side, such as Patrick Gordon-Walker's *The Commonwealth* (London, 1962), or Patrick Maitland's *Task for Giants* (London, 1957) from the Conservative side, it is apparent that the movement of thought in Britain has been away from a closely-knit Commonwealth to an extended one with autonomy as its characteristic. There is still room for hope that co-operation will be widespread and that members will naturally choose one

* Here I am concentrating upon books of a popular character intended for the general reader. The movement in scholarly books has not been so obvious, since scholars of the Commonwealth, such as W. K. Hancock, had a much clearer idea of what was happening to the Commonwealth in the 1930's, and there was less ground to catch up after the war.

another's company rather than that of foreigners, but the trend has been towards the acceptance of the new sovereign state as the hall-mark of the Commonwealth.

It is understandable that, in the post-war period, there should have been more of this discussion in Britain than in the Old Dominions, since Britain had the task of organizing relationships with newly-independent ex-colonies, and they did not: Australia's problem with New Guinea, which may turn out to be as difficult as any British experience, did not become a matter of significant discussion until the 1960's. South Africa's outlook in the matter was always a special one. The shape of the new Commonwealth has been very much a matter of British thinking and British effort. The response from the Old Dominions has been broadly an acceptance of the new situation. The Canadian Government has been en-thusiastic about it; to a lesser extent, so has that of New Zealand. The Australian position has been very much identified with the personality and attitudes of Sir Robert Menzies. Australian in-tellectuals who interest themselves in such matters have taken the same line as their counterparts in Canada; so has the Australian Labour Party, perhaps with some misgivings. Sir Robert has changed his ground to some extent with circumstances. His basic position has been one of regret for the passing of the "Crown Commonwealth". He was disturbed by the new arrangements made for India in 1949, but became accustomed to the Asian members and appreciated the advantages of informal contact with them. However, he was shaken by the experience of African pressure at the 1964 and 1965 Prime Ministers' Conferences, especially by what seemed to be Chinese Communist influence on Tanzania, and opposed strongly suggestions that the new Commonwealth secre-tariat should have executive power in its own right—even though the proposals for a secretariat seemed on the surface to be akin to proposals which he had made in the past.* His general position has involved doubt about the workable character of an enlarged Com-monwealth, along with general support for British aims and policies.

* For some of Sir Robert's earlier views on the Commonwealth, see R. G. Menzies, *The British Commonwealth of Nations in International Affairs* (Roy Milne Memorial Lecture, Adelaide, 1950).

7

DEFENCE AND FOREIGN AFFAIRS
1945–1965

SEEN as states involved in world politics, the three surviving Old Dominions exhibit certain common characteristics. They exercise a practical autonomy in diplomacy, in contrast with their obviously dependent condition before the war; they are guaranteed by the United States; they co-operate closely with Britain; and they are generally hostile to Communism as an international force, although they differ now and then in their interpretation of its virulence and the methods to be used against it. South Africa shares some but not all of these characteristics. In its internal politics and in its government's proclamations about world affairs, it is more stridently anti-Communist than any of the others. But it has not, at any stage, been given the kind of guarantee that Canada, Australia and New Zealand have managed to extract from the United States. Moreover its official relations with Britain have become worse because of its racial policies.

The purpose of this chapter is to consider events since 1945 so as to show how each of the Four has arrived at the position in which it now stands, and particularly to show how Britain fits into its external relations and defence arrangements. From the British side, an attempt is made to assess the significance of each of the Four for British policy. Any realistic description of what has happened to the Old Dominions in their relations with Britain must take account of a number of other developments: above all, of the post-war character of American policy, of the changes in direction of Russian and Chinese policy, and of the rise of new states in Asia and Africa.

It would, however, be absurd to attempt a general survey of post-war events, since this has been done better elsewhere, and there is no room for it here. Nor will there be any attempt to cover the foreign policy of each of the five states in question in any detail, since this would require not one book, but a number.* Instead, this chapter first considers Britain's position in the world, and then looks at relations between Britain and the Four in the uncertain years immediately after the war. It considers the period of consolidation of American guarantees through NATO, ANZUS and SEATO, and proceeds to examine the bases of co-operation of the Commonwealth countries with the United States, before looking at defence and other co-operation between Britain and the Four. Finally, there is discussion of the attitude of Britain and the Dominions to one another in foreign affairs.

BRITAIN IN THE POST-WAR WORLD

We saw in the previous chapter how the Dominions have grown in status and stature within the Commonwealth since the war, and how the pre-war sensitivity about status has tended to disappear. Mention has also been made of the fact that the Four now take part wholeheartedly in the world-wide network of diplomacy and international organization; that they are, in every sense, sovereign states, instead of the doubtfully autonomous bodies they were before 1939. This central fact about the Dominions is of vital importance to this chapter.

Just as important, however, is the position of Britain in the world. When the war ended, Britain was a proud but exhausted victor. Its lack of extreme devastation made it ineligible for American aid on the scale eventually received by a number of continental countries. Its position as a victor gave it continued military responsibilities which it could ill afford to bear. Its leadership of the Commonwealth caused it to undertake tasks, and assume

* There are good surveys from the British standpoint in F. S. Northedge, *British Foreign Policy* (London, 1962) and C. M. Woodhouse, *British Foreign Policy since the Second World War* (London, 1961). Neither says much about the Old Dominions as individual states, though each brings in the Commonwealth from time to time. Canada is best served by books about its foreign policy, in the excellent series on *Canada in World Affairs*, volumes by F. H. Soward, Robert A. Spencer, W. E. C. Harrison, B. S. Keirstead, Donald C. Masters, and James Eayrs (Toronto, 1950, 1959, 1957, 1959, 1959). Australia comes next, with Gordon Greenwood and Norman Harper, eds. *Australia in World Affairs, 1950–1955* and *1956–1960* (Melbourne, 1957 and 1963). For South Africa, see J. E. Spence, *Republic Under Pressure* (London, 1965). New Zealand foreign policy still awaits academic attention for the post-war years, but the annual reports of the Department of External Affairs, Wellington, merit study.

a status, which its economy could hardly sustain. Its custodianship
of sterling made it strain that economy still further by recognizing
wartime debts which, in some cases, hardly merited the name. In
general, its unique position meant that, alone among the powers of
Western Europe, it could not take that temporary dive into men-
dicancy, repudiation and desolation, to be followed by rehabilitation
amounting to a fresh start, that was characteristic of France, Germany and Italy. Like a runner who, on winning a mile race, is told
that there was a mistake and the race is really over two miles, Britain
had to keep on going without getting its second wind.

All these elements made life hard for Britain in the period
immediately after the war. They would have been serious enough
to those who wanted Britain to be a great power; but there were
also factors changing the world in which Britain had to make its
way. Foremost amongst these was the confrontation between the
United States and the Soviet Union. Although the Soviet Union did
not possess nuclear weapons at the end of the war, its power in
conventional forces was so great that only American intervention
could hope to stop it if it wished to march across Europe or force
the installation of Communist governments by intimidation. If
Britain and Western Europe were to be safe against threats of this
kind, they had to have American protection. That protection was
forthcoming as a permanent element in the European situation; it
stopped any prospect of Russian intervention, but it made the United
States the greatest power in Europe. "Europe" disappeared as a
self-sufficient entity which could have its own balance of power, its
own agreements on how power should be wielded in Africa and
Asia; instead, the two super-powers confronted each other across a
Europe which, at the best, could hope only to influence these super-
powers, especially the one allied with West European countries.

The situation described has been alleviated by the nuclear stale-
mate between the United States and the Soviet Union, and by the
complications arising from the split between Communist China
and the Soviet Union; it has also been affected, within the totality
of world diplomacy, by the rise of scores of new nations in Asia
and Africa. The combination of such alleviation with increased
economic prosperity has enabled France to steer an increasingly
independent course, and Britain to exercise many of the functions
of a major power. But Britain is still ultimately dependent on the
United States. Whereas in pre-war days Britain could (if only
notionally) plan for war in both the Pacific and Europe, this is now

impossible. British resources will not allow it. Moreover, the brutalities of nuclear strategy make it clear that Britain, while indefensible against all-out nuclear attack, could not hope to inflict mortal harm on any adversary. Britain's role has thus come to be essentially that of the fighter of non-nuclear "brush-fire" wars in colonial and ex-colonial areas, but always with the backing of the United States; without this backing, as at Suez in 1956, Britain's freedom of movement is cruelly curtailed. It is with a state in this position that the Dominions have had to deal.

POST-WAR UNCERTAINTY, 1946-9

The Dominions were unsure of themselves when the war ended. Status was no longer an issue. They now had bigger things to worry about, especially the amount of notice that would be taken of them, and by whom. They could claim to have been active throughout the war, and to have had as good a record as anyone. But they had experienced the penalties of their smallness, in being pushed aside when many of the major decisions were taken; and this was repeated once the war was over. Australia encountered it immediately over the surrender of Japan and the subsequent peace negotiations, having been, along with the other Dominions, excluded from discussions of the ultimatum delivered at Potsdam. It was first proposed by the British Government that Australian service representatives should attend the Japanese surrender as "attached to" British representatives. This did not satisfy the Australian Government, as indeed it was not likely to satisfy Australians at large. Britain's role in the Pacific War since the surrender of Singapore had perforce been a modest one, and the late arrival of the British fleet in the Pacific, after its European tasks were done, had not resulted in much action. Australia, on the other hand, had experienced hard fighting in New Guinea and the Islands, and had served as General MacArthur's base for his reduction of the Japanese forces. The Australian Government proposed that General Blamey should attend as a "direct" representative. At first this request was turned down by the American Government, but later granted after further representations. Australia also offered to furnish part of the occupation force, but on the understanding that this was offered "not as a subsidiary but as a principal Pacific power which for three and a half years had borne a major share of the struggle against

Japan".* In due course the claims were recognized. But this did not prevent General MacArthur, as head of the occupation forces, from taking little notice of the Allied Council for Japan, on which an Australian sat to represent Australia, Britain, New Zealand and India.†

Canada and Australia experienced similar difficulties over the matter of representation at the conferences to settle the European peace treaties. Here, as at San Francisco, when the nations assembled to draw up the Charter of the U.N., it was made clear that the Great Powers, especially the United States and the Soviet Union, saw no reason to take account of countries which might have been gallant allies but were small in population and opinionated in utterance. The comparative reticence of the Canadians got them into less trouble than the volubility of Dr. Evatt for Australia and Mr. Fraser for New Zealand. Yet all were in the same boat : they might call themselves "middle powers", but to the two greatest powers they were not of much importance. A Canadian historian, looking over this period, explains the difficulties which his country faced :

> "A Great Power could recommend any course it chose, confident that it could protect its interests by its own strength or by its veto in the Security Council; a small Power could advocate ambitious schemes with impunity, confident that it would either not be listened to or at least would not become seriously involved. But a Power of middle rank had to act with considerable caution in taking any initiative, for it might find itself and its resources heavily committed, without the power either to protect itself or to dictate the disposition of its resources."‡

Professor Spencer uses this analysis to explain the lack of a clear-cut, independent policy by Canada, and also its balancing role between Britain and the United States. One could also use it to explain the movement from cheekiness to deference in Australian foreign policy in the decade after 1945.

It is not difficult to see what role dominant elements in the British

* For these negotiations, see R. N. Rosecrance, *Australian Diplomacy and Japan 1945–1951* (Melbourne, 1962), Ch. 2, and *Current Notes on International Affairs* (External Affairs Dept., Canberra – hereafter *Current Notes*), 1945, p. 171.

† Canada did not wish to be included in this arrangement.

‡ Robert A. Spencer, *Canada in World Affairs, 1946–1949* (Toronto, 1949), p. 9.

Government attached to the Dominions once the war was over; it was very much the sort of role they had wished them to play while the war was on. The Defence White Paper of 1946 stated:

"During the war, collaboration with the Dominions and India has been comprehensive, continuous and effective. The long-accepted principle whereby His Majesty's Forces throughout the Empire have been trained, organized and equipped on the same basis, proved its value in the easy and wholehearted co-operation which took place by sea, land and air, in all theatres of war, between men and women of many races. Behind the forces, collaboration in the field of scientific and technical development, and in the production of munitions and supplies of all kinds, was equally close and thorough. His Majesty's Government in the U.K. acknowledge to the full the tremendous efforts put forward in the common cause by the whole of the Commonwealth and Empire, and earnestly desire to continue in peace the full partnership so magnificently established in war. It will be necessary to consider with the Governments of His Majesty's Dominions and India the way in which the lesson of the war can be applied to promote consultation and collaboration in defence matters during peace."*

The notion of partnership with the Dominions was natural to a government which was aware that the adhesion to it of Dominion power would enable it to bargain on better terms with the United States and the Soviet Union. But the British Government was shown in more ways than Australian and New Zealand annoyance over Japan that it must not regard the Dominions as acquiescent partners. In May 1946 it announced the withdrawal of British forces from Egypt, after disturbances there in protest against the troops' continued presence. Mr. Attlee used words which suggested that the Dominion Prime Ministers had "agreed" to this. The next day, evidently on Dominion prompting, he had to state publicly that, while they had been kept "fully and continuously informed", they "were not called upon to express agreement".† The notion of a common front, stated a short while before in the Defence White Paper, was already wearing at the edges; as time went on, it could

* *Statement Relating to Defence*, February 1946, Cmd. 6743, p. 8.
  † F. H. Soward, *Canada in World Affairs 1944–1946* (Toronto, 1950), pp. 225–7.

no longer be sustained, except in special contexts and in regard to particular objectives.

The situation of Canada in this period is the best documented and the clearest to understand. There were forces in Canada which wanted the Government to co-ordinate its policy at every point with that of Britain and to emphasize "imperial" interests at the expense of others, but they were not prominent in the Canadian Governments of Mr. Mackenzie King and Mr. Saint Laurent. The lines of Canadian security, as seen by the Government, ran towards the United States, and these must be made fast first. Once they were, attention turned to the growing problem of Western Europe, apparently open to invasion or the harshest pressure from the Soviet Union; here the Canadian concern was to involve the United States permanently in the defence of Western Europe, and Canadian spokesmen were among the first to call for the kind of alliance which was eventually established in NATO. That alliance, in its turn, brought Canada back into close working relations with Britain in defence matters, but there was no attempt to create a "Commonwealth bloc" of two in NATO: the Canadian Government was there as a power in its own right, and its NATO negotiations, while carried out in the full knowledge of British aims, were essentially Canadian in character, and more concerned with American actions than with British. Once NATO was fashioned, a Canadian could say with relief that "for the first time the Government is sure of itself on questions of external policy".* There were some things which Canada did not do, in spite of its closeness to the United States and its concern for Europe: for example, it did not send forces to take part in the Berlin airlift in 1948, although Australia and South Africa did. Presumably this was because there were still relics of the old caution about active involvement in anything which might lead to a European war. The main thing, however, was that Canada soon slipped into a posture eminently suitable to a "middle power": in between the United States and Britain, in between North America and Europe, in the Commonwealth yet operating extensively outside it to serve Canadian interests. Very quickly it became clear that Canada could not be regarded as part of the British stage army, if anyone should be so foolish as to expect this; the point was made to the United States as well as to Britain.

---

* Professor Eric Harrison, in a preparatory paper for the 1949 unofficial British Commonwealth Relations Conference, quoted in F. H. Soward, *The Changing Commonwealth* (Toronto, 1950), p. 16.

There was, for example, "the storm that brewed up in mid-1947 when it was discovered that a large bell of the carillon being installed at Niagara Falls Bridge was, through the action of one of the Bridge Commissioners, engraved with the names of 'our nations' leaders . . . Winston Spencer Churchill and Franklin Delano Roosevelt'. This, Mr. Chevrier told the [Canadian] Commons, was considered an affront to Mr. Mackenzie King and the people of Canada, and the offending names were removed."*

I am not suggesting that Canada became uninterested in British policy or unconcerned about British or Commonwealth interests; this was not so. But, as the Canadian Government discarded its pre-war isolationism and habitual refusal to be bound by British decisions, it did not automatically drop into line behind Britain; instead, it looked for policies which would safeguard its own position. While these sometimes fitted in closely with British policy (as in the encouragement of India and Pakistan to retain Commonwealth membership), in other fields the incompatibility of interests was revealed. As we shall see in Chapter 8, this was especially so in regard to international trade and finance: Canadian pressure for multilateralism continually conflicted with British caution about the use of the sterling area's gold and dollar reserve.

Australia and New Zealand had a more difficult time than Canada in working out their post-war roles. At the personal level, this was partly because of Dr. Evatt's insistent determination to have an Australian finger in every pie, especially at the U.N. While New Zealand did not support him at every turn, there was enough common ground to enable him to count on New Zealand support in a number of his ventures against authority (i.e. against British and American policy) in the early post-war period.† But there were weightier causes for the difficulties of Australia and New Zealand than Dr. Evatt's intrusiveness. They had been dependent, throughout the Pacific War, upon American assistance. Once the war was over, the Americans went home, metaphorically as well as physically. There was little or no indication, in the first few years after the war, that the United States was interested in other people's

* Spencer, *Canada in World Affairs, 1946–1949* (Toronto, 1959), p. 325.
† Bernard K. Gordon argues in *New Zealand Becomes a Pacific Power* (Chicago, 1960) that in 1944 the New Zealand line on such matters as American strategic trusteeship "was different from the uncompromising line of exaggerated sensitivity which Australia, in contrast with the smaller Dominion, still followed" (p. 221). However, it is clear that the New Zealand and Australian delegations at San Francisco in 1945 were at one in most things.

schemes for Pacific security. Its two concerns were the retention of certain island bases under its system of strategic trusteeship, and the attempt to bring Japan back quickly into the comity of nations. Neither of these was in line with dominant feeling in the Governments of the two Dominions.

The Australian and New Zealand Governments had signed an agreement in 1944 (the so-called ANZAC Pact), in which they laid down some of their aims. Amongst the decisions announced was one (para. 16) which stated that

"The two Governments accept as a recognized principle of international practice that the construction and use, in time of war, by any Power of naval, military or air installations, in any territory under the sovereignty or control of another Power, does not, in itself, afford any basis for territorial claims or rights of sovereignty or control after the conclusion of hostilities.*

This was aimed at the United States, since no other Power could have been intended. It was not received well in Washington, where Admiral King decided not to use Australian or New Zealand forces in operations for the capture of the Marshall and Caroline Islands.† The American Government accepted the joint Australian–New Zealand statement on the assumption that it could be held to apply only to territories which they controlled; they could not bind other countries. But it was over part of Australian mandated (later Trust) territory that the principal difficulty arose after the war. The Americans had built a vast and expensive base on the rainy island of Manus, in the Admiralty group.‡ It may have cost $150 million. American defence authorities put it on the list of Pacific bases which they wished to retain after the war. The Australian Government replied by quoting the declaration above; Dr. Evatt laid down, in March 1946, the conditions under which an arrangement might be made:

"Any consideration of plans for the joint use of any bases in Australia's dependent territories should be preceded by an overall

* Mansergh, *Documents*, p. 1,159.
† F. L. W. Wood, *The New Zealand People at War* (Wellington, 1958), pp. 317–8.
‡ See R. N. Rosecrance, *Australian Diplomacy and Japan, 1945–1951* (Melbourne, 1962). Ch. 5. The Evatt quotation which follows is from p. 61.

defence arrangement for the region of the Western Pacific, including the islands formerly mandated to Japan; as an incident of any such arrangement, Australia should be entitled to reciprocal use of foreign bases in the region, thus providing for an over-all increase in the security, both of Australia and of all other United Nations with interests in the region."

In other words, if the Americans wanted Manus, they would have to pay for it by some sort of general system of guarantee, would have to throw open the Marshalls, the Carolines, perhaps Guam, to the Australians, and would have to share Manus with anyone else the Australians nominated.* This was too high a price. By 1947 the American Government was saying that it did not want Manus after all; and no agreement was made with Australia or New Zealand about continued use of other bases. Practical co-operation at such levels ceased altogether. It was clear that, whatever other ways there might have been towards a Pacific pact involving American guarantees, it was not to be attained through the American interest in bases.

The other sphere of American activity, the occupation of Japan, was also of little help to Australia and New Zealand in obtaining some firm assurance from the United States—although it was eventually to provide this through ANZUS, though not until 1951. As already indicated, General MacArthur took little notice of the British Commonwealth representative on his Allied Control Council. In addition, the United States proved to have little concern for the views expressed by its allies on the Far Eastern Commission. There were disagreements over reparations, trade, and the re-establishment of the Japanese economy. Australia and New Zealand tended to take a hard line on all of these. They were less quickly affected by events elsewhere than was the United States. As the Soviet Union became stronger in Europe, and the Communists gained successes in China, American policy moved towards leniency with Japan; Australia and New Zealand remained for longer in that mental posture in which "Japanese aggression" and "Japanese militarism" were the enemy which defence arrangements in the Pacific would have to meet. The Labour Governments which were in office in both countries until December 1949 continued to speak in terms which recalled the war which they had helped to fight.

* In fact, the Australian Government wanted Britain to share in the Manus arrangement too. (See L. F. Crisp, *Ben Chifley*, p. 283.)

When their opponents came in, they moved rather more quickly than the two Labour administrations might have done to a posture in which fear of China was the principal element; but they too were affected by the sense of condemnation of Japan which had been so widespread in the two Pacific Dominions.

Meanwhile, Australia and New Zealand were still trying to work out the "regional" conceptions which they had espoused during the war, and which it was difficult to reduce to anything clearer than the proposition that the Pacific was important and that anyone who was concerned with it ought to pay attention to Australia and New Zealand. The ANZAC pact had stated (para. 13):

> "The two Governments agree that, within the framework of a general system of world security, a regional zone of defence comprising the South-West and South Pacific areas shall be established and that this zone should be based on Australia and New Zealand, stretching through the arc of islands North and North-East of Australia to Western Samoa and the Cook Islands."

All this really said was that the two countries would defend their own possessions. The New Zealand Prime Minister in 1944 wrote that peace could be preserved "only . . . under a world system of security and not under a number of systems of regional security"; he squared this with the ANZAC approach by recognizing "the practical worth of a zone of regional—in the sense of local—defence as distinct from a zone of regional security for the preservation of peace".* "Regional" was clearly a blessed word. On looking over various statements made by Australian and New Zealand leaders in this and the next four years the following points seem to stand out: the two countries wanted to be regarded as masters in their own houses, i.e. to exercise control over their own areas and those close by; at the same time they recognized their vulnerability, as demonstrated in the war, and wanted American guarantees if these could be got without too many strings; however, they did not wish the world's security to be dependent simply on regional arrangements, but to rest upon a world-wide organization such as the U.N.; and, in the midst of these considerations, they remained closely connected with Britain, and were ready to fit in with British arrangements wherever these were in their interests. It was

* Quoted in F. L. W. Wood, *The New Zealand People in War* (Wellington, 1958), p. 319.

characteristic of their situation that Australia and New Zealand had defence plans to offer the 1946 Prime Ministers Meeting, whereas Canada and South Africa had not. Australian proposals were based upon the country's supply capacity (the Government welcomed the suggestion of a British experimental rocket range in Australia), and upon the idea of a centralization in Australia of Commonwealth defence planning in the South-West Pacific, the organization to include representatives from Britain, New Zealand and India. Mr. Chifley did not at this stage, however, propose an extension of Australian responsibilities into South-East Asia.* The proposals which he made in 1946 bore fruit in the establishment of the Woomera rocket range, and in the association of British and New Zealand representatives with the Australian structure of defence organization.

Whatever could be got from co-operation with Britain in supply matters, however, was not of great importance to the fundamental problem of Australia and New Zealand. If a new aggressive power began to operate on the Asian mainland, or if (as was more often stated) the old one, Japan, got a new lease of aggressive life, Australia and New Zealand would be back in the dangerous position which they had found so distressing after the fall of Singapore. Britain would not be able to help them if conditions in Europe were tense. By the early months of 1949 the Australian Government was trying to bring the United States into a Pacific-wide pact based upon the new and fashionable model of NATO. The American response was bleak, and given only three days after Mr. Chifley had said that planning for the Pacific was proceeding parallel with corresponding planning for the North Atlantic area: the United States had enough on its hands with NATO.† It was two more years before the United States could be brought to drink at this particular water.

The position of South Africa in the three years after the war was comparatively simple. It was a member of no alliance, and was, as always, preoccupied with its own internal problems. External affairs became important largely to the extent that they impinged upon these. Thus, the growth of Russian power was discussed in South Africa in terms of the likely growth of Communist influence amongst South Africa's non-whites; the U.N. was discussed

---

* Crisp, op. cit., pp. 282–3.

† R. N. Rosecrance, *Australian Diplomacy and Japan, 1945–1951* (Melbourne, 1962), pp. 140–41.

almost entirely in terms of the campaign which India had launched in 1946 against the treatment of Indians in South Africa, and of the ins and outs of the South-West Africa situation. A major issue was whether there was any obligation upon South Africa to submit this mandated territory for transfer to the new system of trusteeship, as other mandatories were doing. Under Smuts, who remained in office until 1948, defence and other relations with Britain stayed on something like their wartime footing. It was not in the interests of the South African Government to press for closer relations, since this would provide ammunition for its nationalist opponents; quiet co-operation was sufficient. The British Government saw no reason at this stage to question South African racial conduct; indeed, it supported the South African plan for incorporation of South-West Africa into the Union in 1946.*

It will be clear that there was not much in the position of the Dominions to trouble Britain in the period from, say, 1945 to 1949. The defence of North America was not Britain's business; neither, at this stage, was the defence of any notable part of Asia or the Pacific. British occupation troops were withdrawn from Japan sooner than those of Australia and New Zealand. South Africa's internal rumblings were its own. Britain's preoccupations in this period were recovery in Europe, the problem of Germany, the movement towards NATO by way of the Brussels Pact, the movement to independence in the Indian sub-continent, the settlement of the Palestine issue, and the attempt to fill the "power vacuum" which was said to exist in the Middle East. The Dominions might be concerned with some of these matters, as indeed they were; Canada became part of NATO, and Australia, New Zealand and South Africa were all interested in what was done in the Middle East. But none of the Dominions was fundamental to the difficulties in which Britain found itself. If they were willing to support Britain, as decency might expect, well and good; if not, Britain would manage.

NATO, KOREA, ANZUS AND SEATO

Between 1949 and 1954, the position described in the previous paragraph changed. Asia erupted with the Korean War; it continued

* Gwendolen M. Carter, *The Politics of Inequality* (London, 1958), p. 383.

to cause anxiety through disturbances in Malaya and Indo-China, and to incite speculation and concern over the future intentions of the Communist Government of China. Pacts became the order of the day amongst Western countries. In a variety of ways, Dominion action became a matter of interest to Britain, whether through concurrence (as in attempts at moderation of extreme American positions over Korea) or through divergence (as with the recognition of Communist China and the exclusion of Britain from the ANZUS Pact). South Africa was not a factor of any importance in these diplomatic manœuvres, but Canada, Australia and New Zealand were.

Before considering Asian events, it is appropriate to say something about Canada's position in NATO, since it was NATO that ended the period of comparative uncertainty in Canadian policy. The record of Canadian involvement in NATO* shows that Canadian leaders, including King, St. Laurent and Pearson, soon became disillusioned with the U.N. as a form of resistance to aggression. They had never been as lyrical about its possibilities as Dr. Evatt, in spite of the dutifully evangelical tone in which Canadians habitually speak about international organizations. In September 1947, Mr. Saint Laurent expressed discontent at the U.N. Assembly with a Security Council "frozen in futility and divided by dissension", and warned that nations seeking peace and co-operation might "seek greater safety in an association of democratic and peace-loving states". Pursuing the domestic metaphors which had begun with the famous Canadian pre-war reference to the "fireproof house", he went on :

> "Let us not forget that the provisions of the Charter are a floor under, rather than a ceiling over, the responsibilities of Member states. If some prefer to get even below that floor, others need not be prevented from moving upwards. Two, or more, apartments in the structure of peace are undoubtedly less desirable

---

* Excellently narrated in R. A. Spencer, *Canada in World Affairs, 1946–1949* (Toronto, 1959), pp. 245 ff. It is perhaps worth noting that this, together with other accounts of the situation, is criticized as "the received version" by Kenneth McNaught (in Michael Oliver, ed., *Social Purpose for Canada*, Toronto, 1961, pp. 455–7), to whom the vital point is "the legacy of old-fashioned militarism with which we have been saddled ever since"; it seems to be the "alacrity" with which "the potential internationalism of 1945 was jettisoned" that troubles him. But he does not appear to question either the order of the facts or the sincerity of Canadian spokesmen in 1948–9.

than one family of nations dwelling together in amity, undivided by curtains or even more substantial pieces of political furniture. They are, however, to be preferred to the alternative of wholly separate structures."*

A number of similar statements followed. Canadian leaders can take credit for being amongst the first to talk about the possibility of linking North America with the new West European defence arrangements in what could still be called a regional association. There does not seem to have been any wish to consolidate Canadian security on either a strictly North American or a Western Hemispherical basis. Canada was already assured of American assistance in the event of war; the emphasis of its leaders upon collaboration with Western Europe presumably reflected their concern that war should not start (i.e. that the Soviet Union should be deterred from any attempt on Western Europe by declared American commitment to that area's defence), and also their feeling that an alliance in which Canada was joined with Britain and France, as well as with the United States, would be the most acceptable to Canadian opinion at large. The idea of hemispherical solidarity as part of "the Americas" has been urged on Canada from time to time by friends to the south, but Canadian leaders had shown little disposition to get involved in the tempest-tossed relationship in which the United States stood to the Latin American states.

It was thus by an irony of circumstance that Canadians were led, directly and willingly, into a formal relationship in Europe; was it not of the sort that their leaders had spent the inter-war period in denouncing? But superficial comparisons are misleading, and were widely felt to be so at the time. In entering NATO, Canada was not being dragged along behind Europe's coat-tails; rather, it was helping to institute an arrangement in which Europe would be both safeguarded and, to a certain extent, controlled. Moreover, Canada would have as much say in NATO affairs as any European state, and more than some of them. This was not a case of the Great Power leadership which had elbowed the Dominions aside in the war. Canada was, from the standpoint of the United States, a prize to be valued. Canadian membershp of NATO would moderate the appearance of a single North-American state dominating Western Europe, and help to relieve what might otherwise become an intolerable dichotomy. To the British and the French, on the

* Spencer, op. cit., p. 248.

M

other hand, Canada was also something of a prize, since it might be able to perform the go-between role with the United States that Canadians liked to think suited them so well. Thus Canada, while not in a position of power in NATO, could expect to exert more influence than in any of its previous international associations, and could hope for as effective a voice as an ally dependent on the United States was likely to have. While there were to be mounting problems in working out the most appropriate contribution Canada could make to NATO's physical resources,* these were not so important in prospect as the fact that Canada would combine American guarantees with a capacity to influence European politics, and a voice in the formulation of American strategy.

Although the Korean war began with animosity by one Korean Government towards another, it soon became a matter of Communist China proving its skill and determination in military affairs, and indicating that it was not prepared to let other countries decide the terms on which régimes were to be organized on its frontiers. Korea became, in fact, part of that complex of problems which began with divergencies between Britain and the Old Dominions about the recognition of the new Chinese Government, and continued through the Korean struggle and its long aftermath of negotiation, to the troubles over the off-shore islands, Indo-China, the Indian frontier and Malaysia. The tension set up between China and the United States by the Korean war has relaxed at times, but has not disappeared. Out of it came the guarantee to the Pacific Dominions which they had sought in vain under earlier conditions. Whereas Canada seemed to get NATO almost without effort, Australia and New Zealand had to work hard for ANZUS and SEATO.

The Old Dominions were affected by the Korean war from the start. Australia was represented on the committee which signified to the U.N. that North Korea had been the aggressor. Australia and New Zealand were among the first countries to offer troops. When the various Dominion contingents were put together with Britain's as a Commonwealth force, this was the most substantial committed to the fight, after that of the United States. The four Old Dominions were all represented in the Korean fighting. They

---

* It will not be possible to give details of Canada's problems of decision as a member of NATO, but see especially the volumes of *Canada in World Affairs* by W. E. C. Harrison, (Ch. IX), B. S. Keirstead, (Ch. IV), and James Eayrs, (Ch. II), (Toronto, 1957, 1956, 1959).

were not, however, equally prominent in the diplomacy of the war. South Africa took little part in this. Australia and New Zealand were at times cautious about taking a different line from the United States. But Canada, under Mr. Pearson's skilled hand, played a very considerable part in the matter. Broadly speaking, the Canadian line was very similar to that of Britain : * it concentrated upon finding means of negotiation with the North Koreans and Chinese while not giving up the idea of collective security against aggression; deprecated suggestions from President Syngman Rhee and elsewhere about unifying Korea by force; warned against the consequences of bombing Manchuria, as advocated by General MacArthur; and kept open a ready ear to what India had to say about the reactions of the Chinese. Whereas India's activities in the latter stages of peace negotiations excited much opposition in the United States, Canada was firm in continuing to support a hearing for the Indian point of vew. Following the cease-fire agreement in 1953, the United States wanted the Political Conference (which was to discuss the future of Korea) to be confined on the U.N. side to those states which had actually provided fighting forces, and on the Communist side to North Korea, China and possibly the Soviet Union. However, it was proposed by Britain, Canada, Australia and New Zealand that India, as a neutral, should also join the Conference to help in overcoming deadlocks. They gained their point by a narrow margin, but the scheme never reached fulfilment. It is significant that, after more than three years of fighting and nerve-racking negotiations, these Old Dominions and Britain were still in close contact with the Indian point of view, and largely in sympathy with it in spite of its unpopularity in the United States.

This common ground was not present in another contemporary Asian issue, the question of recognition of the Communist Government of China. Recognition was granted early by the United Kingdom, but the Old Dominions did not follow suit. Sixteen years after the event, they have still (1965) not done so. The reasons are broadly the same for Canada, Australia and New Zealand, for which a number of factors seem to have worked together in varying proportions. The Old Dominions were confronted with something of a *fait accompli* when they assembled at Colombo for a Commonwealth Foreign Ministers' Conference in January, 1950. Britain, Ceylon, India and Pakistan had all recognized the new

* See the interesting comparisons in Keirstead, op. cit., pp. 53–66.

régime in Peking. It is probable that Canada, Australia and New Zealand approached the matter with similar considerations in mind. On the one hand was their wish to keep in step with Britain, and accord recognition if they were not likely to suffer any disadvantage. The British action was being justified on grounds of necessity (in order that lines could be kept open to Peking, thus facilitating negotiation over such matters as British trade with China, and Hong Kong), and also on those of prudence: the new Chinese Government, it was widely argued, must not be left with the Soviet Union as its only major associate. Moreover, there seemed to be little future in any alternative arrangement: Chiang Kai-shek's Government had fled to Taiwan, but its reputation was poor, Taiwan's status was obscure, and no one was at this stage prepared to fight to keep Taiwan from the Communists. Such considerations presumably weighed heavily. But there were points on the other side. The major one was the wish of all three countries to retain American good will. The United States was engaged in its agonizing post-mortem on China; Chiang Kai-shek was unpopular, but the Communists were even more so. They had not only beaten the Government which the United States had backed, but had also shown cruelty and insolence towards American consular officials. The action which the United States took later in 1950—of safeguarding the nationalist régime on Taiwan by means of the U.S. fleet—was not part of its policy in January, but there was a possibility that it might be. There was no obvious advantage in flouting American opinion. None of the three had major trade interests in China. Besides, the Australian and New Zealand Governments were apprehensive about the influence of the Chinese Communists in Asia generally; they were in no mood to encourage the Communists by recognition, even if this were represented as simply a matter of formal convenience. Thus, there was ample reason for the three states to delay a final decision. The outbreak of the Korean war in the middle of 1950 confirmed their inclination to withhold recognition; the course of the war, together with the American guarantee to Chiang Kai-shek, gave further plausibility to a policy of continuing to recognize the Taiwan Government as the Government of China.*

I have tried to weigh the arguments on this matter because it is

* In trying to envisage the situation as it stood in 1950, I have been much helped by Henry S. Albinski, *Australia and the China Problem during the Korean War Period* (Canberra, 1964).

often asserted that the Dominions failed to follow a British lead over recognition of China, because the Americans told them not to. No one can say what pressure was applied by the United States, but, even if there were some, it is not needed to provide a satisfactory explanation of why Canada, Australia and New Zealand differed from Britain. They did not have the same urgent need as Britain to protect trade, investment, nationals and an adjacent colony; their security could be substantially affected by an increase in Communist power in the Pacific area, whereas Britain's could not, except at more than one remove; they could not share the optimistic views of Chinese intentions then being propagated by India; and they were all three anxious to make sure of American help in any Pacific conflict. There were no strong reasons for their recognizing the Communists, and good reasons for delaying until the American position was stabilized. When it was, they needed little or no persuading to adopt it.

However, it would be wrong to assume that the three Dominions, having followed the American rather than the British line on this particular issue, have done the same in all later questions involving China. The reverse has rather been true. In trade policy they have been much more on the British side, especially as regards sales of Canadian and Australian wheat to China; in matters of travel they avoided the absolute ban which the United States has placed on its citizens' visiting China; while receiving diplomats from Taiwan, they sent none in return. Over the Chinese attacks on the off-shore islands of Quemoy and Matsu, and the Geneva agreements on Indo-China (issues of great importance in the mid-1950's) they were very much more on the British side than the American. All three were acutely aware of the need to retain the respect of uncommitted Asian countries, and to avoid complete identification with those aspects of American policy which, through the efforts of Communist and some nationalist propagandists, were given most publicity in Asia. They were deeply suspicious of China but did not wish to take the lead in denouncing it. In taking such an attitude (epitomized by the eagerness with which all three grasped at the idea of the Colombo Plan when put before the Commonwealth Foreign Ministers in 1950), they were close to British thinking and to what later became a stronger strand in American thinking; at the time, however, this sort of attitude looked weak to many Americans in high places.

One obvious result of the Korean War, with its revelation of

Chinese power and determination, was the settlement of the problem with which the Australian and New Zealand Governments had increasingly become preoccupied: how to get a guarantee from the United States. The ANZUS Treaty, signed in 1951 between the two Governments and that of the United States, represented in essence the extension of the Monroe Doctrine to these two countries in the South Pacific; even the language of the Monroe Doctrine was called in to define the position.* ANZUS did not create a special command or exact forces from each member country, as NATO had done, but it gave Australia and New Zealand what was perhaps more important in the circumstances, access to the highest American policy-making levels and to effective military planning. The meetings of the ANZUS Council take place each year at Foreign Minister level; for Australia and New Zealand this is one occasion when they have the ear of the Secretary of State with full authority to lay their strategic problems before him. There are, of course, many other occasions in the course of diplomacy on which these matters can be raised. But the ANZUS Council is a full-dress affair, properly prepared for, and meant to be taken seriously. "The NATO Council is the only fully comparable body to which the United States belongs," wrote the Australian Minister for External Affairs in 1954.†

The ANZUS Treaty came to birth because the Peace Treaty with Japan was doing so.‡ The Australian Government, Labour before late 1949 and Liberal–Country Party afterwards, was, like the New Zealand Government, sceptical of the peaceable and democratic character of the new régime which General MacArthur had created in Japan. It wanted heavier reparations, more restrictions on trade, and a clause in the Peace Treaty which would prohibit Japanese rearmament. These conditions could not be obtained. It was not only

* The vital article IV of the ANZUS Treaty says: "Each Party recognizes that an armed attack in the Pacific Area on any of the Parties would be dangerous to its own peace and safety and declares that it would act to meet the common danger in accordance with its constitutional processes." Monroe stated in 1823 that if Spain and Portugal tried to recapture their possessions "we should consider any attempt on their part to extend their system to any portion of this hemisphere as dangerous to our peace and safety".

† R. G. Casey, *Friends and Neighbours* (Melbourne, 1954), p. 82. For a comparison of ANZUS and NATO, see Sir Alan Watt, *Australian Defence Policy 1951–1963* (Canberra, 1964), pp. 10–27.

‡ See R. N. Rosecrance, *Australian Diplomacy and Japan, 1945–1951* (Melbourne, 1962), Chs. 13, 14 and 15.

the Americans who opposed them. By 1951, the British Government, and others in the Commonwealth, were against a hard peace with Japan. While the Australians' and New Zealanders' suspicion of Japan had persisted, their fear and suspicion of China had grown. The ANZUS Treaty, arrived at after lengthy negotiation, was, in effect, the *quid pro quo* which the Americans paid for Australian and New Zealand signature of the Japanese Peace Treaty. But it was also the achievement of a long-felt wish on the part of the two Southern Dominions. At first the United States Government had wanted to include Japan and the Philippines in the arrangement, but Japan was neither acceptable nor willing, and the Philippines then became something of an embarrassment. In the end, the agreement was tripartite and no more; it has been especially valued by Australia and New Zealand since 1951 for this very reason, since it limits the commitment of the United States to them, but gives them a wide opportunity to call for American help.

Neither Canada nor Britain was a party to ANZUS, though the British Ambassador to Japan took part in some of the early discussion. Canada's omission is easily explained. While it is true that Canadian leaders make statements about the Pacific from time to time, perhaps to show British Columbia that they do not think its sea-coast as illusory as Bohemia's, there is little Canadian interest in schemes of Pacific security as such. Canadian influence on the United States in such matters as the off-shore islands of China, or relations with Japan, can readily be exerted through normal channels; Canada has not joined, at any stage, in the search by Australia and New Zealand for a special Pacific pact. ANZUS excited little concern in Canada. "The Prime Minister, in reply to a question in the House on April 23, 1953, stated very baldly that Canada had not been invited to participate in that treaty, nor had she solicited any such invitation."*

It was otherwise with Britain. Mr. Churchill, after becoming Prime Minister, said in retrospect:

"I did not like this ANZUS pact at all. We did not have an entirely clean sheet in the matter when we took over power. I did not like it at all, and I am greatly in hopes that perhaps larger, wider arrangements may be made which will be more satisfactory

* B. S. Keirstead, *Canada in World Affairs, 1951–1953* (Toronto, 1956), p. 106.

than those which are at present in force. But, as I say, it is not a matter where one can give directions."*

An Australian finds it all too easy to discern an echo here of the wartime determination that Australia and New Zealand should be kept away from the centre of power in Washington, in order that any British Commonwealth allocations might be strained through the mesh of London priorities. The main point of Mr. Churchill's concern, however (and of his predecessors'), seems to have been that, if Australia and New Zealand were to come entirely within the American sphere of influence, the practical arrangements which these countries had with Britain in military planning, supplies, research and the like might lose their force, while Australian and New Zealand forces might concentrate upon operations which ignored British interests. In the event, neither of these results followed. While much standardization of weapons took place with the United States, practical co-operation with Britain, especially in Malaya, continued and was intensified.

Nevertheless, British pride was hurt in some quarters. This was the first time Australia and New Zealand had actually made a defence pact with anyone else; there was something climactic about the occasion, accentuated by the fact that the Governments which negotiated the pact for both Dominions were anti-Labour and traditionally associated with the British connection in its more emotional aspects. It is likely that these two Governments pressed initially for British inclusion in the arrangement, but not very strongly.† They wanted the United States in; Britain's inclusion was much less important. They did not intend to give up their other ties with Britain. There were American objections on such grounds as the difficulty of including British colonial possessions in the Pacific if Britain were in the pact, also of the inclusion of other colonial powers; in the event, the omission of Britain provided a neat and tidy arrangement, in confining the agreement to the three countries most concerned, and its operations to their possessions.

---

* U. K. Hansard, Vol. 516, House of Commons, June 17, 1953, col. 973. There were official British efforts to get observer status at the Honolulu meeting of the ANZUS Council in 1952, but these were a failure. See *Round Table*, Vol. 43, pp. 86–7, and *The Times*, October 13, 15 and 16, 1952.

† There is a useful discussion of Britain's "exclusion" in an article by Dean E. McHenry and Richard N. Rosecrance, in *International Organization*, Vol. XII, No. 3, 1958.

Britain was brought directly into the American system of Pacific alliances in 1954, when SEATO was created. This body need not concern us especially, since it is connected only peripherally with relations between Britain and the Old Dominions.* For some years SEATO seemed to overshadow ANZUS in the estimation of the Australian and New Zealand Governments. They were greatly concerned about the situation in South-East Asia, and welcomed SEATO as a means of associating at least some Asian states in the common resistance to Communism. They contributed enthusiastically to the slender resources assembled in Bangkok at SEATO headquarters, and orientated much of their military planning to take account of possible SEATO requirements. But several factors contributed to SEATO's decline in the latter part of its first decade. One was the lack of substantial Asian representation: only Thailand, Pakistan and the Philippines were members, and Pakistani support eventually became equivocal. Another was the embarrassment of France as a member, when so little help had been given to the French cause in Indo-China; later this changed to worry about France's independence of its allies' professed interests under President de Gaulle. A third was the fragmented character of SEATO obligations: the U.S.A. would fight only against "Communist" aggression, while others did not make this qualification; Australia would not side with Pakistan against India; there were "associated" states, neither in nor out of SEATO, to which the members were in a sense committed; later, Thailand and the United States organized what was, in effect, another alliance inside SEATO. Furthermore, as Australian and New Zealand interest shifted to the help of Malaya against its own Communists, and then Malaysia against Indonesia, the focus of interest shifted further from SEATO, which Malaya had decided not to join.

Britain had never shown much enthusiasm for SEATO, and might have been excluded if a New Zealand Minister had not stated publicly that his Government would not enter unless Britain was a member. The British role remained slight. The Australian and New Zealand interest was two-fold: these countries wanted Asian states to be convinced that they would be protected against aggression, and they wanted the United States involved in South-East Asia. Later events provided opportunities for securing these two

* There is a good account of the negotiations leading to SEATO, and of the Australian approach to these, in Leicester Webb's section in George Modelski (ed.). *SEATO: Six Studies* (Melbourne, 1962).

aims in other ways. The Canadian newspaper which said in 1954 that the SEATO treaty was "a rush job, a makeshift of the kind that history contemptuously sweeps aside" was hardly right, since SEATO is still with us; but it was not entirely wrong. Canada remained studiously aloof from SEATO.*

Thus by 1956, the Suez year which we can treat as something of a hinge in post-war events, Canada, Australia and New Zealand had all provided themselves with the kind of American protection which seemed to suit them best. Their problems were by no means solved, since the United States is no more manœuvrable from outside than any other great power, and since the dangers which these countries felt themselves to face were changing continually with the changes in World Communism, the refinement of methods of warfare, and a number of other variables. Nevertheless, a certain stability had been attained. If it seemed to some people to have been attained at the expense of Britain, this was a mistaken view. Britain could not defend any of the three under any circumstances which could be seriously imagined. They had to re-insure with the United States. This was a big change from pre-war conceptions. But with it went another and perhaps bigger change: they decided on re-insurance in distant lands (in Europe on Canada's part and in Asia on the part of the other two) because danger seemed likely to come from there, and it could be met there with least damage to their own soil. Such major changes in Dominion conceptions called for changes also in the British point of view. In due course it was accepted in Britain that it was better for Canada, Australia and New Zealand to be in good heart because of assurances they had gained from the United States, than to be nagging Britain for military help which it could not supply. Once their safety was assured, the prospect of co-operation with Britain in other military spheres was, if anything, increased.

South Africa was quiescent in this period, except for schemes of technical co-operation with other European régimes south of the Sahara. As we shall see, there was some military co-operation with Britain. But the tides which swept Canada, Australia and New Zealand did not reach South Africa. A different tide was making, but had still to reach its full.

---

* This paragraph owes much to D. C. Masters, *Canada in World Affairs 1953-5* (Toronto, 1959), pp. 96–99.

RELATIONS WITH THE UNITED STATES

In order to see how the Old Dominions' association with the United States has affected their ties with Britain, it is advisable to start with Britain itself. The main hopes and fears which have been engendered in Britain by connection with the United States have been similar to those aroused in the Dominions, allowing for obvious differences in geography and society. For Britain, as for the others, the main aim has been security; necessarily, this has carried with it the wish to avoid "the taint of satellitism, the tinge of puppetry".*

The fundamental fact of Britain's post-war relations with the United States is that of dependence. Britain is no longer a great power, in the sense of being a super-power; it is a major power, with room for influence and manœuvre at levels of international action below the highest, but without the strength to challenge the super-powers. If the United States acts contrary to Britain's interests in major matters, there is little that Britain can do about it. The fact of Britain's possessing nuclear weapons has confirmed its position as a major power but done nothing to ensure its acceptance amongst great powers: British nuclear weapons would not be used as a threat against the United States, because no issue of sufficient seriousness is likely to arise between them; they could not be used against the Soviet Union, because of the certainty of massive retaliation which Britain could neither evade nor parry. Nuclear strength has perhaps increased the area of American uncertainty about potential British divergence, and to this extent increased the influence which Britain might exert; but not even the most unrealistic American policy-maker can believe that Britain would defy the United States in a matter vitally affecting American interests. The only effective form of defiance would be the threat of alliance with the Soviet Union, which, while not entirely unthinkable, is so remote as to be useless as a bargaining counter. So long as there is held to be danger to vital British interests from the Soviet Union and China, Britain is bound to the United States for ultimate protection.

Dependence is tempered, however, by agreement. Britain and the

---

* James M. Minifie, *Peacemaker or Powder-Monkey* (Toronto, 1960), p. 4. This astringent book deserves more attention outside Canada. Even if one disagrees with it, it is a disturbing book to argue with.

United States have fundamentally similar approaches to world problems. Both are, in their own view, freedom-loving democracies; in the Communist view, capitalist states which cannot be trusted to act generously and justly. In spite of manifold differences of view on this or that matter, the two countries have basically similar interests, cemented by their common fund of language. These interests are not simply notional. They have been discussed over long periods by common action and argument. The governmental systems of the two countries have been interlocked for a considerable time. There is, as Mr. Nicholas says in his fine study in this series, "a kind of Anglo-American Gulf Stream whose flow is little affected by the tempests which may disturb the Atlantic surface":* it flows through the myriad conversations of military, diplomatic and civil service people who constantly cross the Atlantic to discuss policy with one another. This process, rather than the fading memories and failing influence of personal wartime contacts, is what constitutes the "special relationship" between the two countries, although it owes much of its inception to wartime events. It has often proved sufficient to deal with what might otherwise become open divergence. One must be cautious about attributing too much agreement to the partnership between Britain and the United States, since this would be to neglect the obvious differences and to adopt the misleading line which President de Gaulle takes when he talks about "the Anglo-Saxons". Nevertheless, there is plenty of agreement; and it seems likely to grow as the cultures of the two countries adapt themselves more to one another.

In the meantime, it is important to recognize that the relationship between Britain and the United States is characterized on the British side, not only by dependence and agreement, but also by resentment. In spite of the fact that the agreement is, to a great extent, natural and unforced, and does not proceed from pressure by the United States but from recognition by the British Government of common interests, there still remains a good deal of feeling against American ways, standards, attitudes and responsibilities. It was typical of a certain kind of opinion in Britain that, having accepted NATO with gratitude, it was incensed by the proposal that, in applying the logic of the NATO agreement, portions of the Royal Navy should be placed under the command of an American admiral. Anti-American feeling in Britain comes from two sides. From the Left, it is obvious and easily discounted, since the

* H. G. Nicholas, *Britain and the United States* (London, 1963), p. 173.

influence of the extreme Left in Britain is fitful and never decisive. From the Right, however, it is more important, since the business of government in Britain is normally carried on by people of the Centre who need sometimes to overcome the prejudices of the Conservative Party, the armed forces, the clubs, the City and kindred bodies; this they do with the aid of the Civil Service and portions of the intelligentsia and the Press. The conquest of anti-American-ism has been one of the great feats of the post-war period, although the enemy is still likely to make an appearance when the United States seems to be operating against British interests, as at Suez in 1956.

One of the most obviously British symbols is the Commonwealth, a term which many older people have found difficult to substitute since 1945 for the Empire. Inevitably, the Commonwealth, especi-ally the Old Dominions, has had pinned to it the hopes which people on the Right traditionally attached to the Empire—the dream of a self-sufficient British group of nations, able to enrich one another and to tell the world what it ought to know. This dream, to which there was never much substance, has had no chance of achievement since 1945. It is natural for some British people to blame the United States, which has taken an unprecedentedly prominent role in British affairs, and which, to some extreme Rightists (and sometimes to irritable middle-of-the-road men) seems to have suborned the Dominions from their rightful allegiance. How much truth is there in this view? Have Britain and the United States been in competition for the attention of the Four?

The answer is that they have been from time to time, but that the competition has not been deliberate. It has arisen in the pursuit of policies sought for other reasons. It is unlikely, for example, that Mr. John Foster Dulles wanted to compete with Britain for the loyalty of Australia and New Zealand when he started to build the ANZUS Pact; his aim was much more immediate, to persuade them to agree to a Japanese peace treaty which they did not want. When it came to detail, he evidently thought it simpler, in military and congressional terms, to leave Britain out. But Britain had never really been in, in spite of Sir Esler Denning's presence at early dis-cussions; ANZUS was an answer to a problem directly affecting Australia and New Zealand and only indirectly affecting Britain. The fact that some people in Britain found the pact an affront was the outcome of sensitivity, and of a wrong assessment of the extent to which the pact would absorb the military resources of Australia and New Zealand.

I am suggesting, then, that competition between Britain and the United States for the attention of the Dominions has been largely incidental to the pursuit of other objectives. The point may be tested by brief reference to two issues in which Britain and the United States have been on opposite sides, the recognition of China and the Suez affair.

In the early 1950's it certainly seemed to many people that the Dominions would recognize Communist China if they were not under pressure from the United States, and that, in submitting to American pressure, they were failing to support a British policy towards China which was markedly different from the American. But, as we have seen, the Dominions had reasons of their own for hesitating about recognition. These increased in weight as the Korean War went on. The forcible Chinese incorporation of Tibet, and the Chinese invasion of northern India, confirmed Canada, Australia and New Zealand in their doubts. From their point of view, the time for recognition has, in one sense, passed (since the international character of the Chinese régime had not been demonstrated when Britain took its early step of recognition), and, in another, has not yet come (since recognition of Communist China now involves abandonment of Taiwan, which the Communists insist must be treated as a rebel province). While it is true that much of the attitude of these three Dominions is coloured by their wish to keep in step with the United States on Asian issues, their reasons arise from their own independent assessments too. As time passes, competition between Britain and the United States becomes more illusory (since it is a long time since Britain pressed hard for recognition), and the independent judgement of the three countries assumes more importance.

In the Suez case there was no intention on either side to ply for support from the Dominions. To the American Government, it was unimportant whether the Dominions supported Britain or not; it was clear that a great many other countries would not. The Eden cabinet seems to have thought it would get automatic support from the Old Dominions, and was grieved when Canada spoke out against it. This was a measure of the lack of realism in the official British approach to the whole adventure. The Canadian Government had deplored the business before it started because it knew that the issue was bound to divide, not only the Commonwealth, but Britain from the United States: the Canadian position, and that of opponents of the Suez action in Australia and New Zealand, was very similar to Mr. Gaitskell's in Britain. It was not a matter of crawling to the United States, but of awareness that divergence between Britain and the United States on such a matter was suicidal. Once again, "competition" between Britain and the United States was incidental to their main aims: Britain's to extinguish President Nasser; America's to prevent the Western world being tarred with the imperialist brush.

The fact of the matter is that Suez was the one glaring exception to the British rule that the Anglo-American alliance must be preserved. Britain must avoid the taint of satellitism as best it can, by the quality of the co-operation and criticism which it brings to bear on its association with the United States.

The Canadian association with the United States is the closest of those considered here. It is, of necessity, a family relationship, and carries with it family quarrels. Mr. Pearson told the Russians at Geneva in 1954:

> "If, indeed, the United States did not respect the rights and interests of others, Canada would not today be an independent power, but merely a satellite of her great neighbour. Her representatives would not be able, as they certainly *are* able, to speak their own minds and stand up for their own views in conferences of the nations, even if this means, as it has more than once meant, disagreeing with some aspect of the policy of the United States."*

This is a truthful statement. But the very closeness of the relationship causes frictions. Some have been directly institutional, arising from the different conceptions of government and different political styles of the two countries. The frigid reception which Senator Joseph McCarthy got from organs of Canadian opinion and from the Canadian parliament was a notable example; so was the Canadian Government's threat to cancel its exchange of security information with the United States over the Norman case in 1957.† Some arise from the problems of sharing the same natural

---

* Quoted in D. C. Masters, *Canada in World Affairs, 1953–5* (Toronto, 1959), p. 13.

† See James Eayrs, *Canada in World Affairs, 1955–7* pp. 153–60 for a lucid account and the text of the Canadian communication to the U.S. Government.

resources, such as the St. Lawrence and Columbia rivers. Some come from a direct clash of economic interests and from the superior strength, politically and economically, of organized interests on the American side: there have been numerous examples in U.S. tariff policy, and also in the difficulties created for Canada by the U.S. disposal of farm surpluses. Some are the product of the substantial investment of American money in Canadian resource and manufacturing industries: there is said to be a traditional Canadian disinclination to invest in equities, and the space has been filled by American investors. Apart from easing the Canadian balance of payments, this process has induced a sense of mingled pleasure, embarrassment and resentment amongst Canadians. When this sense becomes outraged on the side of resentment, Canada recurs to the kind of attitude which has historically been so helpful to the Conservatives, notably to Mr. Diefenbaker in the national elections of 1957. Some come from the tensions of sharing a common culture while being, as many influential Canadians are, anxious to retain a distinctive national identity. Such feelings lead to the attempt to keep certain organs of opinion and culture, such as the CBC and the Canadian magazines, alive as genuine expressions of Canadianism. They have also led to the creation of the Canada Council, with its assistance to various activities which might not otherwise be able to stand against the pressure from the south.*

These irritations find a sort of epitome in the problem of how to organize North American defence. Canada is assured of defence by the United States, but the changes in weapon systems, and the concentration upon the Soviet Union as the enemy capable of striking a nuclear blow at the heartland of the United States, have put Canada in the unpleasant position of being the range across which nuclear weapons might be fired. In the early post-war years, as awareness of the Russian threat grew, Canada and the United States extended their common defence arrangements to the establishment of arctic weather stations; next they were co-operating in three successive chains of radar stations designed to provide warning of the coming of Russian bombers. These culminated in the DEW line (Distant Early Warning), cutting across the far Canadian North and entirely paid for and manned by the United States. Not

---

* On these and other Canadian–American problems, see the two perceptive essays by James Eayrs and John W. Holmes in John Slean Dickey (ed.) *The United States and Canada* (Englewood Cliffs, 1964).

long after DEW was established, the two countries set up in 1958 NORAD, a joint North American Air Defence Command under an American commander with a Canadian deputy. The inexorable march of weapons science soon demanded that guided missiles be introduced into the system, and then that Canada agree to equip certain systems with nuclear arms. It was over this final issue that the Diefenbaker Government fell in 1963, to be replaced by one under Mr. Pearson that recognized a Canadian obligation in the matter. A notable feature of the upheaval was that the U.S. State Department issued a press release at a crucial moment, denying the inferences in a speech by Mr. Diefenbaker, and, in effect, calling on Canada to keep its promises.

In the circumstances, Canada has exercised as much autonomy as any state living next to a great power can, and more than some do. It has not been of the intermittently defiant sort characteristic of the United States's other neighbour, Mexico, because Canada is far closer to the United States in experience, culture, language, living standards and social aims than is Mexico. Canada has absorbed people and ideas from the United States, and has benefited from American technology and productivity in many ways. In spite of occasional demands to the contrary, it is impossible to unscramble the North American omelet. Moreover, it is impossible now, whatever it may have been in former times, to put forward Britain as a substitute for the United States in influence upon Canadian life. British influence upon Canada can be, at the best, peripheral; but it touches Canadian life at points of sufficient importance—diplomacy, monarchy, military affairs, scholarship, education, literature—to enable influence to be marked and memorable. To some extent it can still offset the occasional touch of Americanism that grates on Canadian susceptibilities. In the Norman case, for example, the British heritage of parliamentary government showed itself to be significantly different from congressional government, with a difference in which Canadians could take pride; demonstrations of the relevance of distinctly British contributions to Canadian life, such as this one, reinforce the respect for British ways which is still of great importance in Canada. But the business of living with the United States, day in and day out, is something which Canadians have to manage for themselves.

At the political level, Britain can do something, but not a great deal, to help Canada with its burdens. If a question arises within the NATO context, Britain can help as an ally; similarly at the

U.N. But there is little or nothing Britain can do about major matters. It cannot replace American investment in Canadian industry, for example. In the 1963 controversy over the provision of nuclear arms to Canadian forces, Britain had, if anything, muddied the waters for the Canadians: one of Mr. Diefenbaker's reasons for delaying the fulfilment of promises made by his Government in 1959 was that the NATO position on nuclear weapons had been altered by the Nassau agreement of December 1962 between President Kennedy and Mr. Macmillan. The United States did not think it had, and, so far as one can tell, the British Government did not think so either; but the obscure language of the communiqué, together with the airs of importance with which Britain greeted the agreement, enabled Mr. Diefenbaker to plead that the situation of Canada had changed. The issue was, in fact, a North American one which only Canada and the United States could deal with. The same is true of other major issues between the two countries.

The Australian position is more easily dealt with. While Australian policy is directed towards agreement with Britain, it must ultimately obtain agreement with the United States. The range of manœuvrability open for Australia is smaller than for Canada. Canada is indispensable to the United States; Australia is not. Since 1949 (and at sporadic intervals before then) Australian policy has aimed at getting the United States involved in Asia and keeping it there. The ultimate horror, from an Australian official standpoint, would be for the Americans to return to North America; by definition, this would be a recognition of geography to the Canadians. The Australian Government has been outspoken since 1949 about the need for close relations with both Britain and the United States. "The only hope of salvation for the world," wrote an Australian Minister for External Affairs, "is that we, the British, and they, the Americans, should work together as closely as one blade of a pair of scissors with the other."* His Prime Minister, Mr. Menzies, said sharply in 1955 :

"I have myself met men, some of them occupying responsible positions, who have come to regard any praise for the United States as being anti-British and any work for closer British–American co-operation as being subversive of the British

* R. G. Casey, *Friends and Neighbours* (Melbourne, 1954), p. 41.

Commonwealth relationship. It would be a tragedy if such sorry nonsense became at all widespread."*

In the same speech he said of his government:

"We work incessantly for the closest collaboration between the British Commonwealth and the United States of America who, between them, are the exemplars of peaceful pursuits and of high international ideals, contain the bulk of the military and productive power of the free world, and offer no aggressive threat to others."

It is easy to see why the Australian cabinet was thrown into such confusion when Britain and the United States took issue over Suez.

The basis of the Australian position is clear. The United States is essential to Australia because it is the only major Western power that can give Australia protection against a thrust from Asia, comparable with Japan's in 1941–2. Such a thrust could come from either China or Indonesia. China is already Communist; Indonesia could become so. In 1965 it was on terms with China which were too good for Australian comfort. If the Americans should retire to their own continent and take refuge behind their own I.C.B.M.s, Australia would have little means of defence. Even if the Chinese or Indonesians did not attempt an invasion of Australia itself, they could conceivably threaten it with damage to trade routes, harry it by interference in Australian New Guinea, trump up charges of racialism against it in the eyes of some "uncommitted" countries, and stimulate the growth within Australia of sections with an interest in capitulation to Communist demands. Just how likely this sort of result is, one cannot say; but it is the sort of result which, to the Australian Government and many Australian citizens, might lie at the end of a road which began with the Yanks going home.

An important aspect of the need which the Australian Government feels for American help is its constant insistence that any differences between itself and the U.S. Government should be argued out in private, not in public. Sir Robert Menzies has voiced many times the view that one does not argue with one's "great and powerful friends" in the hearing of one's enemies and those who might become so. He has put it bluntly:

* *Current Notes*, vol. 26 (1955), no. 4.

"True, Australia is an independent nation and has a perfect right to express its views, whatever the result. This is a grand conception, and would be even more admirable if we possessed such population and strength as made us a truly great power, able to defend ourselves in our own right. But the fact is that we are not truly independent, except in legal terms."*

Such statements are maddening to strong-minded Australian nationalists, and to those to whom American policy is a source of anxiety, but the attitude seems to be widely accepted in Australia: it accords too well with experience and national anxieties to be shrugged aside, although its implication of Australian inability to take a separate line on major issues is troublesome.

The Menzies line in regard to communications with the United States is, in practice, confined to questions of foreign and military policy; it does not extend to arguments about trade policy, on which the Australian Government is, if anything, more vociferous than the Canadian when its interests seem threatened—often by the same American policies. In general, however, the Australian Government is less likely than the Canadian to complain in public about American policy in Asia, which is the crucial area for Australia. Much the same is true of New Zealand. Mr. K. J. Holyoake, the New Zealand Prime Minister, put his position in general terms in 1963:

One thing must never be forgotten. New Zealand is a small country. This fact sets very real limits to what New Zealand can do in the international field. It also gives a special emphasis to the manner in which we conduct our international relationships. Any State in determining its actions or attitudes—whether they be reflected in a statement, a vote, or even armed support— must be governed by the national interest. The supreme national interest is security—and the defence of its people. Where a small State is largely dependent for its security on the assistance of powerful allies, it is under a special obligation to weigh with the utmost care the effect which its actions or statements might have.

Traditionally, one of the greatest dangers to international peace has been the tendency of great powers to infringe the rights of smaller powers. This still remains a pressing danger. New

* Melbourne *Age*, July 31, 1958; quoted in G. Greenwood and N. Harper, *Australia in World Affairs 1956–1960*, (Melbourne, 1963), p. 234.

Zealand, as a small power, has always been vigilant concerning the treatment of small States, has resisted aggression against them, and has been particularly insistent on the rights of small States to have access to the processes of settlement of the United Nations.

At the same time, New Zealand has recognized that, in the modern world, a special responsibility lies on small States not to submit the interests of great powers to arbitrary or irresponsible challenge. Wherever there is interdependence, even a small State can hurt another: the greater the interdependence, the greater the power to hurt. Our own modern world is highly interdependent; in it, small States as well as great must accept the responsibility not, wilfully, to shake the international system.*

This is a more sophisticated utterance than that of Mr. Holyoake's predecessor, Mr. Sidney Holland, who at the 1952 meeting of Commonwealth Prime Ministers "spoke without subtlety or finesse, anxious only to express the two uppermost feelings in his head—loyalty to the U.K. and friendship to the United States. He pursued one object and one only throughout his first Conference. He wanted the Prime Ministers assembled to send a joint message of cordial friendship and co-operation to the United States—a suggestion which did not commend itself to Mr. Nehru and had to be tacitly dropped."†

Yet we must not assume too wholeheartedly a devotion to the United States on the part of the New Zealand Government. There is generally a perceptible difference in tone between the statements made by New Zealand ministers and those from Australia. The New Zealand ones are more reserved. Australia is closer to Asia and more directly involved in that continent; Australia's vast size and comparative emptiness make its public men more apprehensive about Asian opinion than those in New Zealand. Perhaps, too, the contrast between Australia's treatment of its aborigines and New Zealand's treatment of the Maoris makes Australians more sensitive

* From an address at the New Zealand Administrative Staff College, August 12, 1963, reprinted in *External Affairs Review* (Wellington), Vol. XIII, No. 8.

† George Mallaby, *From my Level* (London, 1965), p. 146. This book also contains engaging accounts of Holland, Holyoake and Walter Nash, pp. 72–84.

towards Asia; perhaps its immigration policy increases this feeling. At all events, Australian policy, as expressed, is more clearcut in its anti-Communism, more fervent in its devotion to the United States, and more extreme in its denunciation of Chinese intentions. It was a New Zealand Minister for External Affairs who said in 1954 that he was convinced that the absence of China from the U.N. was preventing a lessening of international tension, and an Australian Government that was taken by surprise.* But this should not be regarded as expressing more than a shade of difference; New Zealand did not in fact pursue the matter further. Again, it was a New Zealand Prime Minister who offered to delay the dispatch of his troops to Vietnam in 1965, and an Australian Prime Minister who refused to take his out, when there were suggestions that the Commonwealth Prime Ministers' mission to the capitals of the countries concerned with the Vietnamese war might be prejudiced by the presence of these troops. But here again the New Zealand action represented simply a delay, not a cancellation, and the troops were soon on their way. It may be that the difference in emphasis lies mainly in the fact that Australian diplomacy takes in a wider sweep than New Zealand's, and in the more emphatic nature of Australian politicians. So far as major questions of policy are concerned, New Zealand will be found to agree with the United States in the same way as Australia.

The South African position as regards the United States is different from that of the other three Old Dominions. South Africa is not allied with the United States, and there seems to be no prospect of an alliance. Contacts between the two countries are slight compared with those between the United States and the other three. Yet the United States, as the greatest anti-Communist power on earth, is important to South Africa, the Government of which is more directly anti-Communist than that of any Commonwealth state. The reason for the estrangement between the two is South African racial policy.

American actions towards South Africa have followed a path of gradual hostility. Up to about 1958, the United States had little to say about South Africa; when it had to deal with anti-South African resolutions at the U.N., it usually took the same line as Britain and the three Old Dominions, maintaining that the matters complained of were subject to domestic jurisdiction, and so not liable to intervention by the U.N. But the growth of African

* *The Times*, July 7 and 8, 1954.

nationalism, and the appearance of new states in Africa, changed American policy to a notable degree; further contributory factors, as in Britain, were the greater attention paid to South African racial policies in the world's press, and the shock of the Sharpeville affair in 1960. After Sharpeville, the U.S. State department took the unusual step of issuing a press statement deploring what had happened:

> "The United States deplores violence in all its forms and hopes that the African people of South Africa will be able to obtain redress for legitimate grievances by peaceful means. While the United States, as a matter of practice, does not ordinarily comment on the internal affairs of governments with which it enjoys normal relations, it cannot help but regret the tragic loss of life resulting from the measures taken against the demonstrators in South Africa.*

The statement was made with such speed that the American ambassador in Pretoria was not consulted about it; this did not prevent his being hauled over the coals by Mr. Louw, the South African Minister for External Affairs, next day. From the South African point of view, worse was to come. In the following month the United States joined the majority in a Security Council resolution deploring apartheid and commending some sort of U.N. action through the Secretary-General. Following the change from Eisenhower to Kennedy, there was a quickening of American condemnation of South African policy; and in October 1961 an American representative told the General Assembly:

> "The United States abhors . . . *apartheid* . . . We rejoice in the bravery of the man and women of South Africa who . . . fight on day by day for racial justice. My delegation is happy that one of the most distinguished sons of South Africa, Chief Albert John Luthuli, has just been awarded the Nobel Prize for his fight against *apartheid* . . . We must persevere, remembering that no man, no groups of men, no government is strong enough to resist indefinitely the conscience of mankind. How and when

---

* Statement in Washington, March 22, 1960; quoted in Vernon McKay, *Africa in World Politics* (New York, 1963), p. 299, where the circumstances of issuing this statement from the State department are described.

the South African Government will abandon its hateful racial policies we cannot know, but abandon them it will."*

The United States went on to cancel sales of arms to South Africa, though it stopped short at supporting economic sanctions. There was, however, some ambivalence in the American position, sufficient to enable some South Africans to say that American statements were meant to placate the Negro vote in the United States, and would not be followed up if it meant that South Africa's value as a potential ally was lost to the West. Mr. Louw claimed that just before the statement just quoted, Mr. Dean Rusk had talked to him at length in "a friendly and cordial spirit", and that the statement could not have been cleared with him.† Some comfort could be derived in this way. It is doubtful, however, whether such comfort goes far. South Africa's case for indispensability to the West rests upon its political stability, its high technology, its resolute anti-Communism, its mineral resources, and its strategic position at the southern tip of the continent. The last point would be important in a situation like that of the last war, in which the Mediterranean and Suez Canal were either dangerous or closed to traffic from Britain or Western Europe to India, South-East Asia, Australia and New Zealand, and it was necessary to take the route round the Cape. Under such circumstances, the fact that the Cape was in friendly hands, and the use of Simonstown naval base, would be of major importance. But such a situation could hardly apply to the United States: it is essentially predicated upon the needs of Britain in relation to Asia, Australia and New Zealand. The United States has its own direct supply lines to these places. It does not need South Africa. The point still has importance for some of the United States's allies, especially Britain, Australia and New Zealand: under any conditions of warfare except those of absolute destruction, it would be desirable for these to have a sea route which was not menaced by an enemy. But in their case the point is weaker than in World War II. The Panama route, although longer, would presumably be available, and it would be better defended (by the United States) against Russian and Chinese submarines (the obvious naval enemy) than a route round the Cape. Thus, while they

* Statement by Francis T. P. Plimpton, General Assembly, October 24, 1961; quoted ibid., p. 352.

† Quoted in Thomas Karis, "South Africa", in Gwendolen M. Carter (ed.), *Five African States* (Ithaca, 1963), p. 603.

might be expected to regard the Cape route as worth having if available, they would also probably regard it as expendable; and, in the political circumstances of the 1960's, they would be most unlikely to make alliances with South Africa, especially against the wishes of the United States.

South Africa's minerals, stability and anti-Communism are of diminishing relevance to the United States alongside its bad name amongst Afro-Asian countries. The United States cannot afford to have as allies countries which are hated by a wide variety of other countries with which the United States wishes to be on good terms, unless the advantage to be gained is overwhelming. Moreover, in the South African case there is the possibility that civil war, or armed resistance from the African states near by, might be set off by the continuance of *apartheid*. It is difficult to believe that the United States would knowingly put itself in the position of having to respond to a South African call for help.*

Summing up this section, we can see that post-war developments have introduced a new dimension into the relations of Britain with Canada, Australia and New Zealand, and might have done so in the case of South Africa if it had not been for the intensification of racial policy there. The new dimension is provided by the United States, now an indispensable ally to Britain and the other three. There had been foretastes of this development, clear in the case of Canada, fainter for Australia and New Zealand—although the recognition by their leaders in the 1930's that nothing could be done about Japan's activities in China unless the United States was prepared to step in, was an indication of how matters might develop. What was new in the post-war period was twofold: the fact that Britain itself became dependent on the United States for ultimate defence, and the fact that each country's associations with it were codified in a military alliance. The first of these changes meant that Britain could not "compete" in any fully meaningful sense with the United States, because it was not of equal stature. The second meant that the three Old Dominions, along with Britain, acquired rights of consultation with the United States, together with responsibilities as allies who were expected to be constructive in their criticisms and not openly defiant of American policies. Within this set of conditions there has proved to be room for disagreement and manœuvre. But it is not a totally free situation for

* Cf. the treatment of South Africa's relations with the west in Peter Calvocoressi, *South Africa and World Opinion* (London, 1961), pp. 35–7.

any of those involved: restraints and obligations are built into it. Being so dependent on the United States in the last resort, the three Old Dominions could not construct their relations with Britain on the pre-war basis, even if they wanted to; nor could Britain fulfil the role to which it then aspired. But the very fact of ultimate dependence on the United States has given Britain a special value to the other three. Although itself finally dependent, it is a major power with a notable voice in the world, and still capable of advancing the interests of the Old Dominions. In consequence, there are certain areas of foreign and defence policy in which Britain has come to matter to them. It is time now to consider these.

Here, as in so many other matters, South Africa is a special case.

BRITAIN AND THE FOUR, c. 1950 ON

In this section I shall be largely concerned with defence questions, partly because something has already been said about connections in foreign policy and there will be more in a later section, partly because defence arrangements offer a valuable index of how relations change generally. It will be remembered that this chapter began with an extract from the British White Paper on Defence of 1946, which expressing glowing confidence about the continuation of wartime arrangements with the Commonwealth. By contrast, the 1963 White Paper did not mention the Commonwealth as a factor in British defence. Does this mean that all Commonwealth countries have fallen out of British consideration? The answer, of course, is no. Rather, there has been a movement away from automatic co-operation (or the assumption of it) to voluntary and selective co-operation: this movement has kept pace with changes in constitutional relations and in foreign relations at large.

Since about 1950, British preoccupations in defences have been with the three geographical areas of Europe, the Middle East, and South-East Asia. In Europe Britain has settled down to co-operation with other European countries in the NATO alliance with the United States; despite numerous stresses, especially over the entry of West Germany and the line taken by France under President de Gaulle, the situation has acquired stability. There are arguments in Britain about the quantity of British resources to be devoted to Europe, and about the control of nuclear arms, but Europe is, as it were, fixed. The Soviet Union is not inclined to attack; NATO, in spite of its depletion of forces and complexities over arms, remains in being. In the Middle East, the United States did not become a party to British schemes to the same extent. British efforts to retain a military stake in the Middle East, through negotiations with Egypt over the Canal Zone, and through the Baghdad Pact, reached a disastrous climax at Suez in 1956, and have now faded away to obscure operations in South Arabia and uneasy treaty relations with small rulers in the oil areas. In South-East Asia the United States has taken a much bigger part than in the Middle East, operating something of a division of labour with Britain: while Britain has retained much of the responsibility for the defence of Malaysia against internal terrorism and external threat, the United States has busied itself with Thailand, Laos and Vietnam. Both have taken a keen interest in the defence of India following Chinese attacks upon that country, but this has been in the nature of a watching brief, since formal alliances with India have not been possible.

The parts taken by the Old Dominions in these operations have been various. Canada has been involved only in Europe, as a full founder member of NATO. In any case, Britain's role in NATO is not a leading one in the sense in which its role in the Middle East was meant to be. There, Canada has had no special role since Mackenzie King turned down the proposition that Canadian troops should go to Chanak in 1922;* Canada is not dependent on Middle East oil or the Suez canal, and has not been inclined to shore up British power in the area when long-term trends seemed to be against it. The other three have at times thought otherwise. The 1952 British White Paper on Defence stated:

"A conference of Ministers from Australia, New Zealand, South Africa and Southern Rhodesia was held in London in June [1951] to consider defence problems in regions of common concern, including the Middle East. The defence problems of this area and the related problems of South-East Asia defence were examined in the light of the defence contributions which each of the Governments participating in the conference can make. A continuous exchange of views and information has since been maintained at all levels between the various Governments.

The Governments of Australia, New Zealand and South

* That is, has not played a role in any scenario written by the British; Canada has, of course, been most prominent in U.N. tasks in the Middle East.

Africa have accepted the invitation of the U.K., the U.S. and French Governments to join with them and other interested Governments in setting up an Allied Command Organization in the Middle East."*

The organization projected in the second paragraph was the ill-fated MEDO (Middle East Defence Organization), never brought to fruition. Trouble in Persia and the unyielding position of the Egyptians gave it no hope of success. However, the fact that the Australian and New Zealand Governments agreed to take part in it showed two things : that they still had a keen interest in the Middle East as a highway, and were prepared to back British efforts there; and that they had not yet concentrated their efforts on South-East Asia.† The support which these two Governments gave to Britain at Suez in 1956 was moral, not physical, but it showed the survival of the earlier sentiment. Thereafter, the Middle East largely disappeared from their concerns, except in retrospect.

The failure of MEDO to come to birth prevented South Africa from being directly concerned with British efforts in the Middle East. By the time of Suez, the South African Government had become so cautious as to declare its complete non-involvement and to abstain from discussion and voting at the U.N. However, it is worth interpolating mention of the efforts made by South Africa to associate itself with Britain and other European countries in African defence, during the early 1950's when independent black states were still scarce in Africa. At Nairobi in August 1951, for example, the British and South African Governments convened a conference attended also by representatives from France, Portugal, Italy, Belgium, Ethiopia, Egypt and Southern Rhodesia, the aim of which was to ensure the rapid movement of troops and military supplies to East and Central Africa in the event of war. Again, at Dakar in March 1954, South Africa attended a meeting convened by Britain and France, with much the same representation as at Nairobi, except for the presence of Liberia and of a representative of the United States. Neither conference produced firm public commitments, but defence talks continued between South Africa and Britain for a number of years, culminating in the transfer in 1957 of the Simonstown naval base to South Africa on a promise that it

* *Statement on Defence*, February 1952, Cmd. 8475, p. 13.

† It was not until 1955 that Mr. Holland, the New Zealand Prime Minister, announced (March 24) that New Zealand had been asked to switch her Commonwealth commitments from the Middle East, and would be glad to do so.

would continue to be available to the R.N., and an agreement in 1958 to give South Africa certain overflying and other aircraft rights in the three British protectorates of Basutoland, Swaziland and Bechuanaland. Thus it is apparent that Britain remained South Africa's only dependable military associate up to the time when African pressure against South Africa began to gather; it was afterwards that Britain relaxed these links, under pressure from domestic and foreign opinion.

In the third major area of British military concern, South-East Asia, there has again been no Canadian participation, but Australia and New Zealand have given strong support to British interests, believing that these are the same as their own. Their military arrangements with Britain have not always been fully documented, but, in essence, these date from 1948, when it was agreed to have close and permanent discussions on defence between the three countries. Out of these understandings came ANZAM, a consultative arrangement for extending Australian and New Zealand air and sea power to the defence of Malaya, still a British dependency.* In 1955 Australia and New Zealand agreed to station troops in Malaya. In 1957, when the newly independent Federation of Malaya appeared, the troops were retained as part of a Commonwealth Strategic Reserve, not by distinct treaties between Malaya on the one hand and Australia and New Zealand on the other, but by associating these two countries by letter with the Defence Agreement signed by Malaya and Britain. The same procedure was adopted when Malaysia was created in 1963. The upshot is that Australia and New Zealand have been fully associated with the British position, first in opposition to Malayan terrorists, and then against Indonesian confrontation in Borneo and Malaya. There has been, in fact, close military connection for nearly twenty years between the three countries. Planning is continuous, troops have been committed, command structures are clear, understanding is close, no public differences are aired. In a sense, ANZAM (used as a word to describe the whole complex of British, Australian and New Zealand effort in the Malaysian area) has shown more of the characteristics of a working alliance than either ANZUS or SEATO.

If one looks at the general picture of military co-operation which

---

* There is a lucid account of Australian involvement with Britain and New Zealand in South-east Asia in Alan Watt, *Australian Defence Policy 1951–1963* (Canberra, 1964), especially Part III. See also T. B. Millar, *Australia's Defence* (Melbourne, 1965), Ch. 4.

is so much more important a matter to states than vague sentiments of mutual good will, it is clear that Canada, Australia and New Zealand are still important to Britain—more so, in fact, than before the war, when their active military co-operation was no doubt gratifying in prospect, but had not been actually experienced since 1918. The main point is, however, that this co-operation is not automatic. Canada takes part in NATO discussions because there are Canadian views to be expressed, not because Britain needs an extra hand. Canadian–British defence relations are now diffused; the existence of NATO means that Canada must think of Europe rather than simply of Britain.* The chronicler of Canadian foreign policy between 1953 and 1955, a period of intense Canadian activity in NATO, did not devote a section of his book to relations with Britain, since his judgement was that "in this period neither Great Britain nor the Commonwealth, with the exception of the Asian countries, occupied a place of very apparent prominence in Canadian foreign policy".† Yet the British Government clearly finds comfort in having Canada in NATO. As in other contexts, Canada is not "foreign", and so many of the other members are.

The participation of Australia and New Zealand in British military affairs in South-East Asia is not automatic either. When in 1963 Indonesian confrontation against Malaysia in Borneo was becoming serious, there was British pressure upon Australia and New Zealand to provide special troops or to release for service in Borneo the troops which they had stationed on the mainland of Malaya.‡ Both Governments delayed. It is fairly clear that, whereas they had been glad to commit their troops to operations against the terrorists in Malaya, who could be easily identified as Communists and associated with Communist China, they were reluctant to enter into open conflict with Indonesia, a state much closer to their shores than to Britain's, and one with which they still hoped for good relations. In addition, they seemed reluctant to move in the absence of defined support from the United States, which was pursuing an erratic course in its relations with Indonesia, and had avoided any guarantee to Malaysia. The matter was eventually resolved by their decision to commit forces to Borneo, perhaps under assurance from

---

* I am grateful to Professor Alexander Brady for this particular point.

† D. C. Masters, *Canada in World Affairs, 1953–5* (Toronto, 1959), p. 210.

‡ I have dealt with this matter at some length in "Problems of Australian Foreign Policy, July–Dec. 1963" in *Australian Journal of Politics and History*, Vol. X, No. 1.

the United States that ANZUS covered their operations there—provided that American aid was requested under ANZUS only in extreme circumstances, and not the first time one of their soldiers fell.

The fact that Australia and New Zealand now have minds of their own in co-operating with Britain over defence is perhaps illustrated by the fact that they were visited by the British Minister for Defence, Mr. Sandys, in 1957, and by the Prime Minister, Mr. Harold Macmillan, in the following year. This was the first time a British Prime Minister had visited either country while in office.* No startling changes resulted from either visit. But it was clear that more notice was being taken of them than in the past. Subsequent British involvement in Malaysia has given them even more importance. From their point of view, this involvement relieves them of responsibilities which they would not be able to carry out. If Britain were not prepared to commit large military resources to Malaysia, Australia and New Zealand would certainly feel an obligation to help there, but could not provide what was necessary unless they put their economies on a war footing. They would probably spend much effort in trying to get the United States to undertake the burden which Britain has carried in Malaysia. It would be difficult to get the United States to do this, unless Indonesia, the opponent, were clearly under Communist control. Only time can tell what may result from an eventual British withdrawal from South-East Asia; it is hard to believe that Britain will be there for ever.

Circumstances are otherwise with South Africa's association with Britain.† As we have seen, in the early 1950's British policy was, on the whole, favourable to South Africa. It looked towards continued defence co-operation, and refrained from criticism of South Africa at the U.N. The flow of British capital to South Africa continued unabated. But a change took place in Britain at about the same time as in the United States : South Africa became the symbol of racialism to too many people for the Government to treat it as before. The British Government, to which African problems had become

* Mr. Macmillan's visit to New Zealand is memorably described in George Mallaby, *From my Level* (London, 1965), pp. 67–71. No comparable pen has dealt with his appearance in Australia.

† South Africa's departure from the Commonwealth, together with the attitudes taken by Commonwealth members, is discussed below, in Chapter 9.

increasingly those of granting independence to countries like Ghana, Nigeria, Tanganyika and Uganda without bloodshed and with as much good will as possible, could no longer treat the South African problem as a totally separate one. Resistance at the U.N. and elsewhere was growing; independent African states were soon to appear in large numbers; most important of all, opinion in Britain itself had turned decisively against South Africa, if one could judge from parliamentary debates and the quality newspapers. Mr. Macmillan's "Wind of Change" speech to the parliament at Cape Town on February 3, 1960* marked a genuine turning-point, in spite of its generally mild tone. His statement that

> "As a fellow-member of the Commonwealth, it is our earnest desire to give South Africa our support and encouragement, but I hope you won't mind my saying frankly that there are some aspects of your policies which make it impossible for us to do this without being false to our own deep convictions about the political destinies of free men, to which in our own territories we are trying to give effect . . ."

was a veiled means of serving notice on South Africa that Britain would no longer support it at the U.N. In the following year Mr. Peter Smithers, a British delegate at U.N., went on record as saying that *apartheid* provided circumstances which were "unique"; as a policy it stood "alone in its category". It clearly had "grave international repercussions particularly in Africa, but also in other continents". Referring to the article of the U.N. Charter which safeguards domestic jurisdiction, Mr. Smithers said:

> "While, therefore, the importance we attach to the proper observance of Article 2 (7) of the Charter remains undiminished, we regard the case of *apartheid*, in the circumstances which now exist, as of such an extraordinary and exceptional nature, as to warrant our regarding it and treating it as *sui generis*."†

This was a late conversion for Britain, but a conversion all the same. It marked the withdrawal of overt British support for South Africa,

---

* Conveniently available in full in Peter Calvocoressi, *South Africa and World Opinion* (London, 1961), pp. 45–56.

† Quoted in Bernard Friedman *et al.*, *Looking Outwards* (Johannesburg, 1961), p. 27.

the casting of the die in favour of political association with the black states of the continent rather than with the traditional partner. It also marked the end, for the time being, of the South African Government's dream of co-operation with other states and governments in Africa, on a basis of each recognizing one another's differences.* Since this symbolic British act, there have been the end of Britain's traditional role as a supplier of arms to South Africa, and, under a new British Government, even a cancellation of orders already in commission. The Simonstown agreement remains as it was framed in the 1950's, but could prove the final casualty of estrangement between the two countries' policies.

MUTUAL APPROACHES

Given the background of this chapter, how does each of the Old Dominions look to Britain in the sphere of foreign policy, and how does Britain look to them? I take them in reverse order to that in which they have been taken previously in this chapter.

To the South African Government, the link with Britain must seem tenuous compared with what it was in the early 1950's. There is no prospect of a military alliance, and Britain will not put South African interests ahead of those of present-day Commonwealth members; this has become even clearer since South Africa left the Commonwealth in 1961. At the same time, Britain has taken no coercive action against South Africa, except the stoppage of arms deliveries. Resolutions at the U.N. can be easily borne by South Africa; it has become accustomed to being the whipping-boy there. Britain has shown no inclination to cut off capital or trade. As already indicated, the Simonstown base is still in use, though now under South African control. Britain does not apply any of those restrictions to South African airlines that hostile countries apply. There is still a significant exchange of people between the two countries. South Africa has not intervened in the Rhodesian imbroglio; in a sense the British Government can be thankful that the further factor of overt South African aid and comfort to Southern Rhodesia has not been added to its disabilities in this matter. Thus, basic relations between Britain and South Africa have not changed greatly. The change has been in the British state

* Well stated in papers in SABRA, *South Africa in the African Continent* (Stellenbosch, 1959).

of mind. In South Africa itself, people of British extraction have discovered that they can do without the monarchy without discomfort. In all these circumstances, added to the distaste with which the rest of the world views South Africa, and the turmoil which may be expected to occur eventually there, one can expect a gradual deepening of the existing rift.

For New Zealand, political relations have perhaps changed least in the period surveyed here. As the next chapter will show, New Zealand economic dependence on the British market has remained. In terms of foreign policy, New Zealand has adjusted to the new arrangements of association with the United States, but without the same emotional background as Australia. This is perhaps to some extent because New Zealand troops remained in the European and Middle East theatres in World War II, and were not repatriated to fight in the Pacific War under American leadership, as Australian troops were; New Zealand's associations with the United States were more those of a supply base, although they did involve very heavy dependence upon American naval protection. The sense of reliance on the United States as protector against a rampant Asia, which is strong in Australia, does not seem to have gone so far in New Zealand. As already suggested, its Government's statements are rather more cautious and traditional than those of the Australian Government. References to Britain are more frequent and perhaps more cordial. In any case, New Zealand's preoccupations in foreign policy are still restricted, compared with those of Australia, and incline more towards economic concerns when any discussion of relations with Britain takes place. As the most consciously "British" of the Old Dominions, New Zealand can be expected to prove most sympathetic towards British policies. But this has its drawbacks from the British standpoint. Sympathy implies sympathy. If Britain suddenly produces policies which strike at the root of New Zealand prosperity, which seemed to many New Zealanders to be the case, or likely to be the case, in the Common Market negotiations of 1962,* the shock to New Zealand preconceptions is very great.

The Australian position has already been sketched by implication. Australian policy will support British policy, provided obvious Australian interests, of which the most important is the link with the United States, are not prejudiced. Sometimes, as the Suez record shows, an Australian Government will support Britain even in despite of the United States. But this does not seem a likely event

* There is further discussion of this matter in Chapter 9.

in the future. It is more likely, in my view, that there will be further
Australian scrutiny of British policy with the advice in mind of an
experienced Australian representative: "It is a common and quite
deceptive habit of British politicians to find, in Dominion opinion,
an alibi for any course which they may wish to take . . ."* and that
Britain will have to face a continuation of the hard bargaining
which it has come to associate with Australian negotiators. From
time to time Australian policy-makers will presumably look to
Britain as a buffer against American pressure; this may still be a
possible role for Britain, depending on the issue in question. But
there are certain British policies, implicit in the more recent exten-
sions of Commonwealth membership and activity, which the
Australian Government has found disturbing. It is difficult for an
Australian representative to avoid the fear that, if Afro-Asian
countries are given too much rope in Commonwealth matters, they
may use it to hang Australia for its New Guinea and immigration
policies. Australian sensitivity in these matters is probably often
misplaced. But there may well be reserve in the Australian approach
to British policies involving Africa, partly for the reasons given,
and partly because it is in Australia's interest that Britain should
not devote attention to Africa that might otherwise have gone to
Asia. To an increasing extent, the attitude taken by Britain and
other states towards China may become the test which the Australian
Government applies to the acceptability of their policies. A similar
point might be made about Indonesia.

For Canada, future attitudes towards British policy will, as in the
past, have much to do with the compatibility or otherwise of
American policies. Canada will probably not show the same reserve about the extension of Commonwealth membership as
Australia. The first Commonwealth Secretary-General is a Canadian
diplomat, which can be taken to mean that the Canadian Government supports the idea of a Commonwealth Secretariat and is prepared to go some of the way towards the conception of it put forward by African members. In any case, Canada has no equivalent of
New Guinea, and has long had a revised policy of Asian immigration. The world is accustomed to Canada not having a bad con-
science about anything, except perhaps the United States; there is
no obvious way in which an extension of Commonwealth activities

---

* From an address by the late F. W. Eggleston to apprentice Australian
diplomats, Eggleston Papers, Australian National Library, MS. 297. I owe
this reference to Mr. Eric Andrews.

can harm Canada. It is a consistent Canadian view that extension of the Commonwealth provides means of access to Afro-Asian countries which might not otherwise exist;* this may be expected to continue. Britain, as moulder of the Commonwealth, can thus expect to continue to receive Canadian support. As regards European matters, some division between Liberal and Conservative Governments might be expected in Canada, but it is probable that basically Canadian opinion would be in favour of closer British integration into Europe.

For Britain itself, the one black mark against the Old Dominions is South Africa. It was some release of embarrassment when South Africa left the Commonwealth, but the continuation of British economic connections with South Africa is likely to engender further African opposition at the level of propaganda; whether it will go further than that, and actively damage Britain's credit with new African states, remains to be seen. In addition, there is the problem of the High Commission Territories, to which little or no attention has been given here. British policy, for long one of quiescence, has moved in recent years to one of disengagement, the territories being given increasing self-government, presumably in the hope that their ultimate future will be decided in a triangular contest between South Africa, themselves, and neighbouring states. Disengagement is, in fact, likely to be the general British policy towards South African issues, as it has been since 1960. The most that South African can hope for from Britain is a continuation of existing rights and privileges; nothing new can be expected, and some existing opportunities may be withdrawn.

Canada, Australia and New Zealand do not pose political problems for Britain. Whatever changes might take place in their domestic politics, no likely government of any of these countries will adopt an anti-British attitude on major matters of foreign policy. British anxieties will, of necessity, be largely confined to questions of economic and social opportunity—to problems such as those discussed in the next chapter, of maintaining British "influence" in these countries against the combined effect of their development of cultural and economic self-sufficiency, and of the natural increase of American interest in them. At the political level, they may be expected to applaud British diplomacy which serves in-

* This view has also been held by the Australian Government, so far as Asian membership is concerned; its doubts about African membership are a relatively new development.

terests which they hold in common with **Britain, and** to be critical, but quietly so, when Britain takes steps which they do not like. They will at times look for the support of British pressure against the United States. But anyone in Britain who retains the illusion that these countries are either crying out for British help against the predatory Americans in every field, or are being "Americanized" against their will, cannot hope to be comforted by future events; the reality is less dramatic and more quietly complicated than that.

8

ECONOMICAL AND SOCIAL CONNECTIONS
1945–65

IT was suggested in the previous chapter that Britain's post-war problems of defence and foreign affairs have centred round its decline from the status of a great power to that of a major power ultimately dependent on the United States. Any schemes for substantial British initiatives must take account of this state of affairs. Britain does not have to ask the permission of the United States every time it proposes some new move, but it has to consider its capacity to carry out the move in relation to what it wants to do in other places, and it has to think about the effect on its relations with the United States. Certain obvious consequences have followed for Canada, Australia and New Zealand. They are fully aware that, while Britain may contribute a good deal to the solution of particular problems, their ultimate safety rests upon the United States; and they have acted accordingly. In addition, they have gained more stature and sophistication as sovereign states, just at the time when Britain has been struggling with the difficulties of a decline in power. Their actions are consequently marked by a considerable show of independence, which may or may not fit in with British interests. They are not now bound to the assumption of a common foreign policy which was the invisible concomitant of their undistinguished pre-war efforts to make their way in the world. At the same time, they value Britain's help in spheres in which it is a practical possibility, and are prepared to go out of their way to secure it if it agrees with their interests.

Something similar, though not the same, has occurred in the economic field. Since 1945, Britain has been struggling with balance of payments difficulties, the sign of an economy which is potentially weak in its capacity to provide the resources needed to meet its international obligations. These difficulties were acute in 1945 and immediately afterwards; they were mastered for the time being in the late 1950's; they became acute again in 1964–5. The connection with the Old Dominions is direct, as explained below. So far as the United States is concerned, Britain has been dependent upon

American understanding and good will for support in each of the major crises in its balance of payments. Recovery could not have occurred without the American (and Canadian) loans of 1945, and without Marshall Aid; and the crisis of 1964 could not have been dealt with unless the United States had taken the lead in assisting Britain. In the first of these two cases Britain was subject to very real American pressure to change its trading practices in return for the help it received from the United States;* by the time of the second, American attitudes and world conditions had both changed so much that little American pressure was apparent. If it did occur, it was not on economic issues but on political: British support of the American position on Vietnam was widely regarded as a price paid for American help, though this may well have been a misleading view of the situation. Britain had good reason to support the United States over Vietnam, regardless of what its economic position was. However, whether there was American pressure in 1964 or not, the lesson of 1945 was repeated: Britain would find it difficult to maintain its international economic position without American good will.

The link with the Old Dominions lies in their membership (apart from Canada) of the Sterling Area, and their common interest in Britain's capacity to sustain its position as the financial custodian of the Area; in Britain's capacity to buy their goods (especially relevant in the case of Canada, which, as a dollar country, suffered whenever Britain found it necessary to limit purchases in the world's most widely desired currency); and in Britain's capacity to invest in their economies (again relevant for Canada in the context of Britain's brake on dollar investment; for the other three in the general context of Britain's capacity to spare savings for investment abroad). The period from 1945 to 1958 was one of continual concern by the Four about the state of the British economy. All knew that they would suffer in trade or investment or both if Britain suffered anything like an economic collapse. While the Canadian Government did not hold its national reserves in sterling, it was vitally concerned about the management of the Sterling Area, since restrictions on dollar purchases and investment were aimed at Canada as well as at the United States. It thus became a primary Canadian objective to gain multi-lateralism in British trading policy as soon as possible, and to attempt to avoid the situation in which British financial

* The course of events is described in Richard N. Gardner, *Sterling-Dollar Diplomacy* (Oxford, 1956).

stringency became a reason for providing permanent protection for British home industries (e.g. in the motor industry), or opportunities for alternative sources of overseas supply (e.g. in wheat, salmon or timber), because of the dollar origin of Canadian goods which would otherwise gain access to the British market.

The other three countries did not have the same problems as Canada, since there was never any restriction of British investment in their economies, and Britain did not exercise exchange control on purchases from them, in spite of their local imposition of exchange control on local requests for British currency. They gained, if anything, from attempts to confine British purchases within the Sterling Area during the period of stringency. But they were all anxious to widen their markets, and recognized that Britain was not a sufficient market for their expanding production of export goods. They, Britain and Canada, could readily join together in the 1950's in requests for a lowering of American tariffs and other protective devices (such as those which kept foreign food and fibres out of the United States), and in appeals for new American policies which would make more dollars available to the world at large. The South African nostrum, a rise in the price of gold, never became general Commonwealth doctrine, but might have been acceptable to the other countries here considered* if other means of acquiring American goods had not become available to the world in the 1950's.

The Four have had certain other interests in common with Britain, as regards American policy. Apart from their common desire to reduce American protectionism in those fields in which they might hope to sell to the United States (a point applicable to Canada as well as to the other three Old Dominions), they have also wished to retain the system of Commonwealth preferences in spite of American dislike of it. At certain times the idea of an increase in preferences has been brought forward, but it has failed to gain general support. Apart from the fact that it would need to be negotiated past the GATT obligation to grant no new preferences, it has seemed likely to discourage the United States from taking those steps in reduction of tariffs which, in their total effect, might well give the Commonwealth countries greater advantages than they could get from any manipulation of the preference structure. Moreover, preferences as such have not been of equal advantage to all concerned. A cool-headed American assessment in the mid-1950's was that "existing

* Especially to Australia, also a gold producer.

preferences enable the United Kingdom to protect a declining position, whereas they prevent overseas Sterling Area members from taking advantage of a strengthened trading position".* At the Commonwealth Economic Conference at the end of 1952 Britain brought forward a proposal that all Commonwealth countries should join in seeking release from the GATT rule mentioned above. Some members agreed. Others (of which Canada was probably a leader) "felt that such an approach would not advance the agreed objective of restoring multilateral world trade and the Conference was therefore unable to support it".† Here the wish to tempt the United States into a policy of more generous trading and finance was probably dominant; but there were other aspects of the preference system in the post-war period which dictated caution.

For Australia, South Africa and New Zealand, and to a lesser extent for Canada, the preference system represented a guaranteed, or nearly-guaranteed British market for goods which would be difficult to sell elsewhere. Such industries as fruit and butter in Australia, and wine and fruit in South Africa, were not substantial in the total of the economy, or, indeed, in the balance of payments. Although their contribution to export income was respectable, it could not be compared with the income from wool, wheat or gold. But they were politically important : they represented rural interests with much say in the governments of these countries. In New Zealand the same position applied, except that the dairy and meat industries, which relied on the British market for their income, bulked very large indeed in both the total economy and the balance of payments. Thus, while Australia and South Africa were not dependent on the preference system for prosperity, they wished to retain its effects on certain industries while being reluctant to see it extended if this extension would prevent their selling more freely in such markets as those of the United States, Japan and Germany. New Zealand, heavily dependent on the preference system, would support its retention in all circumstances and its extension if possible. Canada was getting little advantage from the preference system during the 1950's because of British exchange control; in particular, the developments in the Canadian motor trade, undertaken in the 1930's in order to provide vehicles and parts for Britain under the Ottawa

* Philip W. Bell, *The Sterling Area in the Postwar World* (Oxford, 1956), p. 407.

† From the conference communiqué in Nicholas Mansergh (ed.), *Documents and Speeches on Commonwealth Affairs 1952–1962* (London, 1963), p. 405.

agreement, were stultified by the dollar shortage, and it was difficult for Canadians to avoid the view that British motor interests were using the opportunity to obtain effective protection for their own products. Wheat, fruit, vegetables and salmon all suffered in the same way, whether subject to preferences or not. But it was very much in the Canadian interest to retain some level of preference in Britain, against the day when discrimination against dollar goods would give way to greater multi-lateralism. Thus, although Canada did not support a general revival of the preference system, it did not join with the United States in condemnation of it. Moreover, as American capital poured into the Canadian economy in the 1950's, there was a widespread revulsion against the idea that Canada might be "bought" by the United States. Historically speaking, the alternative to American capital had been British, and so Canadian concern for an improvement in the British economic position had another reason to support it.

It is important to balance the account here, and not to give the impression of the Four fending off the United States throughout the post-war period, and looking only for an enlargement of markets within its borders; not to give an impression, either, that the United States has been consistently hostile to economic co-operation between Commonwealth countries. On the first point, it is a fact that each of the Four has been anxious to attract American capital, in spite of the problems which this has created in Canada. American participation in the economies of the other three is never likely to achieve the extent it has reached in Canada; the inflow of American capital represents, for them, sheer gain in resources. In some cases it may be simply a relief to their balance of payments, as when Americans invest in existing enterprises; in others it may represent a net gain in physical resources and technical knowledge, as when American firms exploit minerals in Australia or establish that country's motor car industry. On the second point, it is true that there was much American opposition to the British loan in 1945–6, and a widespread desire to destroy the preference system; but, as suggested in Chapter 5, this was largely an outcome of American and British myth-making in the 1920's and 30's. It became less important in the 1950's. The nearer Britain came to convertibility of sterling, the less was heard about the wickedness of preferences. It is now a dead issue between Britain and the United States. It did arise as an issue in 1961–2, but not because of American opposition. The context was that of Britain's attempt to enter the European Economic Community, which would have meant, in effect, that Britain had to switch its preference system from Commonwealth to European countries—or so the Commonwealth countries feared. Although they had greatly expanded their trade with Europe, Japan and the United States, they were still dependent on British preferential markets for certain politically sensitive products. That is still their position. The standstill arrangement of 1952 remains as the most convenient for all concerned: new preferences might prejudice advantages elsewhere; but old preferences need to be retained, because there is not enough prospect of alternative markets.

THE STERLING AREA SYSTEM

The experiences of the Sterling Area system since 1945 provide something of a conspectus of economic relations between Britain and the Four. The earlier development of the "sterling bloc" has been described in Chapter 5. On the outbreak of war in 1939 the bloc was converted into a more tightly controlled body, the Sterling Area, its object being to pool foreign currencies and use them to the best wartime effect. Each member country adopted exchange control, which it operated along lines approved in broad principle by all. Canada was not a member, but Australia, New Zealand and South Africa were. At the end of the war, with the termination of Lend-Lease, Britain was faced with the combined problem of a grave shortage of dollars, an incapacity to resume civilian exports on anything like the pre-war scale, and massive obligations to a number of Sterling Area countries for wartime services and supplies. The American and Canadian loans of 1945–6 were designed to provide Britain with buying power in North America during the period in which it was getting its peacetime exports under way again. The obligations to Sterling countries (the "sterling balances") should have been, in the view of many people, scaled down or cancelled out, on the analogy of Lend-Lease; but this was not British policy, which aimed at a controlled rate of release of sterling balances, rather than their cancellation. In any case countries such as Australia and New Zealand looked on their balances in London as safeguards against the periodic shortages of international funds with which fluctuations in the prices of their exports had plagued them before the war. It was a combination of inadequate exports and the headlong conversion of sterling balances into dollars (not by Australia, New

Zealand or South Africa) that caused the hasty stoppage of convertibility of sterling in 1947. Thereafter the Sterling Area continued to be operated in something like the same fashion as during the war: its members were in a state of siege against the dollar shortage for some time.

The machinery of the Area in these years was briefly as follows. The members used sterling as a common international currency, settling their accounts with one another and carrying on most of their foreign business in it. Each had its own system of exchange control, designed primarily to preserve its own balance of payments, but also intended to conserve the gold and dollar assets of the Area as a whole. This meant, in practice, discrimination against dollar goods and the critical examination of all requests to transfer funds into dollars. Sterling was freely transferable throughout the Area. Each central bank maintained accounts in Britain into which were paid the ultimate net proceeds of its international monetary transactions. A common pool of gold and dollars was managed by the Bank of England. Members with a net surplus of dollars sold these to the Bank for sterling; those with a net deficit of dollars bought them from the Bank with sterling. The Bank undertook to meet all officially approved demands for dollars, whether they came from Britain itself or from other members-countries.

Such a system required close co-operation between the Bank of England and central banks in other member-countries; it also required some continual scrutiny of the extent to which members were earning and spending dollars. This scrutiny was provided at the official level through central banks and treasuries, and, up to 1955, by two joint bodies in London, the Commonwealth Liaison Committee and the Sterling Area Statistical Committee. In that year the second was absorbed in the first. All Commonwealth members, including Canada, were represented. The material gathered at the official level was made available to Commonwealth Finance Ministers, who met fairly regularly to discuss the Sterling Area's progress. At the summit level, the broad principles of Sterling Area policy were considered by Commonwealth Prime Ministers at their meetings.

Inevitably, the Sterling Area became identified with the Commonwealth, in spite of its containing some foreign members. Canada had a full opportunity to urge policy on its members, though not a member itself. The Prime Ministers issued broad statements of principle about the need to conserve dollars, the desirability of a change in American commercial policies, and the encouragement of dollar-saving industries in the Commonwealth itself. The Area and the Commonwealth could easily be regarded as a combined agency of economic self-help. Its formal advantages to its members were put thus by the Reserve Bank of New Zealand:

"For New Zealand the advantages to be derived from participation in sterling area arrangements are considerable. They include the following:

(a) There are no restrictions on payments from the United Kingdom and most other sterling area countries to New Zealand.

(b) We retain full use of the facilities provided in the London exchange market for multi-lateral settlement of our exchange transactions.

(c) Any deficit in our balance of payments with other countries can be financed by the use of our sterling funds in London. This is particularly important in relation to the dollar area, with which New Zealand normally has a deficit. If we had been outside the sterling area in the period since 1939 (until sterling became convertible for non-residents) we would have had to earn, through our own trade with North America, every dollar we spent, and that would have meant even more severe restrictions on dollar expenditure."*

This represents, as it were, the limiting case, of a small country with few prospects of earning dollars and the need to retain close contact with the British economy. The Australian position was similar, since Australia consistently ran a dollar deficit; but Australia had better prospects of diversifying its trade, and so reliance on Sterling Area machinery was rather slighter. South Africa could adopt a more aloof position. It settled its dollar debts directly with gold, and participated in the Sterling Area only by recompensing Britain with gold for the payments which Britain had incurred on its behalf elsewhere.† This, however, meant that South Africa was using Sterling Area facilities for much of its trading, and was also

* Reserve Bank of New Zealand, *Overseas Trade and Finance* (Wellington 1960), p. 46.
† See Andrew Shonfield, *British Economic Policy since the War* (Harmondsworth, 1958), pp. 135–6.

contributing gold to the Sterling Area pool; it was thus a factor of some importance in sustaining the Area's resources. The common membership of the Sterling Area of these three countries also gave them further advantages than those arising from current payments. The British practice of scrutinizing and restricting capital transfers to dollar countries meant that sterling countries, especially Australia and South Africa, benefited from the movement of capital when there was uneasiness in business circles in Britain. Some of this was "funk money", readily provided and as readily withdrawn, but much of it was genuine investment in manufacturing industry in those two countries. Again, in the years immediately after the war the Sterling Area countries benefited from Britain's retention of bulk purchase for a number of commodities.

In these various concomitants of the Sterling Area's operations one can see how North American eyes, especially in the late 1940's, might descry the attempt to create a closed economic system: the combination of bulk purchases, preferences, restriction of capital transfers, and discrimination against dollar goods, sometimes looked like the extension into the post-war world of the policies of "buying British" which had been hopefully enunciated in the 1920's, adopted in some measure under the stress of the depression in the 1930's, and then carried on in the early 1940's because of the exhaustion of dollar funds and the exigencies of war. The same state of affairs, seen from a different angle, seemed to some people in Britain and Australia an opportunity to bring to fruition that dream of a closed Commonwealth system which had lingered in Rightwing circles for so long.

At all events, the Sterling Area was not to insulate itself from the world economy, and no major effort was to be made to confine Commonwealth resources to Commonwealth needs. The turning-point was in 1952, when, at two Commonwealth economic conferences, declarations were made in favour of multi-lateralism, and efforts were begun at giving sterling a limited convertability to replace the brief, ill-fated convertibility of 1947, forced on Britain by the conditions of the American loan and hastily withdrawn when it proved unsafe. From 1952 onwards, sterling became steadily more convertible into other currencies, including dollars. A number of influences aided this process. The world dollar shortage was eased through American loans and gifts to other countries, through an increase in American investment and military spending, and through some relaxation of tariffs. Europe and Japan revived rapidly as both markets and competitors, diversifying the world trading picture in ways which had seemed remote in the immediate post-war period. The Soviet Union and China became markets for manufactured goods from Britain and wheat and wool from Canada and Australia. There was, in fact, a general improvement in the trading capacity of most Commonwealth countries, including Britain (New Zealand was something of an exception), and a corresponding reduction in the "siege" aspects of the Sterling Area's operations. Along with these external influences, pressing for multi-lateralism in trade and convertibility in finance, went strong domestic influences in Britain itself. Many British writers on finance and economics urged Britain on towards these same goals; some thought the Sterling Area an expensive luxury.* While there were some doubts about the capacity of British industries to withstand competition from foreign goods which currency restrictions had previously kept out, the mass of articulate business opinion was in favour of multi-lateralism. It was felt that the advantages of Britain's remaining the banker for the Sterling Area might be safely combined with purchases and investment over a wider area; and so it proved until 1964.

Whether the Sterling Area will ever regain the cohesion it had between 1939 and the mid-1950's is an open question. So far as Canada is concerned, there is little to be said for the kind of co-ordination and discrimination that marked the Sterling Area's operations then. The exclusion of Canadian goods from markets in which they might otherwise be bought is something which Canadian policy must inevitably seek to avoid; and it is hard to see how a tight Sterling Area could be operated without this being a danger. Unless Canada were prepared to hold reserves in sterling, which seems a most remote possibility, its interest lies in a prosperous Britain with a multilateral trading policy. Australia, New Zealand and South Africa might well wish to see a resurrection of the earlier Sterling Area arrangements, provided they were all in the same difficulties. This seems unlikely. Australian trade is now widely diversified; New Zealand's is not. South Africa's retains its traditional pattern, but gold exports give it access to currencies of every kind; it may need the conveniences of the Sterling Area, but not its support. The kind of trouble which might unite Australia and New

---

* There is a useful contemporary account of these and other British opinions in Susan Strange, "The Commonwealth and the Sterling Area" in *Year Book of World Affairs 1959* (London, 1959).

Zealand with South Africa and even perhaps Canada would be a general slump in the United States, combined with an end to the flow of American money abroad. In such circumstances the United States would be bound to raise tariffs under domestic political pressure. The markets which the Old Dominions had found in Europe and Asia would almost certainly contract under the combined pressure of lowered national incomes and domestic demands for increased protection. Under such circumstances the Old Dominions would all look for help from Britain, repeating Professor Bell's dictum of an earlier decade: "In a world of uncertainty the combination of preferences, stability, and the known concern and knowledge of the United Kingdom with the problems of overseas Sterling Area members is a difficult one to beat."* As in the 1930's, there would probably be a general desire to improve matters by taking in one another's washing. But even greater difficulties would arise than at Ottawa. The washing is now uncomfortably alike in each country. Much greater proportions of the workforce are engaged in manufacturing in Australia, South Africa and even New Zealand than in 1932. The basic exchange of British manufactured goods for Dominion food, whch seemed the obvious choice then, would now be far more difficult to arrange, because of Dominion protectionism and a British wish to buy in the cheapest market. The dream of a closed Commonwealth economic system thus becomes even more delayed than ever, so far as the Old Dominions are concerned. It is possible that Britain might be able to arrange bi-lateral preference or barter arrangements with other members of the Commonwealth with less developed economies; something might be done in restricted fields with the Old Dominions. But any general system would be very difficult to construct.

Thus, there is a certain similarity between the Old Dominions' economic relations with Britain and their political relations. Canada is occasionally restless in its dependence upon the United States, but precluded by circumstances from using Britain as a substitute in substantial matters. Australia does not need Britain for major matters, but finds it still indispensable in certain smaller ones. New Zealand would like to retain something like its pre-war relations with Britain, and has largely done so, but cannot see this as a permanent arrangement. South Africa's position is rather different, since in economic matters it has retained the close connections it has

* Philip W. Bell, *The Sterling Area in the Postwar World* (Oxford, 1956), p. 407.

always had with Britain, but is progressively losing its political connections. All four show more diversified and mature economies than in 1939, just as in the field of diplomacy they have developed their contacts and techniques; they are still, however, dependent economies in something like the same way as they are dependent politically. As small, high-standard countries, they are vulnerable to influences from abroad, and cannot hope to attain self-sufficiency except at very great sacrifice.

Having speculated and generalized about the economic position of the Four in relation to Britain, let us now look at some figures of post-war economic connection.

TRADE

First, the importance of the Old Dominions in British trade can be seen from the following proportions of British exports and imports attributed to them in selected years between, 1938 and 1963: *

British Exports

Percentage going to:

Year	Australia	Canada	New Zealand	S. Africa
	%	%	%	%
1938	8·1	4·7	4·0	8·4
1948	9·1	4·3	3·3	7·6
1952	8·6	5·0	4·5	5·6
1957	7·0	5·8	4·2	5·2
1960	7·3	6·0	3·4	4·3
1963	5·7	4·2	2·8	4·8

British Imports

Percentage coming from:

Year	Australia	Canada	New Zealand	S. Africa
	%	%	%	%
1938	7·8	8·5	5·1	1·6
1948	8·1	10·4	5·2	1·5
1952	5·7	8·0	4·1	1·6
1957	6·0	7·8	4·2	2·2
1960	4·3	8·2	4·0	2·1
1963	4·2	7·6	3·6	2·3

* Derived from money amounts in *Annual Abstract of Statistics* (H.M.S.O.) Nos. 86, 95 and 101.

P

Considering that these figures cover a period in which total British exports rose from £m.470 to £m.4,080, and imports from £m.919 to £m.4,820, one's first impression is that the position of the Old Dominions has not changed very much. They accounted for 25·2 per cent of British exports and 23 per cent of imports in 1938; twenty-five years later the comparable figures were 17·5 per cent and 17·7 per cent. There has been a steady but slow decline in the comparative significance of these countries in British trade; at the same time, when we think of the great changes which have taken place in the world economy in the quarter-century in question, it is remarkable how stable the trade has been. It is ironical that, in spite of Canadian anguish over being shut out of the British market in the 1950's, Canadian trade has been the most stable of the Four. However, certain secular shifts can be discerned. On the export side, it is clear that something of a permanent decline has occurred in the Australian market; this reflects Australia's interest in other sources of supply, especially Japan and other countries which buy Australian wool and metals. New Zealand shows a decline, although in this case the change is more a failure to increase New Zealand buying capacity than a movement away from British goods; that buying capacity, in turn, is affected by New Zealand's decline as a supplier of British imports, in comparison with other countries. South Africa's figure of 8·4 per cent of British exports in 1938 seems unlikely to be approached again. On the other hand, it now provides a bigger proportion of British imports than ever before. Taking the four countries together, one can see that their 1938 and 1948 positions reflected the effect of the depression and of wartime patterns of trade respectively; the figures for later years represent Britain's basic requirements from these countries, and theirs from Britain.

Of the four countries, the greatest changes have taken place in Australia. Here are figures on the importance of Britain in Australian trade: *

* Derived from money amounts in *Commonwealth Year Books* Nos. 31, 43, 49 and 50. Australia uses the financial year July 1 to June 30 for many statistics, not the calendar year.

British Percentages of Australian Exports and Imports

Year	Exports %	Imports %
1938–9	54·4	40·6
1948–9	42·3	50·5
1953–4	36·3	48·8
1956–7	27·9	41·2
1960–1	21·5	31·4
1962–3	18·7	30·4
1963–4	18·3	27·8

The export column reflects the extent to which Britain has been replaced as a market for the major Australian exports—wool, wheat and metals—by Japan, China and European countries; at the same time, Britain remains a significant market for such products as dairy products, sugar and meat, goods for which preferential arrangements are still significant. Australian imports have not shown the same change, but there is a steady decline in Britain's relative position.

Britain's position in Canadian trade is more stable, as the following figures show: *

British Percentages of Canadian Exports and Imports

Year	Exports %	Imports %
1939	35·5	15·2
1947	27·1	7·2
1953	16·2	10·5
1957	15·1	9·3
1960	17·4	10·8
1962	14·7	9·0

It is clear that much of the growth in Canadian exports, especially in the resource fields (such as natural gas and oil) and in lumber and pulp, has been to the United States, which is by far the greatest customer and supplier for Canada. Britain is second in both fields, in spite of the comparatively small percentages of the post-war period. Once the effect of the Canadian loan and Canadian mutual aid passed, Canadian exports to Britain of manufactured and processed goods were unable to regain their pre-war market.

* *Canada Year Books,* 1956 and 1963–4.

Exchange control must have been at least partly responsible. Canada continues to sell a substantial quantity of primary products to Britain.

The place of Britain in South African trade (excluding gold) is seen in the following table: *

British Percentages of South African Exports and Imports of Merchandise

Year	Exports %	Imports %
1935–39 (av.)	36·1	44·2
1948	24·3	31·2
1952	21·8	33·6
1956	29·6	31·6
1960	28·8	28·3
1963	32·4	29·8

Britain is still first as both customer and supplier to South Africa, a point which is important if one is considering the possibility of an economic boycott of South Africa, such as other African states have proposed. The remarkable steadiness of South Africa's exports to Britain indicates the importance of the British market for South African food-producing industries, such as fruit, sugar and wine.

Finally, some similar figures for New Zealand : †

British Percentages of New Zealand Exports and Imports

Year	Exports %	Imports %
1940	88·0	47·0
1950	66·0	60·0
1953	67·2	56·4
1957	58·8	51·4
1960	53·0	43·4
1963	46·0	41·4

* From Nathan Hurwitz and Owen Williams, *The Economic Framework of South Africa* (Pietermaritzburg, 1962), pp. 143–4; *State of South Africa Year Book* 1962 (Johannesburg, 1962), p. 291; and J. E. Spence, *Republic Under Pressure* (London, 1965), p. 131.

† *New Zealand Official Year Book*, 1964.

The obvious change here is New Zealand's increased diversification of exports: roughly half the pre-war percentage now goes to Britain. However, Britain takes nearly all New Zealand's lamb, cheese and butter, and about a third of its wool exports. The encouragement of British agriculture in competition with New Zealand products, and the fear of further British involvement in Europe, have caused New Zealand to look for markets elsewhere, especially in the United States, Western Europe and Japan; New Zealand meat has proved popular in a great many countries. But the staple market for the grassland industries is still Britain. In return, Britain is unquestionably first amongst New Zealand's sources of imports.

Certain agreements have been made to govern trade between Britain and the Old Dominions. The Ottawa agreements of 1932 mostly remain in force. The loosest arrangement is probably that between Britain and Canada: under an exchange of letters between the two Governments in 1947, each has the right to reduce or eliminate the preferences accorded to the other without prior consultation or consent. In the case of New Zealand, Mr. Macmillan's visit in 1958 was followed by a new Trade Agreement, whereby the British Government recognized that the balance of advantage under the 1932 agreement had moved against New Zealand, and agreed to New Zealand having the right to reduce the 20 per cent margin of preference on British goods. All New Zealand's existing rights were preserved; these had, however, been modified by such administrative changes as the British quota system for butter. In general, however, New Zealand remained assured of free entry to the British market for its meat and most dairy products. Australia also negotiated a new Trade Agreement in 1956, preserving its Ottawa rights, and including an assured annual market for a minimum quantity of wheat or flour. The International Wheat and Sugar Agreements, in which other countries take part, but in which Britain appears as a major consumer, have also provided opportunities for the Old Dominions (except New Zealand) to gain special opportunities in the British market.

The complex of trading activities and trade agreements between Britain and the Old Dominions has a number of significant features. In the first place, there is a large area of trade which would probably continue under any system of operation. Britain needs paper-pulp from Canada, wool from Australia, canned pineapple from South Africa and lamb from New Zealand; these things would gain a market under most circumstances. Similarly, Scotch whisky and the products of British engineering industry would make their way into overseas markets. Second, there are certain habits of trade which, while not so assured on either side, would be likely to continue, because of advantages proceeding from language, tradition, the connection of firms with their branches abroad, and the existence of previous trading in the products in question. Thus, there is a sort of minimum level of trade between Britain and the Four which is not likely to be disturbed. But above this much may change, especially in highly dynamic economies which are growing so rapidly as those of Canada and Australia. In these two cases some earlier assumptions about trade with Britain have given way to opportunities arising from trade with the United States and Japan. New Zealand has least of this upper stratum of dynamic trade, because of its small population and restricted resources. Australia and Canada, combining vast exploitable natural resources with an attractiveness to American capital looking for quick returns, have moved to a position in which trade with Britain has become a dependable backlog, not the main fuel for economic advance. From the British standpoint, this sort of development amongst the Dominions was one of the many reasons for seeking further trading rights in Europe in the late 1950's. It was not simply that the Old Dominions were increasingly trading with other countries; it was also that British goods were being squeezed out of their markets by local protectionism, designed to give local manufacturing industries the predominant place in the local market.

INVESTMENT

One way in which British industries could overcome this problem, or alleviate it, was by coming in behind the favourable conditions which the Australian, South African, and, to a lesser extent, the New Zealand Government were prepared to offer. This has been one of the incentives behind British post-war private investment in the Old Dominions. Public investment, which used to be the main part of the British capital flow to these countries, has now largely disappeared or been replaced by the raising of public capital from international institutions such as the I.M.F. and the International Bank. Governments and semi-governmental bodies still raise money in London from time to time, but the operations are small compared with those which are undertaken by private enterprise.

It is not so easy to obtain particulars of British private investment in the Old Dominions as to get details of trade. Moreover, the statistics are not assembled in comparable terms by the various governments. However, there has certainly been a substantial growth of British investment since the war. In *Canada*, by 1961 British investment stood at $m.3,385, compared with $m.1,750 at the end of World War II. The 1961 figure represented some 14 per cent of non-resident investment in Canada, compared with a pre-war figure of 36 per cent before it became necessary to sell large quantities of British securities in Canada to pay for war supplies. 75 per cent of the non-resident investment in Canada in 1961 was American.*

The *Australian* figures of private investment from other countries are made up in the form of the cumulative inflow of private overseas investment in companies in Australia. Between July 1947 and June 1964, the British share of this amounted to £A.m.1,071, which was 54·4 per cent of the total; the combined American and Canadian share was 34·3 per cent.† *New Zealand* makes up its figures in two ways, both different from the Canadian and Australian. They represent "investment change" and "income from direct investment". Taking the latter, it appears that the actual income received by British firms from direct investment in New Zealand rose from £NZ.1,410,000 in 1949–50 to £NZ.13,620,000 in 1962–3. The latter figure represented 57·2 per cent of the income from overseas direct investment; "dollar countries" received 18:1 per cent.‡ In *South Africa* in 1962 the total of British "direct" and "non-direct" investment in the private sector was said to be R.m.1,670, representing 64·2 per cent of overseas investment; this compared with 11·2 per cent by the United States.§ All these figures, it will be remembered, are for private investment only, and do not take account of long-term investment in government securities.

It seems that British private investment in Canada is about 15 per cent of total foreign investment, in Australia about 55 per cent, in New Zealand about 55 per cent, and in South Africa about 60 per

* *Canada Year Book,* 1963–4, pp. 1,034–5.
† Commonwealth Bureau of Census and Statistics, *Annual Bulletin of Overseas Investment Australia 1963–4* (Canberra), p. 7.
‡ *New Zealand Official Yearbook,* 1964, pp. 776–8.
§ J. E. Spence, *Republic Under Pressure* (London, 1965), p. 130.

cent. There has been a steady increase in the flow of capital to these countries since the war, but especially to Australia and South Africa. Most of it has probably been in manufacturing industry, the section of the economy which has got the lion's share of total investment (domestic and foreign) in each case. Traditionally, British investment has been in transport, commerce, government securities and mining. The last of these is still important, especially in South Africa, but the turn to manufactures represents a change in keeping with the comparative maturity of the Old Dominions' economies. It also means that British industries such as the motor industry take a share in the prosperity of Australia by their profits from local subsidiaries, and not, as before, from exporting cars and parts directly to Australia. This introduces an extra complexity into economic relations between Britain and the Four, since the character and extent of these cannot be measured, as in earlier times, by trade figures. The effect of such massive capital transfers on the balance of payments of Australia and South Africa should also be noted. For some years these countries have been able to rely on a flow of British investment which, in each year's accounts, could pay for otherwise unrequited imports. It has been one of New Zealand's special difficulties that the flow to that country has been so much smaller, and consequently of much less help in the balance of payments. No doubt this has meant rather more stability for the New Zealand economy, but in lower gear.

From the British standpoint, investment in the growing economies of the Old Dominions is a means of getting a foothold under conditions which would otherwise favour local firms at the expense of imports. It is also, of course, a means of spreading risks beyond those encountered in Britain itself. Yields have been high, especially in South Africa. But the outflow of private capital represents a drain on the British balance of payments; at times there are doubts in Britain about whether it should be sustained, or whether the capital would be better employed in Britain itself, presumably as a means of increasing exports. If a British Government were to curtail investment abroad, as the Wilson Government thought of doing in 1965, there would undoubtedly be serious complaints from Australia. South Africa is not in a position to make demands on Britain in the same high-handed manner as Australia, but there would be objections from there too.

An Economic Summary

It is difficult to generalize about British economic relations with all four Old Dominions. Canada is an obvious exception. Even for the others, there is not a great deal in common. One can say, however, that Britain has provided both trade and investment which have assisted them to increase their national incomes and diversify their economies. Each is less dependent on the British market than it was, although that market is still of great importance to both New Zealand and South Africa. Despite good intentions on all hands, the proportions of trade between Britain and each Old Dominion have tended to decline; it is fairly clear that none is in a position to gain a bigger share of the British market. A stable or slowly declining portion is what they can look forward to. In these circumstances it is not surprising that they should have made great efforts to find markets elsewhere. A practical multi-lateralism has suited all parties since the latter part of the 1950's. But the British market is still vital to certain sensitive industries. Some products of local political importance can often not be sold anywhere else. There has been a considerable increase in American investment, notably in Australia and South Africa, but Britain is still the main source of external capital to all but Canada.

From the British point of view, it is fortunate that these countries still retain some attachment to Britain and British goods, even though they increasingly buy elsewhere. Even so, they do not provide, between them, more than 20 per cent of Britain's export market. Gains to be made from them are long-term, arising from the profits of industries established within their borders; a good proportion of these profits has to be ploughed back, however, and there may be a considerable interim between the switch from supplying goods to one of the Four and receiving satisfactory dividends from factories established there. The necessarily restricted character of the gains from these countries, the most prosperous in the Commonwealth, was one of the reasons why the Macmillan Government sought increased opportunities in Europe.

The machinery of the Sterling Area is still available for siege conditions, if these should recur, and is useful in facilitating payments under conditions of multi-lateralism. But it is not now the instrument of policy that it was in the early 1950's.

In this summary, something needs to be said about the special problem of Canada.* We have seen that Canadian complaints about the difficulty of overcoming sterling discrimination are not entirely substantiated by the trade figures. Even in the worst period of discrimination, Canada managed to sell a sizeable proportion of its exports to Britain. But the Canadian case is rather that, under more fortunate circumstances, much more might have been sold, and that Canada wanted to make these sales, because of its traditional attachment to Britain and its desire to be less dependent on the United States. There were numerous complaints from Canadians in the 1950's that Britain was not trying hard enough to respond to these Canadian wishes. The generous circumstances of the Canadian loan seemed to have been forgotten; so did Canada's wartime help; the deliberate reduction of the Canadian merchant marine, which indirectly aided Britain, seemed to go unnoticed; Canada's willingness to enter the first International Wheat Agreement at a low price was not given a generous construction. The British action in effectively keeping Canadian cars out of the British market, in spite of the Ottawa assumptions, has already been noted. The reception given to Mr. Diefenbaker's vague 1957 proposals for improvement in trade between Canada and Britain was not encouraging. The proposals may have been childish and far-fetched in many ways, but the counter-offer by the British Government of a free trade area seemed to many Canadians cynical in its calculated disregard of the difficulties which a tariff-minded Conservative Government in Canada would have with its manufacturers. A more modest response, based upon actual rather than millennial possibilities, might have done a good deal to improve Britain's standing in Canada.

MIGRATION

Up to this point, there has been discussion of "markets" and "money", but not of "men", the third element in the trinity of the 1920's. This is because British policy-makers have not tried to relate migration to trade and investment since 1945. Instead of being regarded as part of a trinity of which the development should be planned as a whole, migration has proceeded with little co-operation between the British and other governments. Consideration of its economic effects has been largely confined to the overseas

* B. S. Keirstead, *Canada in World Affairs, 1951–3* (Toronto, 1956), pp. 182–203, is a helpful source.

governments, and been carried on in the context of their domestic economies, not in the "Empire" context of the 1920's and 30's, or even in the "Commonwealth" context in which balance of payments problems were considered by Commonwealth Prime Ministers and Finance Ministers in the 1950's. This state of affairs results partly from the increased autonomy and self-reliance of the Old Dominions, partly from the general enlargement of the Commonwealth (which has meant that activities confined to a few members, such as migration, do not receive the attention from the British Government that they got in pre-war days), and partly from the fact of full employment in Britain itself: there has been no drive to get rid of surplus poor. Nevertheless, post-war migration from Britain has been a substantial and continuous movement of up to 100,000 people a year. There has also been a movement in the other direction, but the net effect has been a significant gain in population for the Old Dominions.

There were proposals for post-war assisted migration to the Dominions during the war;* these were discussed at the 1944 meeting of Prime Ministers. Australia, Canada, New Zealand and South Africa all showed interest in a scheme for free passages for British ex-servicemen. However, all but Australia were extremely cautious about the prospect of assisted migration beyond the limited proposals for ex-servicemen. They were uncertain about post-war economic conditions, and weighed down by their recollection of the disappointments of the 1920's and the unemployment of the 1930's. Australia alone showed interest in a general scheme.

In the post-war period, Australia has been very much the most active of the Old Dominions in promoting British immigration. The Australian ethos of rapid economic development and of population growth as an aid to defence has been the driving force behind these efforts; apart from its vigorous policy of British immigration, Australia has actively sought migrants from Europe, first from the camps of Displaced Persons, later in migration agreements with countries such as the Netherlands, Italy and Greece. The other three Old Dominions have also sought migrants, but with rather less enthusiasm and without the same sustained concentration. New Zealand has looked for British migrants, but has not offered them the same incentives as Australia; Canada has welcomed migrants, but has not had to look very hard for them; South Africa's

* This paragraph owes much to R. T. Appleyard, *British Emigration to Australia* (London, 1964), pp. 33 ff.

reception of British immigrants has been affected by domestic political considerations in South Africa itself. As indicated in Chapter 1, the flow to South Africa has traditionally been small in comparison with the flows to Canada and Australia.

The British Government has not shown much interest in emigration, considering it to be largely a matter for the Dominions to arrange for themselves. If anything, the British attitude has been in the spirit of Winston Churchill's statement to intending emigrants in 1947: "Stay here and fight it out . . . Do not desert the old land. We cannot spare you."* Its first post-war agreement with Australia in 1947 provided for it to bear half the cost of migrant passages; in 1950 it reduced this to a maximum grant of £25 per adult; in 1951 it changed to a maximum annual contribution of £500,000; and in 1954 this sum was reduced to £150,000, at which it has remained.† Australia has cheerfully made up the extra cost. This is because it is getting a bargain: immigrants consist largely of skilled and semi-skilled workmen in early middle life, with their young families. Such immigrants provide labour for Australia's growing manufacturing industries, and children who can quickly be moulded in whatever way is appropriate. Britain, on the other hand, is losing skills and other resources which are only inadequately made up by immigration into Britain from the West Indies, India and Pakistan.

Here are figures of emigration from Britain to the Four.‡

Emigration from Britain to the Four, Alternate Years, 1947–61

Year	To Australia	To Canada	To New Zealand	To S. Africa
1947	14,573	40,401	(1947–8) 6,352	11,611
1949	53,613	20,737	(1949–50) 10,075	n.a.
1951	57,429	31,559	n.a.	5,893
1953	25,767	46,791	n.a.	5,416
1955	36,638	29,382	(1955–6) 11,960	4,444
1957	38,092	108,989	(1957–8) 13,162	4,723
1959	43,959	18,222	(1959–60) 9,738	3,782
1961	46,825	11,870	(1961–2) 12,203	2,323
1963	62,293	24,603	(1963–4) 16,364	n.a.

* Quoted ibid., p. 97.   † Ibid., p. 41.

‡ Sources: Commonwealth Bureau of Census and Statistics, Canberra, *Demography Bulletin; Canada Year Book;* Dept. of Statistics, Wellington, *Population, Migration and Building Statistics;* Bureau of Census and Statistics, South Africa, *Monthly Bulletin of Statistics;* 1963 figures from Cmnd. 2861.

It will be seen that Australia and New Zealand have been fairly steady in their reception of British migrants; Canada has been much more uneven. The huge Canadian figure of 1957 is connected by Canadian authorities with the effects of the Suez affair. Certainly, experience shows that British people are impelled towards emigration, or at least to make inquiries about it, by national crises of this kind; at periodic opinion polls, it has been shown that between 28 per cent and 42 per cent of British people would be interested in emigrating if they could.* They need some stimulus to take the matter further; this may come from international events, from national disturbances such as unemployment or continued bad weather, or from a change in their home circumstances. Dr. Appleyard's investigations of British families proceeding to Australia under assisted passages indicate that they are, on the whole, neither ill-housed nor threatened by unemployment. They are skilled and semi-skilled people who feel that they can do better for themselves overseas; they are drawn not so much by prospects of high wages as by changes in climate, better schooling and opportunities for their children, and a different class structure from the one they are accustomed to. Only about a fifth of them think of setting up in business for themselves; most expect to do the same jobs in Australia as in Britain, but in better surroundings. Unlike the rural migrants of earlier times, they are essentially urban in character, upbringing and expectations.

British migration to the Four is substantial, but it is matched by other sorts of emigration. Here are figures of the permanent arrivals in each of the Four between 1948 and 1957, showing the percentage from Britain : †

Country	Permanent arrivals from U.K.	Total permanent arrivals	U.K. %
Canada	431,993	1,533,494	28·2
Australia	413,836	1,220,613	33·9
S. Africa	71,551	162,345	44·1
N. Zealand	108,612	199,154	54·5

Britain thus provided a minority of immigrants to each of the Four except New Zealand. Continental Europe provided the rest, except

* Appleyard, op. cit., p. 105.
† Ibid., p. 23.

in Canada, where the movement to and fro across the American border creates a special situation.

The effects of migration on relations between Britain and the Four are extremely difficult to estimate. The great majority of those who go are permanently lost to Britain, although they may come back on visits and their children may make the journey out of curiosity in later times. The permanent return traffic is small. The outflow of migrants is offset to some extent by immigration into Britain from the West Indies, India and Pakistan, but the two groups cannot readily be substituted for one another. There is a closer substitution in the quite substantial migration of Australians, New Zealanders, South Africans and Canadians to Britain. While much of this is short-term, consisting of students and young people on working holidays, a significant proportion of these migrants stay in Britain, especially in the professional fields. Sometimes they are attracted by special incentives, like Australian dentists making money out of the National Health Service; more often they find the British environment and the prospects of advancement more attractive than what they could find at home. Britain thus gets a more varied population from the movements to and from its shores. The Old Dominions find, for their part, that British migrants melt quickly into their surroundings. They often come to live with relatives or friends; they have no language problems; their skills are usually highly saleable; and they are mostly immersed in their private affairs, especially their families, and not used to taking a prominent part in anything else. Now and then there are cases of protests from British migrants who think they have been deceived about the new land by promises made before they left; but these are rarer than one might think from reading the London press, and their effect is small.

To what extent does migration help to retain the "British character" of the Old Dominions? The question is worth asking, because this point figures regularly in post-war debates on migration in the British parliament.* There are certainly differences of outlook between British and non-British migrants in such fields as trade unionism and politics at large, and especially on the question of monarchy; a sizeable number of European migrants to Australia have failed to take out naturalization papers because it means swearing allegiance to Queen Elizabeth, whom they regard as Queen of Britain, not Queen of Australia. Those Yugoslavs who are still

* See the references ibid., p. 43.

bitter about Churchill's wartime support of Tito against Mihailo-
vich and the King are disinclined to accept Australia's monarchical
institutions, despite the Government's explanations. No doubt the
same happens elsewhere. If one considers such obvious links as
monarchy to be the effective links between Britain and Australia
or Canada or New Zealand, then these are promoted by British
migration—unless, as in South Africa, more powerful political
considerations cause the ex-British migrants to accept a republic.
The main point, however, is that the societies of the Old Dominions
are now formed in their own national shapes: *all* migrants must
conform to the local stereotypes, whether they come from Birming-
ham or Budapest. The kind of "character" which a migrant finds
when he steps ashore in Canada or Australia is the local character.
The extent to which migration is from this or that country is no
longer likely to change that character; it is now ingrained. To expect otherwise is to invite disillusionment. The misleading novels of
Nevil Shute, for example, with their suggestion that Australians are
at heart more British than the British, are a poor guide to anyone
trying to gauge the post-war character of Australia.

SOME OTHER CONNECTIONS

All the same, the cultures of the Old Dominions are still demon-
strably British in origin, apart from the obvious traditional exceptions of French Canada and Afrikaner South Africa, and newer
colonies of Europeans in the Canadian prairies and in small pockets
in Australia. The common background described in Chapter 1 is
still important, and is renewed by many current connections. These
are hard to catalogue and measure, but some of them may be mentioned.

Education and training are the most obvious. While Britain does
not take in many young people from Canada for further education,
because of closer opportunities in the United States, it takes in a
great many from Australia, New Zealand and English-speaking
South Africa. Post-war increases in university education in all the
countries in question have seen the graduate schools of London,
Oxford and Cambridge jostling with potential Ph.D.s from the Old
Dominions. The flow of British university teachers to these
countries has continued, except for interruption in the case of South
Africa on racial grounds; many posts in English-speaking South

African universities cannot be filled because British candidates are not forthcoming and local products prefer to try their luck in Britain itself. There has also been a massive flow of people from the Dominions seeking training and opportunities in the arts in Britain. Drama, music and the theatre are the most noteworthy. Sadler's Wells and Covent Garden are aware that Joan Sutherland and Marie Collier are Australian, while Inia Te Wiata comes from New Zealand; it is widely known that Tony Hancock's helper Bill Kerr is an Australian, but not so widely known that his hinderer, Sidney James, comes from South Africa. Australian painters, such as Sidney Nolan, have had much success in London.

In the complex of mass communications, comprising press, radio, television, films and books, the links between Britain and the Old Dominions are still strong, though much stronger in Australia and New Zealand than in the other two. The Commonwealth Press Rate still ensures that much overseas news is filtered through London before it gets to the newspapers in the Old Dominions, and British issues are given much prominence. The connections in sport are important: in cricket, athletics, golf, tennis and Rugby football the names of Australians, New Zealanders and South Africans are probably known to more British people than in any other sphere. Only Canada is omitted from this kind of connection, because it is outstanding in no sport that claims British attention. Britain still provides most of the books read in Australia, New Zealand and South Africa.

One can see connections in all these fields; it is much harder to see effects. The main one seems to be simply a continuance of connections which were established long ago and might have been expected to languish under the combined pressure of local nationalism in the Dominions and the attractions of the United States. The reasons why they do not are complex. Local nationalism, for example, works both ways: while it impels young Australians and New Zealanders to find new ways of painting or writing, and not stick to British models, it also impels them to issue a challenge for the attention of an older, more sophisticated and more profitable audience. London is still the place to make a reputation. The kind of tradition which makes even Americans wish to succeed at Wimbledon and Henley leads singers, actors, writers, painters and academics to try their luck in England, in spite of the keenest sense of national self-importance. Again, while the United States is highly attractive in some spheres (such as post-graduate education), it does not provide many of the opportunities that Britain does. Sometimes this is because of lack of facilities (it is much harder to get a national reputation there in music or the ballet); sometimes it is because living is cheaper in Britain, and people from the Dominions can get odd jobs while they are waiting to be noticed. It is also because there are resident colonies of Australians, New Zealanders and South Africans in London, willing to help the newcomer with tips on how to get to the top.

The fact of so much effort to succeed in Britain does not mean that young people from the Old Dominions regard British habits and standards as sacrosanct. It means rather that they wish to show that they can beat the British at their own games. It is also a reflection of the comparative isolation and remoteness of the Old Dominions, separated by great distances from the traditional centres of European culture. Slowly, local habits and standards become paramount. In the ordinary business of living, this process is largely complete. In the arts, which are in any case more truly international in their standards than any other pursuits, local standards are still not good enough. In professional organizations there may be separation from traditional associations for reasons of local politics and local nationalism—as in the conversion of the Australian branch of the British Medical Association into the Australian Medical Association in the 1950's—but connections with Britain remain strong, except in the case of Canada. The same is true of the Anglican and Nonconformist churches. The general effect is to strengthen past ties without hindering the development of local initiative.

SOME CONCLUSIONS

This chapter has been concerned with the ostensibly non-political aspects of the relationship between Britain and the Old Dominions since 1945. One's conclusions must be tentative; we are dealing with changes in things that mostly cannot be measured. But certain points are not likely to be disputed. Britain is clearly still an important country in all the spheres considered here. Only if we assume that *no other* country should be important do we have reason to be distressed—assuming that our aim as British people, or as Anglophile Canadians or New Zealanders, is that British influence should continue. The only other influence of consequence is the

United States, which, because it is rich and speaks English, is re-garded as a danger by many people who wish to maximize British influence. In Canada, obviously, the influence of the United States is paramount. It could not be otherwise. But British influence is still to be perceived, as is the desire to see it increase. Canada is in a different position from the other three overseas countries, because its location alongside the United States means that in so many matters of practical culture it must perforce adopt American ways, whether in sport or television. In South Africa the combination of unpopularity abroad and a determination at home to elevate Afrikaner symbols has meant some decline in the British connec-tion; developments in foreign affairs, as we saw in Chapter 7, are likely to accelerate this decline. In Australia and New Zealand, on the other hand, there are few external influences to compare with that of Britain, although the United States has a natural appeal to these countries, in which climate and society have so much in common with their American counterparts.

In economic matters Britain remains a reliable market and source of supply for each of the Four, though unable to satisfy more than a part of the rapidly growing demands of their increasingly diversi-fied economies. This particular aspect is seen to be most advanced in Australia, least in New Zealand. Only for New Zealand does British trade represent the difference between prosperity and de-pression; for the others it may represent the difference between high and rather lower levels of prosperity. The habits of war and post-war economic co-operation have been largely outgrown in the 1960's; but nothing is normal in economics, and they could con-ceivably be resurrected. If so, it would be in a modified form. It is unlikely that there will be any great leap forward in the co-ordina-tion of the British economy with those of the Four, apart from further growth in industries financed by British private capital. It is possible, however, that a general slump—if one ever comes—could bring the Sterling Area back into its siege condition.

In social affairs, connections remain strong where they were strong before; the flow of migration continues; Britain provides a haven and testing-ground for many Dominion people who might otherwise be condemned to provincialism and insularity at home. In this, as in many other respects, Britain is in the position of an elder brother who helps with his experience and savings, rather than a mother, as in the conventional images of the past. Britain gains from the exchange of peoples, though its gain is on the side of quality (in special skills and professional aptitudes), while the Old Dominions gain also in quantity, receiving people who can contribute directly to the immediate expansion of their economies.

There are, of course, real differences of substance in the economic and social connections of Britain with each of the Old Dominions. To a certain extent, these differences correspond to the development of national consciousness in each of the Four. The British connection is closest in New Zealand, which is widely regarded as having the least active sense of nationalism. Australia is nearer to national consciousness, and stands in a tenser relationship. Canada and South Africa stand farther away still from identification with Britain. But the British strain is both perceptible and indispensable in the societies of all Four.

9

THE CLIMATE OF CHANGE

THIS chapter is intended to give some examples of how relations have changed in the Commonwealth, especially as these affect Britain and the Four, and to indicate the sorts of issues now likely to arise amongst the countries considered in this book. The method is to take four major questions of the past decade—the Suez affair of 1956, the withdrawal from the Commonwealth of South Africa in 1961, Britain's attempt to enter the European Economic Community in 1961–2, and the issue of Southern Rhodesia in 1964–5. Of the three major matters, one is a matter of world politics, one of Commonwealth relations, and one of economics, but each has overtones of all these aspects. The fourth, that of Southern Rhodesia, is a tail-piece or coda to the South African one.

The reason for stressing the climate of change is that each of these issues has brought out relationships and policies which might not have been expected in 1945, certainly not in 1939. To some extent they measure the distances which the Four have travelled in adjusting to the post-war world, especially to the rise of the new nations, both in and out of the Commonwealth. They also show Britain going through the same process. At the same time, they show the prevalence and influence of former interests and ideas.

It seems appropriate at this point, before discussing the actual issues, to interpose another summary of changes in Dominion leadership, following the section in Chapter 5 which brought such events down to about 1949. It is assumed that readers are familiar with the changes in Britain from a Labour to a Conservative Government in 1951, and the subsequent changes from Churchill to Eden to Macmillan to Home, and the replacement of the Conservatives by Labour under Mr. Harold Wilson in the latter part of 1964.

DOMINION LEADERSHIP, 1949–65

In Canada the death of Mackenzie King in 1948 caused no interruption in the smooth operation of a Liberal Government which had been in office since 1935. King was succeeded by Mr. Louis St. Laurent, who had been Minister for External Affairs; it was under St. Laurent that Mr. Lester Pearson, as Minister for External Affairs, scored his most notable successes in the next nine years. The Conservatives, the main opposition party, remained lacking in effective leadership during most of this time. However, in 1957 they managed to emerge as a minority government under Mr. John Diefenbaker, a new party leader and the first Canadian Prime Minister whose ancestry was predominantly neither British nor French. In 1958 Mr. Diefenbaker went to the polls again and won the most complete victory in Canadian political history, securing 80 per cent of the seats in the House of Commons. The Liberals were temporarily reduced to very small numbers. At the next election, in 1962, the position returned to something like its 1957 state: the Conservatives were returned as a minority government, the Liberals improved their positions, but there were sizeable votes for the Social Credit and New Democratic parties. In 1963 the Liberals returned as a minority government under Mr. Pearson. Since 1957, Canada has been the least stable, politically speaking, of the Four.

The Australian situation provides a contrast. The government of Mr. (now Sir Robert) Menzies, elected in 1949, was still in power in 1965. The two parties forming this coalition, the Liberal and Country parties, had shown their capacity to work together with the minimum of friction. The official opposition, the Labour Party, led first by Dr. H. V. Evatt and then by Mr. A. A. Calwell, was greatly handicapped by a split in its ranks in the mid-1950's. This split produced a breakaway party, the Democratic Labour Party, which has consistently supported the Government. While this has not meant the election of any D.L.P. members to the House of Representatives, it has, because of the Australian system of preferential voting, given the Government the benefit of the votes cast for the D.L.P. Sir Robert has had a succession of Ministers for External Affairs, including Sir Percy Spender, Mr. (now Lord) Casey, Sir Garfield Barwick and Mr. Paul Hasluck. However, his own influence in external policy has been profound, especially in Commonwealth matters. In 1966 he retired, to be succeeded by Mr. Harold Holt.

New Zealand, which elected a National Party Government under Mr. Sidney Holland in 1948, retained this allegiance until 1957, when the Labour Party, led by Mr. Walter Nash, was returned with a very narrow majority. In 1960 Mr. Nash was defeated, his oponents being led by Mr. Keith Holyoake, who was still Prime Minister in 1965. New Zealand politics show little prospect of change: the range of issues is narrow, and the country does not have the kaleidoscopic regional and ethnic differences which help to explain the indecision of Canadian politics in recent years.

South Africa, having elected a Nationalist Government in 1948, has retained it, first under Dr. Malan and then under his successors, Mr. Strijdom and Dr. Verwoerd. The main opposition, the United Party, has been reduced in influence with each election; changes in leadership have been no help. Small groups such as the Progressive and Liberal Parties have had only minimal white support. There has been a perceptible shift of English-speaking voters towards the Government.

The period in question has been one of largely unrelieved prosperity in all four countries. Canada staggered somewhat between 1958 and 1962, with an increase in unemployment and devaluation of its currency, and New Zealand experienced balance of payments difficulties for a time; otherwise, however, they have all experienced high incomes and employment, a considerable expansion of their economies, and a steady retreat from the economic apprehensions which characterized them at the end of the war. These conditions and the universal dislike of Communism have caused radicalism to be at a discount, except for those forms which thrive on ethnic differences, such as separatism in Quebec and Afrikaner nationalism in South Africa.

SUEZ

The course of events over Suez is now fairly well known. My purpose here will be to emphasize its Commonwealth aspects, as those apply to the Four.* Briefly, however, here is a summary of the main happenings.

* Students of Commonwealth affairs must be deeply grateful to Professor James Eayrs for his commentary and selection of material in *The Commonwealth and Suez: A Documentary Survey* (London, 1964), on which this section relies heavily. There are also useful documents in Nicholas Mansergh (ed.), *Documents and Speeches on Commonwealth Affairs 1952–1962* (London, 1963), Section II C. Attention must also be paid to Terence Robertson, *Crisis: The Inside Story of the Suez Conspiracy* (London, 1965), since he says "the manuscript was read by officials of Canada's Department of External Affairs who

In 1956 the last British troops left the Suez Canal Zone, following an agreement with Egypt in 1954. At about the same time, the American Government announced that it would not help finance the Aswan High Dam for Egypt, since Egypt did not seem able to provide the necessary resources. A week later, on July 26, 1956, Colonel Nasser seized the Suez Canal Company under a nationalization order and announced. that the Canal (which was due to revert to Egypt in 1968) would help to pay for the dam. There was indignation in both Britain and France, paralleled in the other countries with which we are concerned here: it was widely felt that the canal should not be under the control of one country, but should have some international quality in its management. In Britain, both Government and Opposition expressed grave concern. The question of the use of force against Egypt soon arose, to be widely debated in Britain. The United States proposed a conference of interested nations, which met in London in August without the presence of Egypt. A mission from a majority of these nations, led by Mr. Menzies (who had been nominated at the suggestion of New Zealand) submitted to Colonel Nasser proposals for an international authority, but with no success; the Egyptian Government was adamant that there must be Egyptian ownership and control. It was then proposed by Britain, France and the United States (at the latter's instigation) that a Users' Association should operate the canal; however, the United States had no suggestions about what was to be done if Colonel Nasser would not support the plan, whereas the British and French clearly expected the Users' Association to be able to enforce its demands. Anglo-French military preparations in the Mediterranean were intensified. It is clear now that talks had begun between France and Israel over the possibility of improving Israel's position, and snatching the canal by use of arms. Whether the British Government was privy to these, and, if so, at what stage, is still in dispute. In the event, on October 30 Israeli forces entered Egypt. On the following day, after an ultimatum to Israel and Egypt to stop fighting and to withdraw ten miles from the Suez Canal, British and French forces began their attack on Egypt. The U.N. in New York was thrown

corrected it in detail where Canadian participation is concerned", and that Mr. Pearson also checked its accuracy on the Canadian role (pp. ix-x). Sir Robert Menzies has preserved seven of his statements in *Speech is of Time* (London, 1958), pp. 81–180.

into a tumult of activity and recrimination, resulting in a complete separation of the United States from Britain and France. Largely because of Canadian effort, a proposal for a United Nations Emergency Force was brought into being. Under pressure from the U.N. and the Asian members of the Commonwealth, and faced by a run on the pound and Russian threats, Britain decided on a cease-fire; France agreed. The U.N.E.F. was set up in due course, and took over from British forces in the Suez area. The canal was cleared by a U.N. salvage operation. Egypt remained in complete control of the canal itself, and has continued to be so.

It is clear that the British Government was actuated by the highest motives, although some of its supporters enjoyed the use of force because it made them feel that Britain was great again. To the Government the analogy between Nasser and Hitler was compelling: if Nasser were stopped as Hitler had not been, disaster might be nipped in the bud. If Nasser and the Russians got their thumbs on Britain's windpipe through control of the supply of oil, this could reduce Britain to the most minor status.* To overthrow Nasser might mean the stabilization of the Middle East. The Government does not seem to have been greatly concerned about the prospect of a break with the United States, perhaps because of the consistently bad name which Mr. Dulles, the Secretary of State, had earned in official (and other) British circles; nor does it seem to have been worried about Indian and other Asian opposition. It would have liked to get full Commonwealth support, but did not regard this as essential. It was pleased to get support from Mr. Menzies, and invited him into Cabinet meetings; but it either misunderstood the position of the Canadian Government on the use of force, or did not regard it as important.†

The British Government met considerable opposition at home, once the possibility of its sanctioning the use of force against Egypt became evident. Mr. Gaitskell, the Leader of the Opposition, soon took an uncompromising line against force, and was supported by the kind of opinion represented by the *Manchester Guardian* and *Observer*. Amongst the four countries with which we are concerned, Britain was supported in strong terms by Australia

---

* See Sir Anthony Eden, *Full Circle* (London, 1960), *passim*; see also the revealing conversations by the Canadian diplomat, Mr. Norman Robertson, with Lord Home and Sir Ivone Kirkpatrick, in Terence Robertson, op. cit., pp. 88–90.

† Eayrs, op. cit., p. 89.

under Mr. Menzies; supported in terms a little less strong by New Zealand; not supported by Canada; and not supported by South Africa. No other Commonwealth member supported it. "Support" here means declaring that the British policy was the right one to follow. Let us now look at the policies of the Four in more detail.

The official Australian position was clear and forthright.* Mr. Menzies was in close touch with the British Government throughout; moreover, he had the experience of his journey to Cairo to sustain him. The Egyptian act had been unlawful; the Canal should not be under the control of one man or one country; it was absurd to say that force could be employed only when the U.N. sanctioned it; Britain and France were great powers with high standards and great missions, and they should not be put in the dock at the U.N. Mr. Menzies found a good deal of support for these views in Australia, where Egyptians are not highly regarded.† It was customary to think of the Suez Canal as a "life-line", because trade with Britain went through it. Moreover, Colonel Nasser's receipt of arms from the Russians had been widely publicized. The spectacle of Britain at bay in the Security Council was odious to many

---

* For the debate in Australia, see W. Macmahon Ball, "The Australian Reaction to the Suez Crisis", *Australian Journal of Politics and History*, Vol. II, No. 2.

† The Egyptian case was not aided by the action of an Egyptian crowd which in Port Said tore the Anzac memorial from its granite base and damaged the figures. This memorial, conceived in 1916 as one commemorating the Australian and New Zealand Mounted Division, was erected in 1932. In 1960, after repair, it was re-erected at Albany, in Western Australia, overlooking the harbour in which the first Australian and New Zealand convoy assembled before sailing for Egypt in 1914. The utterance of Mr. (now Sir William) Yeo of the Returned Servicemen's League in New South Wales was not typical in its extreme language, but was to some extent representative in its sentiments: "The Egyptian rabble's recent action in damaging the famed Port Said memorial to Australian and New Zealand war dead was a calculated insult to Australia and New Zealand which ex-servicemen of these countries will find difficult to forgive – and certainly not forget . . . Frustrated by the vigilance and prompt action of Britain and France in their power-drunk bid to seize absolute control of the Suez Canal . . . the Egyptians have vented their own particularly unpleasant type of spleen on the honoured dead of our country. It is difficult to imagine that accomplishment of their hate-inspired defilement of the memorial sated their crazed emotions, but their act has served to illustrate to the whole world the mentality of these people who would have us believe they are capable of administering justly a waterway important to all people . . . For the profanity which they inflicted, they must stand abhorred by all decent peoples." (*Reveille*, Sydney, February 1957.)

Australians, especially of the older generations; they found the idea of not supporting the British case unacceptable.

However, there was also opposition. It has been persistently reported that Mr. Casey, the Minister for External Affairs, was much troubled at the consequences in Asia of the British action; this has not been confirmed. The Labour Party's opposition, as expressed by Dr. Evatt, was based to a considerable extent on his deep belief in the U.N. To him it was a remedy for the world's ills; the idea of decisive action outside it, or of flouting its resolutions, was profoundly disturbing to him. His party tended to hew to this narrow line, rather than to emphasize the damage caused by the rift between Britain and the United States; this latter point came home to the Government when Mr. Casey was refused admission to President Eisenhower in Washington. There was a certain amount of criticism on grounds of the strain which the British action had imposed on Commonwealth bonds, especially with India. It is likely, however, that Mr. Menzies's line was acceptable to most Australians.

The same can be said of the line taken by the Government of New Zealand, which, while milder than Mr. Menzies's, was still resolutely in support of Britain. Mr. Holland was quicker to deplore the Anglo-American rift than Mr. Menzies, and more moderate in his condemnation of Egypt. His Minister for External Affairs, Mr. Macdonald, was rather harsher in tone. But New Zealand, unlike Australia, was quick to see the advantages of the Canadian suggestions for a U.N. Emergency Force, and proposed to recruit a contingent for it. When the New Zealand offer had to be declined by the U.N., the Government accepted the rebuff with a good grace. Mr. Nash, the leader of the Opposition, did not take anything like the same defiant position as Dr. Evatt. New Zealand, in fact, showed itself to be profoundly British in this crisis, but without ostentation.

The Canadian position was the most interesting of all. Here much rested upon the personality and character of Mr. Pearson. Canada tried to act as a bridge between Britain and the United States, a traditional role but one especially difficult in these circumstances:

"Although both Canada and the United States disagreed with British and French policy at that time, there was considerable difference in their postures. The official American demeanour was one of cold anger, and at the United Nations involved a virtual severance of personal relations, but there was much more of sorrow than of anger in the Canadian position. Contacts of the frankest, and in their own way sympathetic, kind were maintained throughout between British and Canadian leaders, and with Indians and Pakistanis as well. As the Americans and British in a critical situation were barely speaking to each other, the Canadian Minister for External Affairs, Mr. Pearson, and his associates, had furiously to interpret. Canada maintained a middle position in the dispute because, although the Canadian Government had been appalled at British and French actions, it became appalled also by the petulant and rudderless policy of the United States as the crisis wore on."*

The essence of the Canadian position was that Britain and France, in using force as they had done, had misinterpreted their whole position in relation to the United States and to the new nations of Asia; they were trying something which could not succeed, and would bring down retribution on themselves and perhaps on others as well. In particular, the Canadian leaders thought the Commonwealth might break apart, leaving adrift those Asian members which it had been Canada's special design to cultivate. The rift with the United States was seen by the Canadian Government as foolish and avoidable; there had been plenty of advance notice that the United States would not acquiesce in the action which was taken. In this matter, as in so many others, Canada was perhaps open to the criticism that it was preaching virtue to others when it was not subject to the same temptations to vice as they were. When the British High Commissioner in Ottawa reflected to Pearson that the world had not realized that Britain would always fight to maintain the flow of oil, Pearson replied, "Canada would never support the use of force to keep oil flowing in any direction."† Canada had oil springing up in its own backyard; it would never be called upon to fight for it. In such circumstances virtue was easy. Nevertheless, the Canadian position was not simply that of condemnation of Britain, in spite of Mr. Saint Laurent's incautious reference to the

* John W. Holmes, "The Relationship in Alliance and in World Affairs", in John Sloan Dickey (ed.), *The United States and Canada* (Englewood Cliffs, 1964), p. 112. Mr. Holmes was a Canadian representative at the U.N. at the time.

† Robertson, *Crisis: The Inside Story of the Suez Conspiracy* (London, 1965), p. 333.

fact that "the era when the supermen of Europe could govern the whole world has and is coming pretty close to an end", which was made much of by his Conservative opponents in the election which followed.* In fact, Canada, while not supporting Britain, did not condemn it either; the Canadian aim was to prevent British isolation at the U.N. turning into outright and repeated condemnation. Mr. Pearson is quoted directly:

> "There was only one course—to do our best to ensure that the British and French action was not examined by itself under a spotlight narrowly focused on recent events alone. I felt it should be examined in the fullest possible perspective against the situation that had led to the intervention, and against the past records of both countries. It was clear even then that if they had suffered considerable provocation at the hands of Egypt, they had endured too the frustrating sequels to what undoubtedly comprised the worst chapter in Dulles's diplomatic career. I regretted they thought it necessary to take the keeping of peace into their own hands, but it was equally obvious that the peace needed keeping in the Middle East."†

This was why Pearson persistently stressed the need for constructive action on a U.N. force rather than mere condemnation of the Anglo-French action; and it is certainly the case that his insistence helped to swing the U.N. away from an orgy of righteous indignation into more constructive channels. The fact that General Burns, a Canadian soldier, was available on the spot to head the U.N.E.F. was a piece of good luck; but the delicacy with which Burns, Pearson and the Canadian Government handled the difficulty of making acceptable to Egypt the use of Canadian regiments with names such as the Queen's Own was an example of fine diplomatic skill.

To those who considered that a Dominion ought to support Britain through thick and thin, whatever the issues, the Canadian Government's actions seemed reprehensible. There were plenty of these in Canada itself. An Australian professor who visited Canada in 1958 remarked that "during some fifteen or sixteen lectures to

---

* James Eayrs, *The Commonwealth and Suez: A Documentary Survey* (London, 1964), pp. 417 and 383–4. See also his *Canada in World Affairs 1955–57* (Toronto, 1959), pp. 182–93.

† Robertson, op. cit., p. 180.

Canadian groups in different parts of the Dominion I invariably found that, during the discussion period, someone in the audience would rise to make sure that I understood how deeply he 'and a great many more Canadians' deplored the weakening of Canada's unity with Britain over Suez in 1956".* It is difficult to tell how much of this kind of opinion was simple traditionalism in English-Canadians, and how much was the product of careful consideration of the actual circumstances. At all events, any coolness which might have existed between Britain and Canada was soon ended. When Mr. Macmillan succeeded Mr. Eden as British Prime Minister, he took action to see first President Eisenhower and then Canadian Ministers at Bermuda in March 1957. The meetings were happy, though there remained some difference of opinion about the value and functions of the U.N.†

South Africa's first reaction to the nationalization of the Canal was that "it is best to keep our heads out of the beehive".‡ This remained the characteristic South African posture. It was traditional South African policy to resist attempts to bring foreign troops into Africa; at the same time, South Africa could have no sympathy with any decisions taken or prompted by the Afro-Asian powers at the U.N. South Africa's actions were practical, in providing port facilities during the period in which the Canal was closed because of Egyptian ships sunk in it. Some years later, however, Dr. Verwoerd said he thought there would be less unrest in the world, especially in Africa, if Britain had been able to go ahead with "the policy which she had believed to be the correct one".§

The attitudes which we have seen the various Dominion governments adopting were framed partly by their basic approaches to the Commonwealth and the British connection, and partly by their sense of national interest and their appreciation of world events. The first aspect is as true of Pearson as of Menzies: while Menzies based his line on co-operation with Britain, Pearson based his upon concern for Britain's future influence and for the preservation of the Commonwealth in its existing form. National interests were assessed in all cases, even that of Australia. To this extent

* Fred Alexander, *Canadians and Foreign Policy* (Melbourne, 1960), p. 138.
† Eayrs, *The Commonwealth and Suez: A Documentary Survey* (London, 1964) p. 379.
‡ Mr. Strijdom, quoted ibid., p. 17.
§ Ibid., p. 394.

there is considerable similarity between the various governments' ways of deciding what to do, in spite of their being impelled in different directions. When one looks at the matter in terms of long-range judgement, however, the greater wisdom seems to lie with Pearson and Gaitskell, not with Menzies and Eden. Pearson and Gaitskell were aware of the consequences likely to follow from the clash with the United States and the loss of Asian good will; both feared the isolation into which Britain was in fact driven. Menzies and Eden, especially the latter, were misled by historical analogies (the Hitler and Mussolini analogies were clearly influential with both), and took a short-sighted romantic view of Egyptian incapacity, wickedness and alliance with Russia, while showing the same romanticism in their apparent belief that Britain's "moment" in the Middle East could be renewed and prolonged.*

So far as the Commonwealth is concerned, the outstanding point is that, of the five countries considered here, only Canada seemed worried about the effect of British actions upon the survival of general Commonwealth good will. British considerations were overwhelmingly domestic, European and Middle Eastern, with overtones of concern (but mostly impatience) about the United States. Australia and New Zealand were limited to their ties with Britain. South Africa made a face about the lack of Commonwealth consultation which had been such a feature of the affair,† but otherwise kept its counsel. Yet, of the lasting effects of Suez, perhaps the greatest was to warn the British Government that actions which could be dubbed "colonialist" ought to be avoided, that Afro-Asian opinion must be wooed, and that the U.N. must be taken seriously, even though it frequently operated in ways which did not suit British interests. The further development of the Commonwealth through the widening of African membership became a prime British concern. None of these results can be attributed simply to Suez; they were already being brought to bear through other causes. But the Suez experience undoubtedly taught the British Government a lesson; and it was a lesson along the line which Mr. Pearson and Mr. St. Laurent had tried to inculcate while the Suez episode was in progress.

* See Elizabeth Monroe, *Britain's Moment in the Middle East* 1914–1956 (London, 1963), especially pp. 202–6.

† See Nicholas Mansergh (ed.). *Documents and Speeches on Commonwealth Affairs 1914–1956* (London, 1963), pp. 519–20 and *passim*.

SOUTH AFRICA'S DEPARTURE

The departure of South Africa from the Commonwealth in 1961 directly affected Britain and the Four. All were faced with problems of decision about the hostility towards South African racial policy of the Afro-Asian members of the Commonwealth. For South Africa, the problem was whether to get out voluntarily or wait to be thrown out; for Britain it was whether to back South Africa as a founder-member, at the possible expense of the loss of new and future members; for Australia, Canada and New Zealand it was which side to choose.

The course of events has been gone over elsewhere,* but a brief recapitulation may help. As we have seen, in the 1950's South Africa's racial policy became the object of increasing execration at the U.N. It was eventually disowned there, and regarded as a matter properly subject to U.N. action, by both the United States and Britain. Within Britain itself opinion had hardened against South Africa as the details of *apartheid* became more apparent. Moreover, a number of British African territories had either acquired independence or would soon do so; the question of future relations with them was complicated by South Africa, since they regarded *apartheid* as an international matter which they, as present or future members of the Commonwealth, had a right to question. The 1960 meeting of Commonwealth Prime Ministers was the first for three years. Two influences focused its attention on South Africa. One was the statement that South Africa intended to conduct a referendum on the question of a republic; the other was that Tunku Abdul Rahman, the Prime Minister of Malaya, was outspoken in his attacks on *apartheid*. The meeting decided that South Africa should seek permission to remain in the Commonwealth on becoming a republic; it also arranged informal discussions between Mr. Louw, the South African Minister for External Affairs, and other representatives, on the whole racial question.

By the time the next Prime Ministers' meeting took place in 1961, the referendum had been held, showing a small majority of

---

* See S. A. de Smith, "The Commonwealth and South Africa" in *University of Malaya Law Review*, Vol. 3, No. 2, and two articles in *Journal of Commonwealth Political Studies:* J. D. B. Miller, "South Africa's Departure", Vol. I, No. 1 and Peter Harnetty, "Canada, South Africa and the Commonwealth", Vol. II, No. 1. Mansergh, op. cit., Section I D. has useful documents.

the South African electorate in favour of a republic. At the meeting Dr. Verwoerd brought forward his proposal that South Africa should remain in the Commonwealth on becoming a republic; as already shown in Chapter 6, other such proposals had been approved. There was intense discussion for some four days. At first it seemed possible that all sections might be assuaged by issuing a joint communiqué in which, while some members stated their objections to *apartheid*, South Africa was allowed to put its viewpoint. But it became clear that this would not satisfy the Afro-Asian members, and that some were prepared to withdraw from the Commonwealth if South Africa stayed in. The minor but telling point that South Africa was not prepared to receive diplomatic missions from African fellow-members of the Commonwealth became a point of substance. In the end, Dr. Verwoerd withdrew the request which had precipitated the discussion, and announced that his country would become a republic and would also leave the Commonwealth.

The attitudes taken by Britain, Australia, New Zealand and Canada were something of an index to what they thought of the Commonwealth. The British position was not fixed, but varied with the movement of debate. It was in some contrast to the determined and untenable position which Mr. Eden had taken over Suez, although the issues are not strictly comparable. Mr. Macmillan's main concern seemed to be to sustain the Commonwealth as an institution in the midst of new problems and situations. If possible, he hoped to retain South Africa as a member, but it is clear that there was no determination to keep South Africa at all costs, especially if this meant losing some of the new members or some who might become members soon. Thus, the British Government was not prepared to uphold the former principle of Commonwealth meetings that matters which any member objected to would not be discussed. Its approach was multi-lateral, not bilateral. It wished to dissociate itself from the practice of *apartheid*; this, no doubt, South Africa would have accepted, and had already accepted in other contexts. It is plain that Mr. Macmillan hoped to combine the discussion of South Africa's racial policy with a generally conciliatory approach, designed to appeal to all members' sense of the value of the Commonwealth in expressing divergence as well as unity; but he and his Government were also firmly attached to the idea of multi-racialism, and they were not to be manœuvred into a position which could be represented as support for South Africa's racial policy. It is likely that, if most Commonwealth

Prime Ministers had supported South Africa's remaining, Britain would have done so too. In the event, the majority against South Africa was substantial, and Britain agreed with a good grace to South Africa's withdrawal—especially since this meant that, technically speaking, no expulsion had occurred. The preservation of the Commonwealth as a body to which black African states could readily belong was a paramount British objective; it was attained.

The Australian position was firm, as over Suez. It was expressed by Mr. Menzies in terms which recalled to many his position on the former issue. According to Sir Roy Welensky, who was presumably the most favourably disposed to South Africa of those present:

> "the way in which this decision was forced by the new members of the Commonwealth and calmly accepted by the old—with the exception of Australia—showed how far and how quickly we had travelled down the road to dissolution. The British Government's policy, for all the fine words in which Mr. Macmillan tried to wrap it up, was one of naked appeasement."[*]

Leaving aside the judgement in this statement, it indicates what was apparent at the time, that Mr. Menzies was Dr. Verwoerd's only major supporter. Mr. Menzies's ground was that *apartheid* was a matter of domestic jurisdiction, and not one on which the Prime Ministers ought to condemn South Africa. He disapproved of *apartheid* as a policy, but thought it was South Africa's business. It is likely that he had in mind the possibility that, if South Africa could be indicted on this point in 1961, Australia might be indicted on its immigration policy in the future. He was evidently not so much concerned about the preservation of the Commonwealth as Mr. Macmillan, if by that we mean the preservation of a Commonwealth in which the black African states would be willing members; he was more concerned about the right of the older members to be preserved from badgering and propaganda by the newer ones.

On this issue New Zealand and Australia diverged. Mr. Holyoake was attending his first Prime Ministers' meeting (Mr. Nash had been present in 1960), and was somewhat strange to the business; his predecessor had taken no clear line on the previous year's discussions, but had, if anything, expressed pleasure that the discussions of *apartheid* took place informally and not as part of the

---

[*] Sir Roy Welensky, *Welensky's 4000 Days* (London, 1964), p. 304.

R

normal meetings.* However, Mr. Holyoake seems to have been strong-minded in his refusal to support South Africa. After the conference he said South Africa's racial policy

> "to most of us seemed incompatible with the multi-racial character and principles on which the Commonwealth is founded. In particular the Asian and African members of the Commonwealth could not ignore the implications of *apartheid*, for them and thus for the Commonwealth as a whole when faced with this specific application for South Africa's continued membership.
>
> I believe the decision that was taken will in the long run strengthen the Commonwealth and enable it to continue expanding and embracing within its membership the new and emergent nations of all races that are rapidly approaching independence. It is a decision which we in New Zealand with our multi-racial population and our opposition to racial discrimination in all its forms cannot cavil at".†

New Zealand had had its own difficulties in regard to South Africa, arising from a decision not to take Maori players on a Rugby Union tour of that country, in case they suffered racial discrimination; this became a major issue, taken up by church leaders and others, and contributed to the generally unfavourable press which South Africa had in New Zealand, as in Canada and Australia. Mr. Holyoake seems to have been glad of the opportunity to support the British position, and, at the same time, demonstrate New Zealand's support for multi-racialism.

The Canadian position was, as at Suez, compounded less of concern for Canada's immediate interests than of concern for the future of the Commonwealth, in spite of the change from a Liberal to a Conservative Government under Mr. Diefenbaker. The Canadian Prime Minister stood out amongst the white representatives as a firm oponent of the South African position. He had not given much notice of this at the previous year's meetings, when he had been concerned to maintain the principle that the Prime Minis-

---

* *External Affairs Review*, Vol. X, No. 5, p. 25.

† Ibid., Vol. XI, No. 3. It is perhaps significant that, while this issue carried statements by Mr. Macmillan, Mr. Diefenbaker, Mr. Nehru and Sir Abubakar Tafawa Balewa, and by Dr. Verwoerd, it carried none by Mr. Menzies. I am afraid that I misrepresented the New Zealand position, through ignorance, in the article cited at the head of this section; I hope the quotation from Mr. Holyoake will make recompense.

ters should not interfere in the internal affairs of other Commonwealth members. During the interval, however, he reacted sharply to a kite flown in South Africa to the effect that, if South Africa became a republic, the Prime Ministers of Britain, Canada and Australia had said they would give a lead in retaining South Africa in the Commonwealth. He said "most unequivocally" that he had said nothing to justify such a view.* It became increasingly clear that he intended to take action against South Africa at the coming conference; what form this would take was not clear, but it was suggested that he might propose a Commonwealth Declaration of Rights, along the lines of that which he had long pressed for in Canada. In the event, Mr. Diefenbaker took a lead in combating the South African arguments, and maintained strongly that there could be nothing automatic about consent to South Africa's remaining; it had to be contingent on better behaviour in racial policy.

"I pointed out that we were opposed to racial discrimination and made it clear that I could not approve any formula or solution which did not maintain beyond any doubt that non-discrimination in respect of race and colour is an essential principle of the Commonwealth association."†

In particular, Mr. Diefenbaker sided with Nigeria and India in calling for stronger condemnation of South Africa's policies in the draft communiqué which, it was hoped, the Prime Ministers would be able to issue; this was one of the deciding points in determining the South African withdrawal.

Mr. Diefenbaker did not escape criticism from South Africa. Dr. Verwoerd referred to racial discrimination in Canada in one of his final statements, and Mr. Louw said soon after of Mr. Diefenbaker: "He has been losing ground in Canada and is pandering to the anti-South African campaign carried on in the Canadian press as well as in clerical and ultra-liberalistic circles."‡ This may have been so; but the widespread support which Mr Diefenbaker got from both sides in his parliament when he reported back to it (very much in contrast with the stormy time Mr. Menzies had) suggests

* Peter Harnetty, "Canada, South Africa and the Commonwealth", *Journal of Commonwealth Political Studies, Vol II*, No. 1, p. 37.
† Canada, *House of Commons Debates*, Vol. 105. No. 70, March 17, 1961.
‡ Quoted Harnetty, op. cit., p. 41.

that Canadian opinion was more unified in this matter than Mr.
Louw believed, and that Mr. Louw's criticism met no answering
strain in Canada itself. No doubt Mr. Diefenbaker's stand was moti-
vated in part by his keen interest in questions of civil rights. But it
was also in line with that determination to see the point of view of
the Afro-Asian members of the Commonwealth, and work with
them whenever possible, which had been characteristic of Mr.
Pearson over Suez. What enabled Diefenbaker to take the line he
did in 1961, while attacking Pearson's in 1956, was that in 1961
there was no desertion of Britain in supporting the Afro-Asians.
The British Government's position was, in fact, very much like
Diefenbaker's, but not expressed with verve until after the conference was over, by the Commonwealth Secretary, Mr. Sandys:

> "Everywhere else outside South Africa, governments are trying,
> more or less successfully, progressively to eliminate racial dis-
> crimination between their citizens. In South Africa, on the other
> hand, discrimination and segregation have been elevated into
> a principle, an objective of policy, something to be proud of,
> an inspiring ideal.
>
> Anyone who attended the Prime Ministers' Conference last
> week must have felt that on this subject Dr. Verwoerd was talk-
> ing a totally different language from that of the rest of his col-
> leagues. He is deliberately trying to swim against the whole
> current of world thought. He is trying to put history into reverse.
> It may be said that, however wrong and ill-conceived *apartheid*
> may be, it is South Africa's internal affair and does not affect her
> external relations with other members of the Commonwealth. It
> must, however, be recognized that *apartheid* has aroused deep
> emotions throughout the world, and has ceased to be a matter
> of purely domestic concern."*

The complexities of the British position are, in fact, the most
interesting aspects of this question. Was it "naked appeasement",
as Sir Roy Welensky said, and did it mark "the road to dissolution", as he suggested? The answer is yes, only if we assume that
the Commonwealth's essential nature was that of an association of
white settler communities with their mother country, the sort of
association which white Rhodesians found acceptable. It had been
that sort of body; it was now changing rapidly; from the British

* *Hansard*, March 22, 1961, cols. 528–9.

Government's standpoint, there was more value in the new form than in the old. A published statement by Mr. Julius Nyerere, to the effect that he could not expect to bring Tanganyika, his country, into the Commonwealth if South Africa was there, had a notable influence on the conference.* South Africa had become an increasing embarrassment within the Commonwealth. Legal and economic connections with Britain could be (and were to be) safeguarded by special action if South Africa left the Commonwealth. There was, in fact, nothing for the British Government to gain from keeping South Africa in. Much the same reasoning prevailed in Canada and New Zealand. The main effects of the 1961 crisis were to free these countries of an embarrassment, and the English-speaking South Africans of a vestigial "loyalty" which was no longer vital to them.

BRITAIN'S ATTEMPT TO ENTER THE E.E.C.

The question of British entry into the European Economic Community, which preoccupied those concerned with Commonwealth relations in 1961 and 1962, was a different sort of question from the two examined above. No single clear issue was involved. Instead, it was a matter of continual discussion at two levels: one the cloudy level of high policy, entailing speculative forecasts about the future of Europe and of the world; and the other the humdrum level of hard bargaining over the advantages to be gained or lost over things such as pigmeats and tapioca. Australia, New Zealand, Canada and (to a much lesser extent) South Africa were involved in close consideration of numerous detailed points, each of which affected some particular domestic interest. They and Britain had to weigh one economic possibility against another, and then to weigh economic against political possibilities; moreover, this had to be done in an atmosphere in which, as in most trade talks, the minutest details seemed to take up all the time. Very real political issues were latent in the situation, but they were distant and difficult to see with any clarity; moreover, they had to be expressed with so man "ifs" and "buts" and "assumings" that it is no wonder a great many people were bewildered by the whole affair.

* See J. D. B. Miller, "South Africa's Departure" (*Journal of Commonwealth Political Studies*, Vol. I, No. 1), for this point and the text of the Nyerere statement.

Another aspect of Britain's attempt to enter the E.E.C. was that, unlike the Suez and South Africa affairs, it tended to unite the old and new members of the Commonwealth against Britain. When the Commonwealth Economic Consultative Council met at Accra in September 1961, its communiqué was quite unlike those usually issued at Commonwealth meetings: it openly stated a series of objections to the course which Britain intended to pursue.* Apart from Britain, "all other Commonwealth representatives expressed grave apprehension and concern regarding the possible results of the initiative taken by the United Kingdom"; "most Commonwealth countries questioned whether the United Kingdom . . . could possibly secure in the proposed negotiations an agreement which would protect Commonwealth interests adequately and effectively"; "because of the inseparable nature of economic and political relationships within the Commonwealth and because of the political and institutional objectives of the European Economic Community and the terms of the Treaty of Rome, it was feared by the other Commonwealth countries that United Kingdom membership in the European Economic Community would fundamentally alter the relationship between the United Kingdom and Commonwealth countries, indeed this relationship might be so imperilled as to weaken the cohesion of the Commonwealth as a whole and thus reduce its effectiveness as a world instrument for understanding, prosperity and peace". Ministers from Canada, Australia and New Zealand set their hands to these disturbing sentiments.

The reason was that all had something to lose if Britain entered the E.E.C. in terms of the Treaty of Rome, which had been drawn up to provide for an economic community of six countries in Western Europe which would gradually achieve free trade within its borders while keeping barriers against goods from outside; and which would operate a common agricultural policy, whereby food from outside would be admitted only after all the food grown within the community had been satisfactorily disposed of. This latter point was the most disturbing to Canada, Australia and New Zealand. As we have seen, they were not dependent on the British market to the same extent, New Zealand being the most affected; but they all grew food ("temperate foodstuffs", in the language of E.E.C.) which had free entry to the British market

* See the extract in Nicholas Mansergh (ed.), *Documents and Speeches on Commonwealth Affairs 1952–1962* (London, 1963), pp. 650–51. The section contains a number of other helpful documents.

and in many cases enjoyed preferences. If Britain joined E.E.C., preferences would be exercised against them in favour of French farmers in particular. So the Australian Minister for Trade, Mr. John McEwen, thundered to his Country Party Conference in June, 1961 :

"It would be unthinkable for Australians to contemplate that foreigners should obtain a preferred position in the United Kingdom market; that, by any contrivance, foreigners should receive higher prices for the same commodities as the Commonwealth countries sell to Britain."*

This was the basis of their concern about Britain's entry. The Asian and African members of the Commonwealth had different concerns again, about tropical products and textiles; but they could join with the three Old Dominions in a common dislike of the intended British move.

From the standpoint of the British Government, these were troublesome objections, but they were not sufficient to prevent an attempt at reconciling British, Commonwealth and European interests. Britain's trade with Europe was growing at a faster rate than its trade with the Commonwealth; moreover, the E.E.C. was a going concern which would steadily raise its tariff walls against British goods unless Britain got in behind them. There were difficulties about agriculture, both British and Commonwealth, but perhaps the rapid economic growth of Europe would take care of these, by providing an expanding market in which all could share. The matter was not simply economic. There were political gains to be made too. Mr. Macmillan used to tell his Commonwealth critics that he had seen two wars start in Europe and wanted to prevent a third; if Britain became part of Europe, economically first and (in an undefined way) politically later, British influence could help to keep the nations of Europe at peace. Britain needed Europe, and Europe needed Britain.

The British decision to apply for membership of the E.E.C. was announced by Mr. Macmillan on July 31 1961, shortly after he

* Speech of 21 June, 1961; *Current Notes*, Vol. 32, No. 6, p. 53. Mr. McEwen's use of the term "foreign" is selective. When speaking of other countries getting into the British market, he calls them "foreigners"; when objecting to the growth of overseas capital in Australian industry, most of which is British, he calls it "foreign".

had sent Mr. Sandys to see the Australian, New Zealand and Canadian Governments. Negotiations would proceed with the E.E.C. Commission over the difficulties arising from Britain's obligations to the Commonwealth and European Free Trade Area countries, and from the position of British agriculture. These negotiations continued for sixteen months. They were stopped because President de Gaulle, convinced that Britain would not become a good European because of its American and Commonwealth ties, imposed a veto. During the negotiations a number of matters concerning Canada, Australia and New Zealand were considered, but only a few solutions were arrived at. The E.E.C. Commission reported after the talks concluded that there had been agreement with Britain on manufactured imports from these countries, which were to cease to gain preference by 1970; a *décalage* would occur in the level of preference in the intervening time.* A "soft *décalage*" had been decided for processed foodstuffs, except for canned salmon, canned fruit and dried grapes, which mattered considerably to Canada and Australia, and had still to be agreed upon. This was not a very promising start; when it came to "temperate foodstuffs", the nub of the matter, there was even less to report. The Old Dominions wanted "comparable outlets" if they could not retain their British markets, and Britain agreed. But the Six took the view that there could not be "a permanent solution by means of specific measures in favour of those countries alone. A permanent solution could only be sought within a world-wide context". They were, however, willing "to seek transitional solutions taking into account any real difficulties which might arise and thus permitting a progressive adaptation of the Commonwealth countries concerned to the new situation created by Great Britain's entry into the Community". In pursuit of this principle, it was tentatively agreed that an international conference in 1963 should try to reach world-wide agreement for cereals, meat, dairy produce and sugar. A scheme was sketched for a phasing-out of British preference on cereals; it might be possible to sketch similar schemes for phasing-out in regard to meat, sugar and flour. The British had asked for consideration also of pigmeats, eggs, apples and pears, tobacco, wine and rice, but all these products "might still have raised difficulties, even though

* E.E.C. Commission, *Report to the European Parliament on the state of the negotiations with the United Kingdom* (Brussels, 1963), pp. 32 ff. A *décalage* is a process bringing something down to zero. When it has a number of steps, E.E.C. calls it a "soft *décalage*".

the broad lines were already laid down".* The Six recognized the special case of New Zealand, but did not agree on what should be done about it; and they had not discussed it with Britain when negotiations broke off.†

If these were the best results that the E.E.C. Commission could produce for the European Parliament, a body predisposed towards European Union, it is not surprising that Canada, Australia and New Zealand were apprehensive about the negotiations while they were going on. Represented in Brussels by some of their sharpest economic diplomats, although they were not parties to the negotiations, they watched with anxiety the British attempt to pierce the armour of the Six over matters which involved vital interests, especially those of France. To a large extent, France had joined the E.E.C. because it saw an opportunity for its farmers to provide the food which Europe wanted; now their reward was to be endangered by proposals that cheaper food should continue to come in from the Old Dominions. The mood of those Old Dominions' representatives was a mixture of respect for Britain and anxiety about where and how the British would crack on temperate foodstuffs. Suppose imports from Canada, Australia and New Zealand turned out to be the one remaining difficulty standing between Britain and the Six: how would Britain respond? Would a government committed to the idea of entering Europe allow this one strand of kinship to prevent it? This melodramatic possibility did not eventuate (though it might have; the issue was a very stubborn one),‡ since President de Gaulle settled the matter for the time being on other grounds. It is clear, however, that the three Governments were deeply concerned.

Mr. Diefenbaker's Government put out rather muffled signals. It was a protectionist Government which had stressed the importance of preferential trade ties with Britain; at the same time it had a Canadian tradition of concern for Europe to uphold. American policy was in favour of Britain's joining. After its consultations with Mr. Sandys in July 1961, the Government indicated that it assessed the situation differently from him; it felt "grave concern about the implications of possible negotiations between Britain and the European Economic Community, and about the political and

* Ibid., pp. 60 ff., 110.
† Ibid., pp. 66–67.
‡ See James E. Meade, *U. K., Commonwealth and Common Market* (London, 1962), pp. 26–27.

economic effects which British membership . . . would have on Canada and on the Commonwealth as a whole."* At the Accra conference Canada was well in the lead in expressing concern. At the Prime Ministers' meeting in London in September 1962, which considered the whole question after a year's experience of the Brussels negotiations,† Mr. Diefenbaker continued to express dissatisfaction: "substantial further improvement will be needed in the terms of entry in the light of the undertakings that have been given regarding the safeguarding of Commonwealth interests". He was not happy about what had been achieved on British imports of Canadian manufactures and on temperate foodstuffs. He wanted, it seemed, a world trade conference to settle wider issues, and there may have been a hint that Britain should wait for this before deciding its final position on the E.E.C.‡ Mr. Pearson, as Leader of the Opposition, had said it was deplorable that Canada should be "ganging up" with those interests which for a variety of reasons were criticizing Britain's proposed entry; "there should be no doubt", he said, "about our sympathy with the aims of Britain in seeking to join the Common Market".§ To a certain extent, these two men were reproducing the positions of Bennett and King in 1932.

Canada's economic position was so poised as to make a decision about the effects of British entry into E.E.C. very difficult. This was also true of Australia, though not to the same extent. Whereas Canada's preferential trade with Britain had been stunted by dollar shortages, in the 1940's and 50's, Australia's had continued without interruption. The Australian industries which traditionally depended on a sheltered British market were still in that condition. There were prospects for them elsewhere (notably in Japan), and home consumption continued to rise rapidly with continued immigration, but Britain still mattered for meat and dairy producers, fruit growers and others. The Australian Government, headed by Mr. Menzies, had the leader of the Country Party, Mr. McEwen, as its Minister for Trade. It was in his interests, in both capacities, to stress the damage likely to be done to Australia if the advantages

---

* Communiqué at the end of Mr. Sandys's visit, July 14, 1961; *External Affairs* (Ottawa), Vol. XIII, No. 8, p. 278.

† Extract from communiqué in Nicholas Mansergh (ed.) *Documents and Speeches on Commonwealth Affairs 1952–1962* (London, 1963), p. 656.

‡ *The Times*, September 18, 1962.

§ *The Times*, September 13, 1962.

of preference were lost. The same view was not held to the same extent by all Ministers. One of them, Mr Bury, went so far as to say that the potential effect on the Australian economy had been greatly exaggerated, and that any material fears that might be entertained were relatively trivial; the political implications were much more far-reaching. For this he was called upon to resign by the Prime Minister, on the ground of Cabinet solidarity; from Mr. McEwen's point of view, Mr. Bury was cutting the ground from under the feet of the Australian negotiators in Brussels. However, it was clear that, while the likely loss to Australia was hard to calculate, there would certainly be some loss, although it might be mitigated by giving Japan further privileges in the Australian market at Britain's expense. There was probably some readiness in Australia (as in the other countries affected) to adjust the existing British preferences there if Britain abandoned Australia's preferential advantages in the British market.

Perhaps it was this economic uncertainty that led Mr. Menzies to concentrate more upon political than economic possibilities in trying to assess the effects of Britain's joining. At all events, he made a number of wise and tolerant statements on the political side; they remained as, in many ways, the most notable utterances of the whole episode.* His main aim was to throw discussion forward to the time when Britain had joined the E.E.C., and forces there were pressing for a closer political union, perhaps in the form of a federation. What would then be Britain's position in the Commonwealth? It might be possible to retain the Commonwealth association, but Mr. Menzies had grave doubts.

New Zealand was the limiting case amongst the countries considered here. Britain's entry into the E.E.C. promised immense difficulty. Mr. Holyoake said in May 1962 :

"We are fighting for our very livelihood, because 91 per cent of our exported butter, 94 per cent of our cheese, and 94 per cent of our mutton and lamb is sold in the British market. This presents the greatest problem affecting the future of our country. . . .

New Zealand is not seeking guarantees that our products will in fact be purchased by other countries. What we want is an opportunity to sell on a fair basis and without fickle changes in

* These will be found in *Current Notes*, Vol. 32, Nos. 7 and 8, and Vol. 33, Nos. 8 and 10. The last is perhaps the most thoughtful.

import policies to which we have all too often been exposed in the past."*

For fifteen years, from 1939 to 1954, the whole of New Zealand's exports of dairy produce, meat and wool, had been sold to Britain under bulk purchase schemes. Since 1954 New Zealand had experienced the cold blast of competition in the British market, especially in butter, and especially from surpluses dumped there from Europe. This state of affairs had given New Zealand ministers great trouble; they had appealed without much success to Britain for policies which would safeguard their farmers. The E.E.C. proposition was a kind of last straw. Yet the New Zealand Government remained quiet, tolerant and understanding in the face of possible disaster. When Mr. Sandys visited Wellington in 1961, he got a much more accommodating reception than in Canberra.†

South Africa, having left the Commonwealth, had no standing in the discussions which Britain had with the E.E.C. about Commonwealth arrangements. It is likely that, if satisfactory conditions had been arranged in regard to the other three, South Africa might have benefited from them too. But Britain was not under the same obligation to safeguard the interests of South Africa.

The point which emerges most forcibly from a consideration of the Old Dominions' situation, especially in terms of British public opinion, is the old-fashioned character of much of their argument, and its practical irrelevancy. It was not old-fashioned or irrelevant to them (although the case of Mr. Bury illustrates that it was possible for them to go on repeating old shibboleths without being aware of how these fitted the immediate circumstances), since it arose from the existence of clearly-defined economic interests. But it had both these qualities for many articulate and influential people in Britain. Dominion argument seemed often to assume that nothing had changed since 1932 at Ottawa. Dominant opinion in Britain was aware that everything had changed. The obsession of many organs of opinion with the possibilities of "going into Europe" meant that the element of relevancy in the Dominion case often went unregarded; the fact that Lord Beaverbrook implanted his kiss of death on the Dominion position meant, to many people,

* *External Affairs Review*, Vol. XII, No. 5, pp, pp. 22–3.
† The contrast can be seen in the communiqués, in Mansergh, op. cit., pp. 635–8.

that there was no position worth considering.* The British Government was not as contemptuous as this. But the Old Dominions' position (except that of New Zealand) must have been hard for the Government to regard as vital. Canada and Australia were rich countries which had continually put barriers in the way of British imports; they were not so deserving as the newer countries of the Commonwealth, in which under-development was so manifest; they were stubborn in defending their rights, but reluctant to grant rights in return; in any case, their trade, while important to Britain, was nothing like so important as European trade promised to be. Since the matter was settled in the end by President de Gaulle, no one will ever know how far the Government would have gone in pursuit of safeguards for the Old Dominions. It is possible that opinion in Britain itself might have hardened against entry on other grounds. But if the position had been reduced to satisfying the Old Dominions or joining the E.E.C., few people would have expected the British government to choose the Old Dominions.

The difficulty of estimating what might have happened is increased by the fact that, in Britain at the time, the problem was often presented in the misleading form, "which should we be in, the Commonwealth or Europe?" The entry into E.E.C. did not involve leaving the Commonwealth; it did involve endangering certain economic interests in Commonwealth countries. This might have led to worse relations with those countries. But E.E.C. as such did not provide a political alternative to the Commonwealth; it was the possibility of a European federation, to which many of E.E.C.'s designers hoped it would lead, that provided the political alternative. The actions of France have shown that a strong-minded member of the E.E.C. can stultify moves towards a political union. Britain might have been able to do the same, given a British Government which wanted to. In any case, only some parts of the Commonwealth stood to lose from Britain's joining the E.E.C. Sierra Leone and the independent Caribbean countries were prepared to consider associated status in regard to the E.E.C.; India, Pakistan and Ceylon had been offered trade treaties which they were prepared to accept, provided that their existing arrangements with Britain continued up to the time when these treaties came into effect. Canada, Australia and New Zealand were the hard cases in economic terms,

* I have attempted to deal with some of the intricacies of British opinion on the E.E.C. question in "Britain without Europe" in Coral Bell (ed.), *Europe without Britain* (Melbourne, 1963).

Ghana and Nigeria in political terms. However, no member country was prepared to leave the Commonwealth because Britain entered the E.E.C., if the 1962 Prime Ministers' meeting was any guide. In sum, Britain was not being asked to drop the Commonwealth when it entered the E.E.C.; but it might have had a difficult choice at some future time if the political integrationists in the E.E.C. had been lucky.

Nevertheless, in our context the outstanding point about the argument over Britain's attempt to enter the E.E.C. is the extent to which Canada, Australia and New Zealand were prepared to use Commonwealth symbols and conventions in order to try to gain their ends. While not content to allow the British Government to argue their case with full knowledge and good will at Brussels, they were also not content to keep the matter confined to their own direct relations with Britain, as Australia and New Zealand (not Canada) had often been prepared to do in the past. They attempted to deploy the full weight of the Commonwealth mystique in defence of their cases. They were also happy to make common cause with the newer members against the British position.

SOUTHERN RHODESIA

The question of Southern Rhodesia is a coda to the South African issue. It can be stated briefly.

With the dissolution of the Federation of Rhodesia and Nyasaland, two new black African states came into being within the Commonwealth: Zambia (formerly Northern Rhodesia) and Malawi (formerly Nyasaland). This left behind the self-governing colony of Southern Rhodesia, a paradoxical survival in that it had had internal self-government since 1923 when the other two territories did not even have representative institutions. Southern Rhodesia was a survival of the kind of colony that the several Australian states, Natal, Cape Province and New Zealand had been —a small settlement of white men who had been given the sort of control over their internal affairs that it was customary to grant a British colony in the nineteenth century. In this case, however, the white men reigned over a much greater number of black men. Moreover, they did so at a time when the climate of opinion, in Britain and in the world at large, was vastly different from what it had been at the beginning of the twentieth century. The internal self-government of Southern Rhodesia was an anomaly which drew increased attention when the Federation was dissolved. In an Africa moving rapidly towards independence, Southern Rhodesia's similarity to South Africa became ever more obvious. Its practices were attacked at the U.N., and raised at the 1964 and 1965 meetings of Commonwealth Prime Ministers.

The British Government's position was embarrassing. It insisted that the right of the British parliament to legislate for Southern Rhodesia's future remained unimpaired. At the same time it showed no disposition to exercise that right in defiance of the white minority in Southern Rhodesia, since the convention had arisen that such a grant of internal self-government as Southern Rhodesia had received should not be withdrawn. In any case, the Southern Rhodesian Government said it would only be moved by force, and force would be difficult and distasteful for the British Government to apply. Yet Britain was under pressure from Afro-Asian members of the Commonwealth to reorganize Southern Rhodesia so as to give the black majority control. It was argued that Britain had not hesitated to revoke internal self-government in British Guiana when racial trouble broke out there; racial trouble was already present, if only in solution, in Southern Rhodesia.

We are here concerned with the attitudes expressed by Canada, Australia and New Zealand. None showed any inclination to defend the Southern Rhodesian position. They differed somewhat in the extent to which they were prepared to make suggestions about what should be done—Sir Robert Menzies confined himself largely to maintaining that the problem was Britain's, and Britain should not be given too much advice, while Mr. Pearson made a number of suggestions*—but they did not attempt to prevent the expression of stronger views from other Prime Ministers, and they made it clear that they would not recognize a unilateral declaration of independence by Southern Rhodesia.

In the Australian case, support for the British Government over Southern Rhodesia seemed largely a matter of caution about the pushfulness of some of the new African Commonwealth members; in the Canadian case, it seemed to arise more from an assessment of the world situation, especially of the position in Africa, and

---

* Sir Robert Menzies's comments on the two conferences are in *Current Notes*, Vol. 35, No. 7, and Vol. 36, No. 6. Mr. Pearson made suggestions about a constitutional conference and about the release of African leaders from gaol. See his statement to Canadian House of Commons, July 17, 1964.

was accompanied by pressure for a Commonwealth declaration against racial discrimination. The New Zealand position was somewhere in between. The three countries had in common their readiness to recognize the importance of the colonialism issue to their new colleagues,* and their wish to help Britain out of a difficult situation. They also had in common, however, a negative quality of even greater importance: none seems to have attempted, or thought of attempting, a defence of the Rhodesian white settlers on that "kith and kin" ground which is often present in Right-wing Conservative discussions in Britain. They were presumably responsible in some degree for the reference in the 1946 communique to "the necessity for giving confidence to the minority community in Southern Rhodesia that their interests would be protected";† but this is a reference to the need for justice, not a case for the Southern Rhodesian whites in the terms which they would like to see other white men adopt. In effect, the treatment of Southern Rhodesia by the remaining Old Dominions is the end of a chapter in white settlement and its political effects.

Looking at the four issues which the Old Dominions have had to face since 1956, it is clear that they are going through a process of movement away from traditional attitudes towards cool-headed selection of issues and positions. This movement, which we saw in Chapters 7 and 8 in the contexts of foreign policy and economic change, has been most obvious in Canada, as one might expect. It has been less obvious in Australia, except in the economic sphere: Australia was probably the most active of the three in trying to secure concessions from the E.E.C. negotiators at Brussels. The most uniform attitude towards Britain has been that of New Zealand, but even here the movement towards an independent position is discernible. The climate of change is towards more sophistication, more selection, more awareness of the world at large, and more recognition of the Commonwealth as a device to be used for the advantage of an individual Commonwealth country. The process has also been characteristic of Britain itself. The simple-minded evocations of "unity" which were still prevalent in 1945 have given

* "The first thing that a Prime Minister of the old Commonwealth has to adjust himself to", said Sir Robert Menzies after the 1964 meeting, "is that although this is not his vocabulary and these are not his ideas, they do exist and they must be received and understood . . . The personal relations between all representatives were extraordinarily good." (*Current Notes*, Vol. 35, No. 7, p. 36.)

† Ibid., p. 28.

way to a flexible acceptance of the Commonwealth as an institution in which unity, while agreeable when it can be found, is not a prime characteristic. Each of the countries considered here would like to see Commonwealth "unity", if that means acceptance of its own position; each is resigned, however, to accepting that this cannot always be the case.

South Africa has figured little in this chapter, except as the man in the dock. At the 1964 Prime Ministers' meeting, the leaders of Britain, Canada, Australia and New Zealand, with the others present, "reaffirmed their condemnation of the policy of *apartheid* practised by the Government of the Republic of South Africa" and "were unanimous in calling upon South Africa to bring to an end the practice of *apartheid*, which had been repeatedly condemned by the United Nations and was deplored by public opinion throughout the world".* South Africa has a climate of its own making to contend with.

* Loc. cit.

10

THE FUTURE

IN the mid-1960's, Britain's relations with the Four are more distant than they were, but still basically good, except for South Africa. How will they develop from now on, in the three related fields of cultural, economic and political connection?

Culturally, British influence can be expected to remain strong, but as part of a general English-speaking culture in which the Four participate in varying degrees, rather than as aphorisms and instructions gratefully accepted by children from an indulgent mother. The Four still have provincial cultures, but they are not so provincial as they were; moreover, they draw increasingly from the wealth of ideas and attitudes in the United States, as does Britain itself. We may expect that, as time goes by, it will be possible to a smaller and smaller extent to recommend ideas, statements and institutions to the people of the Old Dominions, simply because they are British. As I have suggested earlier, this is not just because of influence by Americans. It is due much more to the growth of national feeling in each of the Four. In some cases, as with the Afrikaners and the people of Quebec, this is a self-conscious nationalism, deliberately cultivated on the basis of another language than English, and utilizing symbols which are not connected with Britain. The more important kind of national feeling, however, is that which grows from the local soil and the interaction of people who live there. The British strand in it is strong and vigorous. But the sense of deference to British origins which, for example, the early New Zealand settlers showed in such measure has now disappeared. Local standards and customs are what matter; if British contributions can enrich these, they will be accepted. But they will have to make their way in competition against local and foreign rivals. There are, of course, brakes on this process, originating from the essentially British character of many Dominion institutions at their establishment. In the practice of the law in Australia and New Zealand, for example, it would be difficult to dislodge British precedents and practices. In the organization of the Anglican church in each of the Dominions, English standards will continue to carry weight. But in all that is characterized by rapid movement and the flow of fresh ideas, British efforts to influence the Four will need to be strong in themselves; they will not be able to rely on the ebbing force of traditionalism. When they are strong, however, they will find a much wider acceptance in Canada, Australia and New Zealand than in other Commonwealth countries which are still subject to British influence. The power of education in English, which in India and Nigeria reaches only a selected few, is universal in Australia and New Zealand, and effective in the greater part of Canada. Even migrants from Europe have to educate their children in English. While they may never come under the spell of the Queen and the Church of England, they cannot withstand Shakespeare. It is the *lingua franca* of English that offers Britain the opportunity of future cultural penetration.

In economic terms, it is most unlikely that the Old Dominions' former degrees of dependence on Britain, either for markets or for basic manufactured imports, will ever recur. The diversification of their exports and the growth of their own manufactures make it unlikely. Britain is still significant for Dominion export industries which were specially shaped to serve the British market. The future may be expected to see a gradual lessening of the importance of the British market, unless Britain goes into Europe on the basis of the Treaty of Rome, in which case the sudden loss to Dominion farm industries would be substantial. To suggest, as above, that the Old Dominions will never be dependent again on imports of basic manufactures from Britain is not to say that they will want nothing from the British manufacturer. In fact, Britain can expect to provide knowledge and equipment for new industries, as well as capital. The sterling system will continue to be a help in this regard. But the rapid economic growth of each of the Dominions means that British contributions to their technology will need to be new and effective, and able to withstand international competition; the level of technical criticism grows significantly higher all the time in an advancing industrial society, which is what each of them, with the partial exception of New Zealand, has developed. The efficacy of the sterling system depends upon a significant flow of transactions between Britain and the Dominions. If the trade and payments position of any of the others approaches that of Canada, sterling will not remain an acceptable base for its currency. The curious, often entertaining, aspect of the Old Dominions' economic position in relation to Britain is that, although they trumpeted their attachment to the practices of Ottawa when they objected to Britain's entry into the E.E.C., they are in fact greatly removed from the whole situation in which their Ottawa agreements were arrived at. The dwindling significance of preferential trade was brought into false prominence in 1961–2 (not false for New Zealand, but false for the others); it does not seem to have a future. The future may be expected to show an increasing multi-lateralism in the international dealings of all concerned, provided there is no crisis of international trade and payments, arising from a failure to cope with liquidity problems.

Chapter 7 showed that each of the Old Dominions except South Africa shares considerable common interest with Britain in political matters. The South African position will probably deteriorate. Only a massive change of heart either in South Africa itself or in the countries which constitute the Organization of African Unity could change this likelihood. The coolness of the United States towards South Africa is an index to what may be expected from Britain and from the other Dominions. Whether the situation will deteriorate to the point at which Britain administers economic or military sanctions against South Africa is impossible to determine now; but the possibility exists. Nothing like this is going to happen between Britain and the other three.

Canadian interest in a future British connection lies in the prospect of common pressure on the United States, and in the opportunities which Commonwealth membership provides for influencing Afro-Asian countries. In this latter connection, the link with Britain will be significant in itself; in the former, Canadian effort may be expected to show itself more in multi-lateral European situations than in teaming up with Britain to restrain the United States. The North Atlantic Triangle still exists, but its eastern point hovers over the English Channel, ready to move to Paris or London or Bonn as occasion demands; it is no longer firmly planted on London. In Commonwealth matters, Canada may be expected to continue as before.

Australia and New Zealand have a similar interest to Canada's but the business of exerting pressure on the United States will necessarily be less multi-lateral for them. Asian countries with which Australia and New Zealand may ally themselves cannot be expected to show the same cohesion and initiative as European countries. In facing China, Australia and New Zealand might get Japanese help, but it would certainly be equivocal if it did not become dictatorial.

They would like to have British assistance if it can be got, but its provision depends upon a set of variables which no one is yet able to assess accurately. The extent to which Britain will wish to continue to be a force in Asian affairs depends upon commitments in Europe, conceptions at home, and connections with the United States. If Britain is to be mainly a European power, it would be ridiculous to have an extended British defence effort in South-East Asia, whether based on the Asian mainland or on northern or western Australia. On the other hand, if Britain is to adopt a deliberate policy of maintaining mobile defence forces to deal with "brushfire" outbreaks in Asia and Africa, not interfering with American efforts but supplementing them, then this demands the permanent commitment of resources; it also involves an enlargement of ANZAM arrangements with a wider field to cover. The situation for Australia and New Zealand is delicate. They cannot expect Britain to defend them in the literal sense, as it is possible to imagine the United States defending them—by nuclear or some other massive attack on substantial forces from China; Britain does not have the strength to manage such a manœuvre, nor would it be likely to have the inclination. To this extent the United States remains fundamental to the defence of Australia and New Zealand. But Britain is a valuable aid in the expensive and extensive operations in Asia which have been pre-figured in the defence of Malaysia against Indonesian confrontation. If the price of continuing this sort of aid is substantial contributions to the outfitting of future British bases in the area, Australia and New Zealand might pay some of the bill. Just how much would be the subject of much haggling. If, on the other hand, Britain does not attempt a long-term commitment to Asia, it may be expected to become less and less important to Australian and New Zealand defence, but to return even more of that diplomatic importance in general world politics which it has for Canada.

In the Introduction, it will be remembered, I quoted Mr. Auden in identifying two kinds of British reaction to the Old Dominions. One was the snooty aesthetic attitude that the Dominions had produced no art and did not contain many aesthetic people. The other was the commonplace attitude that people in the Dominions were just like the British in a suet-puddingy sort of way. Both of these were true of certain times and places in the past. Neither is true now. Dominion art is worth attending to (especially New Zealand poetry and Australian poetry and painting), but it is, on the whole, not attended to in Britain because the lines of selection by publishers and their equivalents in the other arts have gone out to Europe and the United States, not beyond. Population and sophistication grow rapidly in Canada, Australia and New Zealand; art grows with them, albeit in fits and starts. The suet-pudding side is even more false. Different climates cause different practices in food, clothes and shelter. Moreover, as we saw in Chapter 8, the populations of the Old Dominions are being significantly affected by immigration from places where they do not eat suet-pudding. Yet it is still the case that large stretches of the life of communities in Canada, Australia and New Zealand—even in South Africa— have a strong British tone and are easily traceable to their origins. All the same, there will be no effective repetition of those scenes and attitudes associated with World War I, and epitomized by Graham McInnes in describing his school days in Melbourne:

"In the chapel at Scotch College hundreds of reedy voices rose in unison towards the rafters as they sang another song which catches forever the extraordinary mood of passionate love for a Mother Country. This song had the added merit in our eyes of having been written by a Scotch Old Boy, J. D. Burns . . . Burns had enlisted with the A.I.F. in 1914 as a second lieutenant and had been killed in France. He was one of the many Scotch collegians who gave their lives, but to us his poem *The Bugles of England* irradiated him with the same magical light as Rupert Brooke. It was set to music in mournful minor cadences and it is impossible to hear it in the mind's ear today without a constriction of the throat. The boys who sang it often wept unashamedly for its nostalgia, its innocence and its heartbreaking might-have-been:

> *The bugles of England are blowing o'er the sea*
> *Calling out across the years, calling now to me.*
> *They woke me from dreaming in the dawning of the day*
> *The Bugles of England; and how could I stay?*

> *The banners of England unfurled across the sea*
> *Floating out upon the wind beckoning to me.*
> *Storm-rent and battle-torn, smoke-stained and grey*
> *The banners of England; and how could I stay?*

Oh England, I heard the cry of those who died for thee
Sounding like an organ voice across the wintry sea;
They lived and died for England and gladly went their way
England, oh England, and how could I stay?

There is in this song no mention whatever of Australia or of the fact that in rallying to the flag these young men were defending Australia and creating a nation. It was sufficient in those days that the Mother Country was in trouble."*

If Britain were attacked now, Australia, New Zealand and Canada would go to its aid; South Africa presumably would not. They would do so with some diminished sense of kinship, and with a fuller awareness of the strains of international politics than in 1914. They would be accompanied by the United States. A network of treaties and obligations to other countries would surround them; there would be much talk of national interests. But there would still be something of the sentiment of 1914, though it would be expressed in a manner which the men of 1914 would have found strange and which they might not relish.

* Graham McInnes, *The Road to Gundagai* (London, 1965), pp. 281–2.

INDEX